We Were
IN
AUSCHWITZ

We Were
IN
AUSCHWITZ

6643 JANUSZ NEL SIEDLECKI

75817 KRYSTYN OLSZEWSKI

119198 TADEUSZ BOROWSKI

TRANSLATED BY ALICIA NITECKI

Welcome Rain Publishers
New York

Armii Amerykańskiej,

która przyniosła nam oswobodzenie

z obozu koncentracyjnego

Dachau-Allach,

pracę tę poświęcają

autorzy

i wydawca.

The authors and the publisher

dedicate this work

to the

American Army

which brought us freedom

from concentration camp

Dachau-Allach

We Were
IN
AUSCHWITZ

FROM THE
PUBLISHER

Is this book necessary? I don't know. Whatever will be said about it, however, one thing is irrefutably clear: the art in it must be separated from the documentation.

Certainly this book is not needed as an artistic act. But as a document it is very distinctive.

In a fairly straightforward way, the book gives the history of a certain concentration camp, commonly known in Europe as Auschwitz, and in Poland as Oświęcim. Obviously, it does not subsume all of the circumstances of this camp, but very cautiously, and, one is tempted to say, intimately, it gives a few fragments of what the authors themselves experienced and saw with their own eyes.

This book is difficult and terrible, as terrible as only a crime committed against people can be. Perhaps this book will be useful to a doctor or a psychologist and, perhaps, to an artist who will seek in it material for an epic about our era.

False legends are being created around many aspects of this war. This book removes one of them: the legend of the concentration camp. There is in it the naive amazement that a person forced to live in a criminal system can become so base, an amazement with which we are still filled. And there is in it an indifference, characteristic of our time, toward acts of evil which do not affect us directly.

We have tacked the label *fascism* to a certain body of crime committed by man. A myth of the superiority of man over man; collective madness; bands of party members; very well-nourished, athletic, educated criminals and their families making very good business on the black market; the murder of many millions of people; gas chambers; prison cellars, and common graves for hostages who had been shot; the thoughtless destruction of Europe from Cherbourg to the Volga — all this we have called Hitlerism. We have cursed the ethic that, in the name of race, nation, and the party, ordered one man to rob, imprison, and murder another man. We are those to whom this ethic was applied. We are those who were sent to the camps because we did something, because we didn't do anything, because we were — in the thinking of this ethic — guilty, or because we were innocent.

We Europeans, if we fought for anything, it was not for a change in etiquette, but for a new, anational, classless, and apolitical ethic. In any event, not for a change of ethic. And not so much for the word *democracy*, which has as many meanings as there are national systems in the world, but for its inner meaning, the fundamental concept of freedom and law. We live on the cusp of two worlds. If we find an ethic that will have as its goal the welfare of man and not economic profit or the selfish interests of some race, nation, or social class, then, perhaps, we will be able to clear the rubble from our continent and provide education and comfort to people who crave housing, work, and books more than uniforms, guns, and tanks. If, however, we attach deluding ethics to evil, which can outlive the criminal, perhaps we will then find ourselves in the midst of a world so criminal and a life so terrible that the world and the life described in this book will appear to have been not so bad.

This book is a modest fragment of a story about the life that millions of Europeans lived until not so long ago. Perhaps it doesn't have any great artistic value. But its documentary worth is indisputable, because this book, portraying the pathological changes in the soul of these Europeans, is an eloquent testimony to the fact that one of the worst of human crimes is that of striking out the fundamental ethical principle that "God created man free."

191250
ANATOL GIRS

PREFACE

We were people like all other people in the world. We had a family, friends, our own home, our own yard, and a dog in the yard. Our generation was raised in the here and now and took ideals for granted, like everything else that was our due. And when our here and now and our ideals crumbled along with the walls of our city, we went out in search of them.

Here is the history of a certain unsuccessful expedition.

One of us went across the "green frontier," fled the country, made it to France, and when he came back carrying a password and the codes of a special mission in the dirty pages of a greasy notebook, and with a Browning camera stuffed into his pocket, fell into an ambush in the Carpathian mountains.

The second one was arrested, together with his companions, transporting weapons at one of the stations near Warsaw.

Five of "them" waited for the third one in a small apartment on Puławska Street. They took lots of worthless papers and a half-read book about the features of European culture out of his briefcase.

Auschwitz brought the three of them together. Auschwitz, the meeting place of the whole of Europe, a sliver of earth where the living were gassed and the dead burned. We were united by commonplace, pitiless death, not death on behalf of the nation or honor, but death for worn-out flesh, boils, typhus, swollen legs. Years of lying to death, cheating her, slipping by her stealthily, bind us as tightly together as if we'd fought battles in the same trench, even though these were not heroic years.

We saw millions of people go apathetically and without resistance to the gas chambers. We walked across the mountains of riches they had brought with them from Europe. We destroyed piles of clothing, sifted fistfuls of gold; we stepped on money from all the countries of the world. We stepped on people who had fallen from hunger, and we were stepped on ourselves when, exhausted, we fell to the ground, onto sticky, putrid mud.

We saw people killed for stealing a couple of raw potatoes, and we saw cars filled with food stolen for the families of the SS men. We saw women who gave themselves for a piece of bread, and we saw people who bought themselves lovers with gold belonging to people who had been gassed.

We saw, and we think that we have the right to talk about this without subterfuge, openly, as we remember it. Confinement in the camp, destitution, torture, and death in the gas chamber are not heroism, are not even anything positive. It was defeat, the almost immediate abandonment of ideological principles. A primeval battle remained, waged by the solitary, debased prisoner for his existence against the equally debased SS and against the terrible force of the camp. We stress this strongly because myths and legends will arise on both sides. We did not fight for the concept of nation in the camp, nor for the inner restructuring of man; we fought for a bowl of soup, for a place to sleep, for women, for gold and watches from the transports. The savagery of the SS went far beyond the call of duty. Their lust for murder, delight in killing for its own sake, sadism masked by nothing, triumphed over any human scruples they may ever have had and burst out of them unchecked. We survived, though we were neither better nor worse than those who died. But we do not want the dead to be forgotten.

We were evil, hard, and cruel; we often renounced our humanity because we wanted to survive. But the dead and the living, the good and the bad, were bound by a boundless contempt and hatred for the Germans and a mystical faith in a better, more just world. We, to whom survival was given, look at that good, just world with enormous bitterness. Our family home was burned, our friends were murdered, our country destroyed. But that is not what hurts us. What hurts us is that in the world that was supposed to be our redemption, the same rules of life that we came to hate so much in the camp still exist — looting, robbery, swindling.

We cannot allow ourselves the luxury of forgetting. We also cannot bring ourselves to split hairs, to laboriously sort out the good and the bad Germans, because that division does not exist for us. In our prison stripes we measured the Germans lengthwise and cross-wise and we know the soul of that nation better than tourists armed with binoculars and Kodaks do. The memory of the camp will go with us throughout our lives, although we are people like all other people on earth.

But our arms have been tattooed with a number as a sign that we were slaves.

AT THE JUNCTURE
OF THE SOLA AND
THE VISTULA

Oświęcim — the famous *KL* Auschwitz. The German concentration camp near the little town of Oświęcim, which lies about forty kilometers west of Kraków on Polish land grafted on to the Reich and created at first as an extermination camp — *Vernichtungslager* — only for Poles.

In the spring of 1940 came the first transports: about a hundred long-term prisoners from German concentration camps, mainly professional criminals, who were assigned to assume all the camp functions and who were given unlimited power over the prisoners, and about a thousand Poles from the prison in Tarnów. These were almost exclusively "tourists" captured on the Hungarian border on their way to the Polish army in France. Shortly afterward the first and second "Warsaw" transports arrived, altogether about two thousand people. These had been taken off the streets during the first roundups in Warsaw, which in their incongruity had created, at the beginning, such a terrible sensation in the city. In the fall, Auschwitz accounted for six thousand, and then in spring 1941, ten thousand people. At first the prisoners were kept in former army barracks, and then a *Lager* — a camp — was built, the ground was leveled, ponds filled in, local houses demolished.

The area, idyllic and peaceful till now, became depopulated, deadened. Within a radius of many kilometers, within reach of the guards and beyond, no one from the free world can gain entry. Houses stand empty, fields unsown; in the marshes and the ponds neighboring Lagers arise. Huts, and next to them the penal colony for women, Harmenz, *Ogrodnictwo Rajsko z Instytutem Botanicznym* — the Rajsko nursery gardens and Botanical Institute — and, above all, the terrible Birkenau begins to grow, crematoria are built, the railroad comes up to the camp and an "internal" ramp arises, intended for transports. No one from the outside will now see people going to the gas.

In fall 1941, transports of "the fruits of war" arrive, (Soviet

POWs) numbering about ten thousand (in 1942, only a few hundred of them remained, and in 1944, around fifty). In 1942 part of the camp was fenced off and reserved for women. At about the same time, typhus broke out; many thousands of people died of it.

In spring 1942, a new camp was opened, the so-called Auschwitz II, situated on the land of the Rajsko estate near Brzezinka — Birkenau, three kilometers away from "Old" Auschwitz. In this same period, Auschwitz's fantastic career begins: an "internal" Polish camp nobody knows changes into an enormous extermination camp for many millions of European Jews.

In 1943 four huge crematoria began to work. Previously they had gassed people in an ordinary country barn, appropriately sealed, that could hold up to five hundred people at a time. In June 1943, a record was reached: within a period of twenty-four hours, twenty-three thousand people were gassed. They were burned in ovens and on enormous pyres. Children, the elderly, and the sick were thrown, alive, into the fire. Human screams from behind the famous little birch forest could be heard without interruption for whole weeks at a time.

Numbers assigned to ordinary prisoners — *Schutzhäftlinge* — rose above the twenty thousand figure, and with that, one must remember that in a certain period numbers belonging to the dead were reassigned. Numbers given to ordinary prisoners of Jewish descent — Series A — twenty thousand, and as many in Series B. These numbers started to be given out in June 1944. Numbers given to Soviet POWs in the eleven thousands. Numbers given to the men and women in the Gypsy camp in the eleven thousands with the letter Z for *Ziguener*. Temporary prisoners or *"Erziehungshäftlinge,"* educable ones, in the several thousand. The numbering of women — *FKL Frauenkonzentrationslager* — at one hundred thousand. The transports arriving from the evacuation of Warsaw after the Uprising were only given numbers at first.

Altogether, there were about 400 thousand numbered prisoners. Probably around twenty-five thousand remained alive, that is 6 percent. Around 4.5 million unnumbered were burned. Auschwitz was planned for about three hundred thousand living people, and for how many dead ones is not known.

Money, valuables, shoes, gold, the entire personal wealth of the murdered went to Germany for the internal needs of the nation.

WITH A BAEDECKER
AMONG THE WIRES

I was a political prisoner in Montelupich Street prison in Kraków. Despite isolation from the world, despite heavy guard, gossip, news, and, sometimes, papers seeped through the prison walls. There, I got to know Pomorska Street where the Gestapo was; I learned the name Bielany, a place of execution. There, I heard for the first time about the newly established camp in Auschwitz. Slowly, from hints from the guards, from smuggled letters, from attendants' tales, we forged for ourselves some kind of image of a concentration camp. It was not a complete image, an impression, rather, of something as terrible as it was unknown.

A few months later, I was to compare that impression with the reality. I was transported to the camp in November 1940. I left Auschwitz in October 1944. Auschwitz was built while I was there; while I was there, they began to liquidate it. It seems to me that I got to know well the structure of that modern feature of European culture, the concentration camp. With Auschwitz as my example, I will try to capture that structure in words.

A concentration camp consists of a certain number of "residential houses," most frequently wooden, known as Blocks. These Blocks are laid out symmetrically along the camp streets, and they surround the *Appelplatz*. On the Appelplatz, roll calls are held to ascertain the number of prisoners, these are called *Appel*, and work details, *Kommandos*, in other words, assemble there before marching out to work. The camp is surrounded by two rows of electrified barbed wire, which are illuminated at night by powerful lamps. A three-meterwide neutral strip runs the length of the wires. If a prisoner finds himself in this strip, the guards have the duty to shoot him without warning. Behind the wires, a guard tower can be found, equipped with machine guns and reflectors, independent of the system of lamps. There is only one gate, guarded day and night by SS men. By the gate, may be found the guardhouse, known as the *Blockführerstube*. In Auschwitz, there were two-story brick buildings, and on the other side, where the civilians were, a large cement wall was built. Birkenau was completely wooden, apart from some of the Blocks in the women's camp.

The leading authority in the camp is the *Kommandant*, whose right-hand man is the so-called camp leader. To him, in turn, report the director of the camp Appels, and, finally, the leaders, or more precisely, the superintendents of the Blocks, the ordinary SS men. Apart from these basic leaders, others existed in the camp, ostensibly answering to the Kommandant, but possessing a certain independence. This arrangement allowed the cleverer prisoner to navigate between bad authorities and unpleasant orders. There was the work office, directed by the *Arbeitsdienstführer*, which means the leader of the workforce; there is a camp hospital, which answers to the camp doctor, whose subordinates are the nursing chiefs, the *SDG*; a kitchen and warehouse, having their own completely independent administration and control; there is an all-powerful "Building Administration" with a *Bauleiter* at its head; and so on.

At the same time, there exists a prisoners' self-government, which serves to help the German powers and is appointed by them. All the positions conform strictly to the positions of the SS who administer the camp. The *Lagerführer's* assistant, then, is a prisoner who supervises the whole camp, and who, to distinguish him from the others, is equipped with a black band with white letters *LÄ* for *Lagerältester*. The *Raportführer* is assisted by the camp scribe, the so-called *Raportschreiber*, who also wears a black band with beautifully embroidered letters. He runs the entire camp office, he manages the prisoners's files, the death books, writes down the new arrivals, prepares roll calls, supervises the conditions of the Blocks, is the camp's main bookkeeper. The actual administrators of the Blocks are the *Blockführers*. The *Lagerältester KB* stands at the helm of the hospital, the *Krankenbau*. The assistants to the SS man in charge of labor are the *Arbeitsdienst* men, and so on. The work details are directed by the *Kommandoführers* through their Kapos and Unterkapos. These wear yellow bands with appropriate inscriptions on them and with the name of the Kommando.

The power of prisoner over prisoner was absolute, softened only by protection or friendship, and, in later years, by the ever-present threat of an end to the war. Nearly always, these positions, these "functions," were attained by people totally devoid of all scruples; people blindly devoted to the SS men; sadists; or those who either out of desire for the comforts and privileges associated with their position, or in order simply to save their own lives, did not hesitate to murder hundreds and thousands of their companions, to walk, as was said, on corpses. For this reason the name Kapo or *Lagerältester* was nearly always a synonym for the vilest murderer and torturer.

One has to also dispel the myth of the German political prisoner. He differed in nothing from the criminal. He was always a sophisticated murderer and, nearly always, a homosexual — ruthless toward prisoners; servile in the extreme to an SS man, always loyal to him, always under his care, always enjoying his complete trust. He constituted the aristocracy of all the camps and was of inestimable help to the SS. These people were hated as much as the SS and aroused as much fear. There was no chance of coexistence between them and the rest of the prisoners. Rumors of crimes they had committed in Sachsenhausen, Buchenwald, Flossenbürg, Dachau followed some of them into Auschwitz. . . . On the basis of our experience in Auschwitz, we maintain that a great part of the responsibility for the prisoners from Europe who were murdered in German concentration camps falls on the shoulders of German political and criminal prisoners.

Prisoners arriving at the camp were, first of all, given serial numbers that after 1942 were tattooed on the left forearm, and then they were shaved, deloused, bathed, and dressed in striped clothes made out of nettles. In later times, when the number of new arrivals sometimes reached ten thousand a week, it was permissible to use civilian clothes, but only in the area of the so-called Birkenau. These clothes were marked with a red stripe of insoluble oil paint.

Of personal belongings, one could own only glasses and a belt. There were times when owning a spoon and a handkerchief was also permitted. In the period when receiving packages was allowed, the food constituted the property of the prisoner.

After leaving the showers, last name and first name vanished at the recorder's table; all that was left was the camp number and, something fairly important, your profession. Depending on what crime the prisoners had committed, they received a triangle in the appropriate color, which was worn on the left breast next to the number. Political criminals had red; professional criminals, green; saboteurs, black; homosexuals, pink; and students of the holy word, violet. National origin was identified by a black letter on the triangle: P=Polish, F=French, and so on. The Germans did not wear any letter.

"Work makes man free," announced the sign on the camp gate; therefore, everyone in the camp had to work. The prisoners were divided into work units. Only a small number of them were employed in their own professions; the rest performed manual labor with a spade, a pickax, a tip-wagon. When there was no work in the camp, the prisoners performed unnecessary work, for example, turned the snow over from one side to the other, so that it took twice as long to clear the area. At first in Auschwitz, there were the following Kommandos: the famous *Bauhof*, where around two thousand people performed the hard and exhausting work of unloading, sorting, piling, and moving all kinds of building materials, tools, and machines; then agriculture, about a thousand wagon drivers, dairymen, swineherds, and so on, working hard but having the possibility of "organizing" food; a total of three thousand people in mechanical and shoe warehouses; the famous *Holzhof*, the Kommando for the weak, and many other Kommandos that there is no need to name here. Work lasted twelve hours in the summer, until twilight in the winter. During work, it was prohibited to talk, even in a whisper, to sit or to squat, to stand idle or to walk slowly. There were no work quotas, but performing the work slowly brought with it punishments.

"Anyone who does not steal, or who does not allow someone else to steal for him, will rot in Auschwitz in no less than half a year," said Aumeier, camp Kommandant, and the expression became a proverb, because it was true. With a twelve-hour workday, on their feet for eighteen hours, the prisoners in their striped uniforms, received half a liter of black coffee or mint tea in the morning; at midday, one liter of soup (depending on the season of the year, rutabaga, turnip, carrot, pumpkin, less often, *kasza* or potato); for dinner, about 300 grams of bread; fifty grams of fat, sausage, or marmalade; and half a liter of coffee, with sugar in it on Sundays. Twice a week, "a supplement for the hard workers," altogether a kilo and a half of bread, and around two hundred grams of cold cuts. And nothing else. Nothing. It was an amount that was absolutely insufficient to live on. After a few months, the strongest and the most resilient person lost his strength, and fell sick, went to the gas chamber, or died immediately under the SS man's or the guard's whip. In this manner, many thousands of Greek Jews from Salonica died. Of these, after several months in the camp, there remained only fourteen.

Against this background, the necessity for "organizing" — which was as much a feature of camp life as the Appel, the work, the SS, and the crematorium — becomes clear. Organizing is the procurement of the means of survival beyond the portion or the ration.

A thief steals a portion of bread from under his colleague's head, the organizer steals it from the storeroom, and steals more: loaves of bread, margarine by the carton. A thief steals a piece of cake from a friend's package, the organizer brings gingerbread from the ramp or the crematorium. The ordinary prisoner slowly dies of hunger and writes home for packages; the organizer sends his family assiduously saved banknotes.

Patently, organizing has various shades of honesty. The purest organizing hurts no one, comes from the main food warehouses, from the SS kitchen, from the farmwork, from the crematoria, and from the "Effects" — the stores of things robbed from those gassed. The trading in the warehouses in individual parts of Birkenau, were less obviously pure, while completely dirty dealings went on in the Block offices and among the food suppliers of the Blocks and so on. They cut the portions of margarine, stole sausage and bread.

There were a great variety of organizers. From the Gypsy who acquired a broom and brought it from the field to the camp in order to sell it for a bowl of soup; from the Jewish woman who sold herself for a portion of bread or for lisle stockings, through the traders in spirits carrying a flask in their trouser legs, to the bleary-eyed Jews in whose pockets lay a handful of several-carat diamonds. The organizer is not hungry, helps his colleagues, but as a result doesn't have day or night enough for business. Long after the evening gong, he comes out to the wires calling to his friend in a neighboring area to throw him the acquired goods, spirits, or eggs across the wire. He knows the value of the dollar and of gold teeth yanked out of the mouths of corpses; he knows many other camp secrets. But he keeps quiet because he knows how to value life.

The significance of organizing did not diminish at all in the period when it was permitted to receive packages. In the fall of 1942 — at the time of the breakthrough battle of Stalingrad — came the first distinction between the "Aryans" and the Jews: the Aryans were allowed to receive packages. The summer of 1942 was a period in which the work area of Birkenau knew absolutely no hunger, while twenty meters to the right, and two hundred diagonally across, forty thousand Hungarian-Jewish women died of hunger.

In order to make it difficult for prisoners to escape, three times a day, at first, Appels took place, assemblies of all the prisoners, the aim of which was to check on the status quo. The Appels (the first, at four or five o'clock in the morning; the second at noon; and the third, about seven in the evening) were held according to Block, and, when the camp first opened, lasted from forty-five minutes to forty-eight hours, in the later period from twenty-minutes to several hours. The *Blockführers*, after arranging and straightening their group, gave the command, "Attention! Caps off!" (the same command in a snowstorm as in a heat wave), and they reported the number to the *Blockführer*, who, after checking a few Blocks, reported it to the *Raportführer*. Only after that came the command, "Hats on! At ease!" A successful Appel ended with this. If, however, something didn't tally, something didn't *schtimmt* — jibe — as reported, they counted a second time, sometimes several times, and waited for the Kommandos who were late. In such cases, the Appel lasted several hours. For example, in the fall of 1941, the Appel regularly ended when it was completely dark at nine or ten o'clock. If someone was still missing, it meant that he had escaped, or, as often happened, he had been miscounted, and we stood for the whole night in order to march out to work the next day without having been given food. The longest Appel in Auschwitz (1940) lasted forty-eight hours, which means that several thousand people stood completely still outside in orderly rows. Several hundred people fell to the ground on that occasion.

For escapes, collective responsibility was introduced. If the escapee was caught, he was murdered on the spot, or in the camp; it more rarely resulted in execution by firing squad, or hanging, in the later periods. Before an execution, the condemned, dressed in a clown's costume, walked around the camp several times, beating loudly on a drum. Above him was carried a sign, "Hurrah! Hurrah! I am here again!" If, however, they just brought the body back, then it was exhibited, tied to a pole or propped up with spades, by the gate under an appropriate sign, didactic in meaning. If the escapee was not caught, then ten people, chosen by the Kommandant at random from among the prisoners occupying the same Block as the escapee, were hanged. I was present twice at these selections. Two of my neighbors, young and healthy people, were taken. Then, in addition to the colleagues, the Kapo of the Kommando and the group leader were hanged. When that didn't help and escapes continued, they began to bring in and hang the escapee's closest family: his parents, wife, sisters, brothers. Only in the last period was the punishment for escape reduced and limited to beatings and the penal company; in practice, however, the beating led directly to the crematorium.

For breaking camp rules, slowness at work, lack of energy at drill, talking at work, or else a reckless loud word on the Block, the prisoners were punished immediately with beatings by the SS men, *Blockführers*, Kapos, or group leaders, or else reported to the camp Kommandant. The beatings varied: a blow to the face with a fist; a kick in the stomach or groin; a strike with a switch across the back; but also crushing blows with a pole; the knocking out of teeth; the breaking of ribs; the cracking open of heads. Some trained themselves to beat so that they could kill a man with a single blow.

At the Appel, obviously, to explain yourself without authority, or to present your case, led either to corporal punishment (from ten to a hundred lashes, administered by the ordinary SS or one of the officers), or to punishment on the stake. That punishment consisted of tying the hands of the condemned behind his back and hanging him with handcuffs to a gallows. The best-exercised man might endure this position for a few minutes, after which the muscles weakened and the shoulders, dislocated from their sockets, slowly turned above the head. The tortured man fainted, of course; he was then lowered, water was poured over him, and he was beaten until he regained consciousness, and, then, he was hanged again. The third punishment, was to be sent to the *SK*, the penal company, where there was particular rigor; the *Blockführer* and the Kapo were specially chosen, and the work correspondingly arduous, often lasted longer than in the rest of the camp. At the beginning of Auschwitz, the life of a man in the penal company did not last longer than one month. They say that there was a custom in the first years of the penal company of hanging a noose in the doors of the Block after the evening Appel, and prisoners voluntarily hanged themselves while the whole Block sang in chorus, "*Góralu, czy ci nie zal* — Moutaineer, aren't you sorry?" There was always a crowd by the noose.

The punishment preliminary to the penal company, other than beating, was the so-called bunker, a cement cage 30 x 50 x 200 in which the prisoners were locked — whether after work for one night, or continuously for several months — and spent the whole time in one position without moving.

There was no gradation of crime. Hanging for a loaf of bread and for attempted escape; punishment with the bunker for diamonds and for collusion with the SS men; the *SK* was given for a piece of worn blanket used to wrap the feet, or for lighting a cigarette during work.

A separate element of camp life was the transports of Jews from the whole of Europe to the gas. Old people, children, pregnant women, the sick, mothers, and children were gassed; the healthy and the young, on the other hand, went into the camp.

It also happened, however, that whole transports wandered immediately and without selection to the chimney (among them many transports of Hungarian Jews). Completely inexplicable, but nonetheless true, is the history of the transports from Theresienstadt which, after a six-month stay in the camp, were completely annihilated in a single night. It was then that the Kommandant of Birkenau, Schwarz Hubert, sent his lover to the gas chamber, and, yet, it is said, he loved her very much. And although the Germans stressed the difference between the Aryans and the Jews very strongly, one must not assume that a quick "humanitarian" death was an exclusively Jewish privilege. Polish transports also met their end in the gas chambers. I know the fate of a certain transport from the Lublin area, around one and a half thousand people, that arrived and perished on one dark winter night (1942–43).

The Jewish transports brought with them great wealth. Gold, diamonds, clothes, food. Some of these things sneaked into the camp through the well-known system of organization, saving — what a paradox — many people from death through starvation. Some of the prisoners grew enormously rich by burying their acquired treasure in the earth.

Above all, however, the SS men were the ones who grew rich. There was not a single one among them who didn't profit from the gassed. They stole directly on the ramp; they stole at the crematorium; they stole from the Effects; they stole stolen goods, too — from prisoners. They bought with vodka, with newspapers, with leniency, and by turning their eyes away. They sent their families hundreds of thousands of marks and foreign currency, scores of watches, kilos of gold, and dozens of diamonds. Their wives, their mothers, and their children wore, and still wear, the underwear and clothing of people who had been gassed; ate, and still eat, bread bought with money stolen from them, with gold teeth extracted from them.

However, neither theft, nor lovers recruited from among imprisoned women, nor the selling of vodka and news brought the SS man and the prisoner closer to each other. On the "human" level (the administrative one), when it came to organizing, functions, camp intrigue, or women, the relationship could be trusting, even friendly. On more than one occasion, the SS man made possible some camp collusion for a prisoner, carried a letter, or gave news from above. At the same time, however, when it was a matter of the "divine" order (the political one), of a question of politics, of one step taken beyond the line of guards, of gassing a lover — the SS man would shoot his administrative friend without hesitation and would murder the woman. Murdering, stealing, and peddling, the SS man never stepped beyond the bounds of his mission or neglected his duty. He committed evil and, with an unusual knowledge of human psychology, knew how to blame it on others.

The prisoner who colluded with the SS, on the other hand, had only one desire: freedom and peace. An equally dominant feeling was the desire to avenge the dead and the living.

There are many camp secrets that will never be revealed. Those who died of hunger, the strangled, those killed with a club, will never speak. The millions from the gas chambers will not give their impressions. They will not express their amazement that this — is the truth. A truth in which they did not believe even up to the last moment on the threshold of the *Gaskammer*. The descriptions of writers will be regarded as poetic license, as calumny. But even the living don't know everything. You didn't impart news about the camp; to do so threatened death. Everyone had to acquire knowledge about the Lager for himself. Thousands of prisoners don't know the names of the camp's Kommandants or *Blockführers*. Thousands of them don't know the behind-the-scenes parts of the camp. They know only the nameless official scenario: gas, work, horrendous fatigue, hunger, beatings, rain and snow, disease, and, again, the gas. They know lice, fleas, bugs. They know boils, phlegmon and bloody dysentery.

A smaller number, whether because of the position they occupied, or because of the long time they spent there, know many aspects of the camp. They know names and facts, numbers by heart; they remember the faces of the murdered and of the murderers. For years, they stared at the faces of the SS men. They had to build with their own hands the wooden horse stables in which they lived, surround them with electrified wire, erect crematoria. With their own arms they carried the corpses of their friends. They stood in selections.

There is no exaggeration in what they say.

And there isn't a single German town by which a camp wasn't built. There isn't a single camp in which people were not killed. This earth isn't German earth because in it lie the people murdered by them.

Let time turn back so that those who do not believe might enter through the gates of the camp at Birkenau, see with their own eyes Lager Five, Mauthausen, Neuengamme, Majdanek . . .

Let them question the people from the gas chambers and the lime pits. The gassed, the shot, and the dead from hunger.

And then let them try to ask for mercy for the Germans.

HOMO SAPIENS
AND ANIMAL

The term *muzulman*, denoting a frail, hungry human, depleted to the edge of his physical limits, arose in concentration camp Auschwitz and spread from there to other camps. The term arose from the similarity between the movements that the weak and notoriously frozen prisoners made to warm themselves and the monotonous swaying of, precisely, the muslims at prayer.

The muzulman's mentality is quite different from that of a normal person. Out of all the interests a formerly intelligent "civilian" had, there remains only one: food. To eat, swallow, stuff your stomach — it doesn't matter what with or at what cost. I saw barrels of soup out of which seconds were being given; to restore order, the Kapos beat everybody, including, for the fun of it, those receiving soup. The muzulmen willingly paid for half a bowl of soup with a broken nose, a torn ear, or several bruises. I saw how the crowd fighting for access to the barrel knocked it over and gathered drops of soup out of the gutter with trembling hands.

The muzulman's second characteristic is fear. Fear — in fact, a justifiable fear — of the SS man, the Kapo, the Block Elder, of every person who looks healthy, of a stronger muzulman. Out of this fear arises a hatred for everything that lives, that can threaten or consume his food. Every muzulman who could would murder his neighbor. The hatred and determination leads to macabre scenes: two muzulmen lie on the ground; they are so exhausted that it's only from time to time that one of them lunges at the other and strikes him with the bowl he holds in his hand. Between them, a couple of spoonfuls of spilled soup. They are fighting only about licking the valuable drops that were spilled during a brawl.

The muzulman isn't a human being; he's an animal who is ready to give his life and his freedom for a rotting turnip.

In the four years I spent in the camps, mixing with people from many nations and of all social classes, I never met any who, in that physical state, thought or behaved differently.

* * *

. . . I knew that I was a muzulman but I had not realized I was quite as bad as that. After a six-month illness, several illnesses actually, during which both the doctors and my colleagues in the neighboring bed tried to convince me I'd die, I was transferred to the Block known as convalescence.

After the "paradise" of the hospital, it was terrible. Fifty of us lay on straw mattresses that covered the whole floor of a not very large room. We could lie only on our sides, all of us facing the same way, and we could turn only in unison with our companions. Something was hurting everyone; everyone had inflamed, open wounds. But we could lie down and that was good. After two weeks, however, I was released; I was declared well and transferred to a working Block. I weighed forty kilos and felt as good as I weighed.

I was transferred to the same working Block I had been in before my illness. The Block was the same, but the people were different. The clerk, slender and brown-haired, sat at the table taking down personal data from the *Zuganger*, the new arrivals on his Block. He stared at me intently.

"You . . . lousy dog, why aren't you shaved?" he asked through clenched teeth as he gnawed his pencil.

Of course, I made a mistake: I started to explain. I reported that in the hospital Blocks they only shave once a week, and unfortunately four days had elapsed since the last time. The clerk leaped from the table and came up to me. Amid a barrage of horrendous curses, I learned what he, *Schreiber* Stefan Wierzbica, thought about the hospital, muzulmen, useless animals and, then — then I saw only that my right ear was on my left, my nose was broken, the stove was standing on the ceiling and everything was swirling at an ever-increasing speed. Had some merciful supervisor not thrown me out into the corridor by means of a deft kick to my stomach, my camp career would have come to an end. After I had washed and been shaved, I had to report back to the terrible *Vertreter*.

On the following day, I went out in a Kommando. Immediately after the morning Appel, when the shout came: *Arbeits Kommando formieren* — Work details assemble! — pushed and shoved, I pressed through to the gong where the *Arbeitsdienst* was assigning "appropriate" Kommandos. Along the way, of course, I caught several kicks and blows from the Kapos and Block Elders who were beating everything in their way in order to hasten the assembling and to create empty paths through the seething crowds. They had already taken all the stronger and healthier ones — a veritable trade in prisoners — and only a few of us were left, when a tall young Kapo arrived, breathlessly reporting that he needed two men. Without asking very much, he grabbed me and another weakling and started to run back, with us following behind him. We fell after a few paces, and the Kapo picked us up by our collars like two large chickens and dragged us to the Kommando. The orchestra played a march, and the division moved in the direction of the gate. I fell out of step, I couldn't keep up, and I was altogether very unhappy. It took a couple of well-aimed kicks from the *Vorarbeiter* to bring me back into line.

On the other side of the gate, it was possible to communicate in a whisper with colleagues in the same row. I had gotten into the *Holzhof*, to chop down and saw wood for fuel — a muzulman Kommando but comparatively gentle and good. Chopping was out of the question: I couldn't lift the ax, never mind hit with it. We cut old telegraph poles with a lumberman's ax. After a few days, the wounds on my leg opened again. The pain was unbearable. It is very hard after lying down for six months to stand in one place for twelve hours at work. I very cleverly threw the chopped blocks of wood around me, and stood one, about the height of a stool, in such a way as to be able to lean my knee against it. When somebody dangerous appeared on the horizon, which was always carefully guarded, all I had to do was stand up normally and the Block fell over, arousing no suspicions by its position. But one day, the Kapo came up from behind, saw my crutch, kicked me in the appropriate place and added:

"I understand, but you know it's not allowed. And if it's not allowed, that means it's not allowed."

He was a good guy, even though he was German — he didn't report me and he didn't beat me. And he could have killed me, after all. It was worse with the chamomile. Wild chamomile grew by the fence. I picked it and ate it raw; it was quite good. My group leader saw me and started to blackmail me. I preferred to give him the portion of bread he demanded than lay myself open to a report, the bunker, and the penal company. It was a good Kommando, but, unfortunately, the woodcutters who had worked in it came back from the hospital and I had to leave it.

I was given a different assignment. I got into the beet-weeding Kommando. The work was hard, but not the worst. We marched for three or four kilometers beyond the camp and then we were divided in the fields. A group took up the entire width of the field; everyone got one row of beets to weed. We moved forward, we were allowed to squat or "even" kneel on one knee pulling weeds and grass and spacing the beets thirty centimeters apart. If somebody left a weed, or pulled out too many beets, he was regarded as a saboteur and the Kapo beat him with whatever came to hand. The same thing with the ones who were slow. The good part of the work was that when the guard's back was turned we could take the opportunity to eat a sorrel plant or a young beetroot. Unfortunately, after a few days of this good work, an accident happened — with terrible results. Next to the field in which we were weeding the aforesaid beets ran a railway line, and along that railway line masses of trains often moved. Once, when a train carrying wounded German soldiers drove by, a few of us expressed our pleasure at the sight a little too obviously. Two hundred prisoners were immediately transferred to the penal company (only a few of them survived the camp), and the rest were left to work in a punishment Kommando.

In the morning, we went to work at a run. In the evening we returned to the camp at a run. The edges of the fields smelled of approaching summer. Birds flew across the azure sky. I twisted my aching feet in the hot wooden clogs and thought that I would not live through the day. Because how was it possible to live through it when an SS man with the handle of a spade in his hand was walking slowly along the rows? I know what will happen: he's going to beat everyone, one after the other, on the back, on the buttocks, on the shoulders, on the head. If a beaten man hissed or moaned, or tried to bend down, the SS man hit to kill, and if a prisoner was too tough and didn't die immediately, the SS man called the Kapo. They would drag him to the side, into the rye, and then his body would be placed very neatly by the side of the road along which we returned to the camp. It usually happened that the group leader, a Gypsy, held the man while the SS man beat. The Gypsy grabbed the prisoner by the throat and it was the prisoner's fault if the Gypsy strangled him. Several people were finished off in this fashion every day. It was not a pleasant Kommando.

I knelt, bent over the furrow, and out of the corner of my eye saw the SS man's silhouette. He was approaching me. At regular intervals, I hear the regular sounds of beatings. Suddenly, the hissing of the beaten, and the rhythm is lost: a tempest of blows descends. The beaten man moans out loud and without hope: he has lost. The

SS man walks on, drawing ever closer to me. I know that one mustn't move or look around, because that will make it worse. I stay hunched over; a century of seconds goes by. I lean to the left, just a little, so that he won't notice — perhaps I'll protect my left shoulder blade, which hurts terribly from yesterday's beating. At last — the swish of the stick — just don't hiss, just don't let him hit on the nape of the neck. I got it on the back — on the spine to be exact. He must have broken my vertebra, but at least the thick wooden handle of the spade broke. I didn't hiss.

"Damned swine!" the SS man muttered characteristically, and with regret for his broken club.

And so it went several times a day, day after day, for long weeks. Coming back to the camp for dinner and for the night, we carried with us the bodies of our murdered colleagues. It really wasn't a pleasant Kommando.

But after a month, the camp Kommandant grew interested in the Kommando. Something had reached his ears about the weeding of beets. Perhaps he recognized that the punishment for joy at the sight of carved-up Germans had been exacted; perhaps he had quarrelled with the *Kommandoführer*, for whatever reason, the instructions changed and the people changed. A new SS man arrived on the following day, new guards. The *Kommandoführer* summoned the Gypsy and, pointing to the weed basket that lay several meters on the other side of the sentinels guarding us, ordered him to fetch it. The Gypsy hesitated, but seeing a threatening gleam in the SS man's eyes, went. We all watched him: we knew what would follow. When the Gypsy bent down for the basket, the SS man made a sign to the guard. The guard took aim and brought to the ground an "escaping" prisoner.

That day we returned to the camp carrying only one corpse.

I AM AFRAID
OF NIGHT

Practically every prisoner going through the changing fortunes of the camp experienced a critical moment when no hope of survival remained, and his body, diseased and weakened by work, refused to cooperate. For the average prisoner such a moment usually arrived within a few weeks of arriving in the camp and often ended in suicide at the wires or "normal" death in the Block, at work, in the hospital.

Such a night was not the fleeting night of an individual man. This night was the eternal night of tens and hundreds of thousands of people.

I am truly afraid of night and all afternoon I await it with mounting dread. How I envy those who are able to sleep and not see its nightmares. For me, night is a sleepless agony, a feverish delirium on a hard, disgusting bunk on which after a minute every position becomes unbearable, and my aching flesh, and the narrowness of the straw mattress, allow no movement. But the worst are the fleas. I can feel thousands of them crawling over me. The stinging bites are like the pricks of red-hot needles. They demand tremendous effort, a constant flexing of every muscle. I try to bend my legs; to pull them out from under the heap of legs belonging to my companions; to protect them with my arms. I scratch them with my rough palms, I feel relief, an easing of tension, but now they are stinging me on the face, the neck, the chest. I direct my hands quite automatically to where the itching is most annoying. The insane battle with the fleas goes on endlessly. Sometimes it seems to me that I won't be able to endure it anymore, that I'll go mad; I want to scream, cry, ask someone. I go numb; I haven't the strength to move any more. My head drops onto the hard beam off which a scrap of blanket has fallen. I no longer hear the rattle of the Dutchman dying next to me; has he stopped dying? I don't feel the sharp, wrenching pain in my leg; I move my palm along my shin: it's still there. To sleep. Nothing but sleep. I haven't slept a night in two weeks. Suddenly, a bite on the lip forces me back into consciousness. Sand and rubbish rattle, and the wood full of rusty nails from the top planks of the bunk squeaks. How do I know, I wonder, that the nails are rusted? A foot moves over the edge, terribly thin and covered with scabs, and, rummaging uncertainly in the air, seeks a resting place. I look at it with disgust; I feel, I know, that at any minute it will step on my face. Damned Greek! Attention! Ah! I grab it with my hands; I pull it with hatred. Curses fall from above and another foot steps on my head. I beat blindly behind me with my fists; I want to topple him, to throw him down. Aloysha, sleeping beside me, wakes up and starts to swear:

"*Malczi, bladzki Palak!* Let me sleep!"

The Greek who is clutching onto the top bunk is kicking and stepping on us, unable to find the plank. He slips on the Dutchman's face, which is covered with spit and foam, he hits Aloysha in the nose with his foot, and, finally, captured by him crashes down onto the cement. Exhausted, I again fall into numbness, into a feverish sleep filled with nightmares. I see the Greek crawling toward me holding his broken-off, bony foot in his hand; I see hatred shining in his eyes. I know that he wants to kill me. He approaches slowly, he extends his huge, clawlike hand and gropes blindly for my head. His eyes glisten hypnotically; I can't move. My heart leaps into my throat, his paw feels my head and squeezes me by the throat, strangles, strangles. I am out of breath, a sharp pain pierces my chest. My heart beats like mad, I catch my breath sporadically; so this is it? This is death?

I force myself to open my eyes. The Greek's hideous paw isn't there, but my heart beats quickly, so quickly . . . my heart? No, someone is running over me. No, it's me running, fast, fast, as long as it's faster, as long as I run farther away, don't trip, don't stop; to stop means it's the end. But why is my heart pounding like this? Perhaps I'll try to sit down, to lift myself up, up there, where the air is clean and cool. I lift my head slowly; it's so heavy, so hot; what can I do about it? I'll ask the Dutchman, perhaps he'll hold it for me.

"*Kamerad, Kamerad!*"

Is he asleep? Perhaps he won't be angry if I rest my head on his chest? I grab him with my hand:

"*Kamerad! Kamerad!*"

His hand falls useless onto my face. It's cold and cools my burning forehead nicely. Carefully, so as not to waken the Dutchman, I lay it under my head. Oh, how comfortable it is: perhaps I'll fall asleep at last? But what is it that I need to remember, desperately, desperately? My heart beats nervously, helplessly; if it stops, I won't be able to remember. I know! I'm thirsty.

"Nachtwache! Water!"

I shout. I shout in a hoarse whisper. Somewhere, far off, at the other end of the corridor, the night watchman is sitting cooking something on the stove — what is he cooking? I know, tea with lemon for me. He'll bring it to me in a moment for sure, but first, he has to brew it and sweeten it. . . .

Slowly consciousness returns, and with it, feeling, pain, fleas. I rub my itching skin with my palm and come upon something sticky. Yes, it's pus. It has seeped through the paper bandages, and a stream of thick, putrid stuff is flowing down my leg. And I can't have it rebandaged until the day after tomorrow. The day after tomorrow will probably be too late. This is the last moment. Just one more hour or two and I will be lying as peacefully as this Dutchman. I just don't want them to drag me onto the truck through the mud. It's disgusting. . . .

A terrible thirst extinguishes all thoughts. I grope for the bottle that Aloysha usually hides under his head. I know that he'll kill me if he catches me, but it's all the same now anyway. It's here! Slowly, slowly, I drag it toward me. Carefully, I open it under the blanket and sip the warm, sickly drink in little gulps to the end. I throw the bottle blindly onto the lower bunk. It breaks with a crash against the brick walls between the bunks. Suddenly, a yelp of curses and swear words bursts like a thunderbolt out of the gloomy, dumb silence. The *Nachtwache* runs up and beats those who are fighting on the lower bunk with a hot poker.

"Ruhe, verfluchte Schweine," he curses in German.

My neighbor raises his head and rummages uneasily under the blanket.

"Aloysha, Aloysha, listen, they stole your bottle, and now they're fighting over it underneath us! Go, get it back!"

"Hold your trap, muzulman," shouts the *Nachtwache* running up with the poker. A torrent of blows falls onto the Russian. Aloysha hides himself under the blanket and curses in quiet.

"Ja jemu sawtra pakazu! A ty czemu mienia pierwej nie skazal? Ach ty durny, durny, i wady niet i butelki nie ma. Czortowa zizn."

A deadly silence descends again. The silent moans seep into it as into a huge, black sponge.

Clutching onto the bunks with their hands, the sick drag themselves to the toilet. They trip on others who are lying on the cement. I have to last until morning. Kolka will come in the morning and

24

carry me there on his back. I can't go there by myself; I'd rather give him a piece of bread than end up under the bunk where they throw the filthy *Durchfall*. No, I don't want to die like that. Oh, God, when will this terrible night end? Millions of fleas crawl along my flesh, burrow into my flesh, my heart is pounding, burning like a glowing coal. Let it stop beating; it's enough, enough. . . .

THE FIFTH HUNDRED

The order came from above: "Annihilation through work," and in the concentration camps work became an excellent supplement to hunger and beatings. The Bauhof *— the warehouse for building materials — was one of the many hard Kommandos in Auschwitz. The fifth hundred is a memoir about that Kommando. It provides a picture of the work performed by most of the prisoners in the camp. Those of them who survived it, got into a different and better work group and sometimes only saw from afar the work of the "newcomers" at the spade and the pickax.*

Schieben, schieben, feste schieben!

Chanted in a *Kapo*'s hoarse voice, German phrases cleave deep in the memory — for the rest of one's life.

Schieben, schieben, feste schieben!

The shouts, now closer, now farther away — repeated by group leaders armed with clubs — fly by, torn by the gusty wind, which rushes in an icy stream down the length of the train. How difficult it is for the hundred hungry and frozen people to move the heavily loaded train. The wagons are slippery, the evil-smelling boxcars stand as though frozen to the tracks. Already the shouts from the front, which set the rhythm of the work, change into a terrible torrent of curses, thuds from clubs hitting against human flesh, and suppressed moans.

In spite of myself, I lean farther down, rest my other hand against an iron screw that is sticking out through the covering of the train and, by bending my body, try as well as I can to feign effort. I am careful to lower my head as deeply as I can between my shoulders. When he strikes with the club, he'll get my shoulders, not my head. The din from the front draws closer. Buffeted by a feverish effort, the privates of the wagons start clanging. The crashing of the buffers moves rearward, returning in a fierce, metallic echo. Then it dies down. Nothing.

Behind me, I can feel the breath of the man standing next to me. He's not pushing either. I'm sure. No one's pushing. And the train is standing still.

Schieben, schieben, feste schieben!

A couple of SS men run up, kicking and beating in all directions with their fists. The group leaders club the bent backs with renewed energy. They possess the power of life and death over twenty people. And they know how easy it is to lose it. They know how easy it is to become a hungry muzulman again and how much hands ache from cold metal in the frost and the rain. They know it is better to beat than to be beaten. The crazed-with-rage shriek of the Kapo, however, lords it over all. It doesn't matter whether you are honestly pushing, or pretending. The Kapo has been a slave for years, and now that he's landed on top, he walks the length of the wagons beating everyone in turn, without exception.

The train vibrates again. Slowly, slowly, the wagons start to roll onto the siding at the *Bauhof*.

Karol, a companion from my bunk, is walking in front of me. He's heavily bent over, and he's kicking the gravel up with his feet. He really is pushing. My muscles tense with anticipation, fear paralyses thought. Out of the corner of my eye, I see the dark figure of the Kapo emerging from behind the wagon. He raises the hand holding the club. Karol bends over as though he wants to run away. He doesn't pass him by. Now me.

Kapo Kurt!

The shout that has been passed from mouth to mouth reaches me together with a hoarse scream: *"Kommt schon!"* and, repeated, moves away from me.

A release of tension. My knees shake. I was lucky. I look around carefully, hide my hands in my overly long sleeves. I walk with my side plastered to the wagon. I can't stand the feel of the frozen iron anymore.

"Roll call!"

Stumbling over the stones, I run down the embankment, spotting the group leader on the road, his hand raised, calling his people.

"Fifth hundred, third group, *Antreten*, damn you!"

I want to hide in the middle of the row where it's safest. There are five people in front of us already, but the two in the middle are swaying on their feet and holding on tight to those next to them. I pull one of them back, Karol seizes the other, and we jump into their places. The group leader who is counting throws himself in our direction:

"Dołaczyć, pokryć, you Schweinehunde!" I don't look behind me, but I can hear him beating heads.

"Stand up when I count you damned *muzulman!*"

He counts us. We move back again to the end of the train. We are to unload a wagon of bricks.

"*Dali, dali, los,* quickly."

"Look how he thumped me," Karol complains, showing me the bloody lump on his head.

"What can you do about it; his time will come," I reply, blowing into my hands. We are standing by the wagon. A couple of stronger people throw themselves at the doors and open them with a clang of the bolt and a grinding of rusty metal. They scramble inside. We have to carry. Oh, if just for once I could climb inside! It's easier to be handing it out.

"You, Karol, lift me up onto the edge."

I catch onto the cold railing and scramble up. Through the open door of the hut attached to the wagon, I notice a crust of bread lying on the floor. My hand moves quicker than thought, but from below I can hear a whisper:

"Get down, a Green is coming!"

I waiver. Perhaps, I'll have time to cross the surface and get inside?

"Hurry up!"

Slipping on the muddy steps of the wagon in my wooden clogs I slide onto the ground.

"Show me what you've got."

So he noticed! Reluctantly, I show him my find. I give him a crust. He jams it in his mouth and looks at the rest greedily. He's stronger than I am. I divide it all in half. It comes to three crusts and a little piece each. I let him choose, and at the last minute notice that the pieces are uneven. He immediately sees this, and takes the bigger one. Bastard! A piece of brick breaks with a thud against the metal of the wagon right next to us. We jump away and cower, not even looking to see who was throwing it at us. Curses rain down on us from the neighboring wagon.

Our group makes a chain handing bricks out of the wagon right to the top of an enormous pile behind the road. I run to the end, to that pile. Someone on the road kicks me; I don't look to see, maybe it's the group leader? I stop only when I get to the base of the pile. I climb up it. The sharp wind goes right through me at the top. I take the bricks I'm handed and arrange the weird fire-clay cubes on the heap. I arrange row after row.

"What do they need these fireproof bricks for?" I don't know.

They make a dry, bricky sound as I arrange them higher and higher, creating a barrier on the side facing the road. It's cold here, but it's not too bad. There are lots of holes and cracks between the bricks that can't be seen from below. At one point, I take a chance, and, when those who are handing them up can't see, I squat in a deep crevice behind my barrier. It's quiet and peaceful here. I can hardly hear the distant shouts from the wagons and the muffled sound of the bricks being arranged. I warm my frozen hands in my pockets and fondle the crumbs of dry bread that I am about to eat. I chew them for a long time and deliberately, and then I turn my pockets inside out and carefully pick out the tiniest crumbs. The sound of the bricks from behind the barrier grows clearer. As usual, the muzulmen are talking about food; they don't know how to think about anything else.

"So, councillor, a little coffee with cream for breakfast?"

"Cocoa, cocoa, dear sir, and a roll with caviar, but only red caviar! And thick with butter . . ."

"For me, a goose wing, and something spicey with it . . ."

"Who on earth eats goose for breakfast?"

No, there's nothing left in my pockets. Karol had to notice that! Well, it's better to live on good terms with him. He speaks German. He's the soup distributor's assistant. Maybe he'll give me some peelings again? Yes, it's Tuesday today, there should be potatoes. And for the portion of *Zulag*, the supplement for the good workers? Perhaps, I could buy potatoes for half a piece? They should give five or six, and if they're small ones, seven. I'd eat them with margarine, bread and marmalade, and kielbasa to finish. But, perhaps, it would be better to buy gloves? The Ukrainian from the second bunk is selling them cheap, for half a *Zulag*, double ones, they won't rip quickly. Where did he get them from? He probably stole them. . . . But he's got something to eat. . . . And maybe if I . . .

It's cold when you're not moving. Through the gap, I can see the sky, pale with frost. Somewhere, low over the horizon, the sun spills over in a misty stain, and on the other side a gray curtain of snowy clouds moves. What time is it? Probably around ten. Six hours left.

Through the hole in the bricks on the right-hand side, I can see the red Blocks being built on *Neubau*. A huge crane lifts wagons of stuff every few minutes and drops it on the building. White smoke billows out of the train's engine car and freezes in the air in puffs, like beaten egg whites. The wind has abated, and a milky steam hangs for a long time over the ground before melting and soaking into the air. It would be nice to work on the locomotive. . . .

The lazy, mixed murmur of bricks being arranged grows fast and nervous. I should look out to see what's going on. I crawl out onto the surface with the bricks in my hand. Something really is happening. In the middle of the road, between us and the wagon, an SS man is kicking a Serb, who is lying on the ground, in the head and the stomach. Nearby, on a broken brick, stands the group leader, his mouth bloody. A hat is lying on the ground. He got it good.

The SS man stares at the Serb to make sure that he isn't moving, kicks him in the stomach again to make sure, and then turns to the group leader:

"You dumb dog, I'm going to teach you how to guard people so they don't ruin the materials! I'll give it to you for sabotaging!"

And once more, in the face . . .

"*Herr Rottenführer*, I told him, but he didn't listen . . ." Once more in the face.

"I'll give you a *Meldung*, I'll report you. *Numer?*"

Trembling, the group leader shows the number on his chest so it can be recorded.

"Are you German?"

"*Jawohl*. I'm a *Volksdeutsch*."

"You stinking swine, you're going to the *SK*! And now call the *Appel, aber los!*" We form ourselves into rows in silence. They're going to give it to us now. . . . The group leader, pale and bloody, runs from front to back counting us time and again. There should be twenty of us. Seventeen of us are standing there, one is lying down, there's the group leader — nineteen altogether.

"So, it doesn't tally? One has escaped, no?"

The SS man is whistling through his teeth and slowly moving his pistol from the side to the front.

"*Kapo Kurt*," he shouts and whistles again.

The group leader searches through his pockets feverishly for the cards with the numbers, and in a broken voice begins to shout out our numbers.

Suddenly, Karol steps out of the first five and, his cap in his hand, reports:

"*Herr Rottenführer*, I know where one of them is hiding. A Pole from my block, I know him!"

The huge lump with its dried blood shows up on Karol's shaved head.

"Where? Show us!"

Karol points with his hand to the pile of bricks.

"Go first!"

He goes first; the SS man, pistol in his hand, follows, and, far behind, the panting Kapo.

Karol climbs onto the pile with a sure step, and pointing to the barrier I had built, says:

"He hid in there, in that hole!"

I feel my heart starting to pound feverishly, and a thousand thoughts come into my mind. A dreadful fear chokes everything. . . . If the Kapo says that it's me, they'll beat me anyway. As through a fog, I watch the Kapo who, having climbed onto the top, is looking in the crevices. Below stands the silent SS man and Karol, straightened to attention.

"Kapo, he's there, he's there!"

A thin, bent figure emerges from behind the pile of bricks. The muzulman is holding by his hands his trousers, which are falling down, and he doesn't know what to do with himself. He wanted to retreat, but the Kapo's shout arrested him· "Stój!" He stands stupefied, trembling; his bony hand drops the trousers. Watery feces trickle down his thin white legs.

Kurt runs up to him, grabs him by the throat and starts to shake him. It seems as though his head is going to drop off at any minute, like a pear off a branch. . . .

Now they start on us. The former group leader gets fifteen strokes of the club. Karol takes his place. I avoid his gaze. Hide behind the others.

"Run! Run! Fast!"

Again, we unload the same wagon. But now we don't hand the bricks to one another. We carry them at a run onto the pile.

Time and again, a traffic jam forms by the doors. Everybody is rushing for the next load, just to avoid the club.

"Why are you standing there? Lazy pigs! I'll show you! You! Climb onto the wagon and throw the bricks down from above, understand? And you, catch them from below! But fast!" shouts Karol, hoarsely, interweaving the orders with German curses and chasing those standing by the wagon with his fists.

The Kapo looks on contented, dusting off his nicely pressed

trousers, which are covered with brick dust. Both of the SS men are smiling.

I can scarcely stand on my feet. When no one is looking, I press a completely bloody rag to my face. The blood keeps flowing out of my swollen, cut lips. I lick my teeth with my tongue. The top canine on the right moves like a piano key, the incisor, too, but a little less. How did it actually happen? I know that I was catching the bricks that were dropping from above. One of them must have hit against the wagon and, instead of dropping into my hands, fell on my face.

The sounds of a march reach us from afar, from the camp. We stand on the road between the *Bauhof* warehouses, waiting for the other Kommandos to pass by. I shake with cold and exhaustion. My cut lip stings in the frost. The pain rises and falls with the pulsation of my blood.

Next to us stands the column from the warehouse. Their faces fat and well fed, their clothes unbuttoned despite the cold, they joke and laugh in lowered voices. I look at them with hatred and envy. They move forward first. They are the first hundred Kommando; they don't carry the dead behind them. How I hate them! They will survive the camp.

I want to survive as well. I know I have to get myself out of the fifth hundred; I won't survive here.

Yes, my friend. Two days later, I dared a heroic step. I reported to the office as a sculptor. Notice that I had never held a chisel in my hand. But sculptors and painters were valued for their output in the camp. So they placed me in a better Kommando. When it transpired that I hadn't a clue about wood carving, they left me on the new Kommando as a carpenter's aid. I survived the worst of winter in the workshop, and then we moved to neighboring Birkenau to build a new camp. Spring came very early that year. By the end of February, the sun had completely melted the snow. But now we were no longer so afraid of the famous Auschwitz mud. Experts! Carpenters! We erected the barracks of the future hospital by the forest. It's true we had to walk through the mud to fetch bricks, but we had somewhere to warm up and dry off. Obviously, if there's enough wood, a fire can be lit. I warmed myself in the spring sun nailing tiles to the roof. I absorbed the rays as if they were food. It was good on the roof. From time to time, the wind carried the smell of the burning pyres to us.

The guard who stood on the tower all day in that abominable smoke swore at us terribly.

The beaten and driven transport column dragged along the road next to us churning the mud. Losing their wooden clogs in that mud, which was as thick as dough, the muzulmen each carried five yellow bricks from the distant ramp to the fourth crematorium which was being built in the woods. The fifth hundred from their Kommando gathered for the midday meal at the nearby, finished barracks. They left their bowls under the walls of that Block and piled their dead there. They often raised their heads and looked up at us sitting comfortably on the warm, dry roof.

I survived the camp and have retained a souvenir of the fifth hundred — a small scar.

Look — here!

I DON'T RECOMMEND
GETTING SICK

Auschwitz I, the recollections of a muzulman, 1942

In the first period of Auschwitz, the period of German victories on all fronts, only the odd individual survived the camp for more than a few weeks. Thousands perished almost instantly from bullets, phenol injections, the SS man's and the Kapo's club; died of cold or of heat, from the wind and the rain, from thirst and from contaminated water. To drink a mug of unboiled water meant dysentery; to scratch lice-bitten skin meant dying of phlegmon; to take one step out of line, to drop a spade, meant to perish under the club.

A score or so of people in the camp were well nourished. Thousands ate soup made out of turnips and nettles and dreamed of getting a refill.

There was a hospital in the camp. Thousands died on lice-filled straw mattresses in there, went to the "needle," or to the gas.

Only individuals returned cured to the camp Kommandos and, a few months later, went back again to the hospital.

The most fortunate remained in the hospital as "functionaries," as nurses, orderlies, clerks, and gained a hundred times greater chance of surviving the camp than their colleagues in the "Lager."

I am going to tell you what *ulcus cruris* is. *Cruris* sounds like the growl of a ferocious dog. In Polish, it is medically known as "an inflammation of the shank." Even without its scientific name, it would hurt in an ordinary human way. A lousy, the lousiest, wound under the sun, which doesn't heal for months, for years.

I left the *KB*, chopped wood and weeded beets, and the sores came back. The wounds reopened, covered with a very thin membrane. I don't know why. The slightest scratch, blow, rub is sufficient. A tiny scab forms, which instead of drying up, softens and bursts from the pus that collects underneath it. The pus and blood dry out in turn, forming a slightly bigger scale. And then that swells, enlarges, bursts. The wound grows bigger, and a tiny speck becomes the size of a coin. The swollen, red edges pull away to reveal an ever-larger surface. I saw sores ten centimeters wide encircling legs. I saw wounds on the thigh that could barely be covered with two hands.

One wound opened on the inside of my left ankle right along the surface of the bone. Another on my right tibia. The left one was especially painful. My leg throbbed horribly, the skin looked like an overblown balloon — shiny, dry, the slightest scratch creating a deep crack. It is strange that it still holds, doesn't explode and fall away like a useless, dirty old rag. The wound burns and itches, and becomes unbearable after a few hours of standing up at work. The pain can drive you crazy at the evening Appel. I make the most of every moment, and when no one is watching, I go down on one knee, ready to leap up again at the first sign of danger.

Even though the wound is unbearably painful, even though you can't walk, can't sleep, can't think, they don't admit you to the hospital for such trivia. So I go to have it dressed at the clinic and risk a lot in doing so — supper. Someone may notice that I have gone to the hospital, will give my number, take my portion. Or the *Stubedienst* won't give a latecomer his share. He'll tell the Block Elder that I am trying to get seconds, that I am a "rebellious pig," and beat me into mincemeat, like Cichocki, in whose Block I am, a few days ago. The pain is unbearable, however; I have to take the risk. I go to the clinic. The sick are ranged in two columns in rows of five, in classic camp manner, waiting hopelessly. The large group of "dressings" moves exceedingly slowly. But I know the hospital and all of its ways; I stand with the "outpatients"; there are only a few of them and they go in more quickly. They stand on less ceremony here with a sick stomach or pneumonia than with some ulcer that has to be dressed.

I finally make it inside the clinic and quickly get myself into the line of those waiting for dressings. I maneuver so as to get into the line of an orderly I know. Tired and crumpled, I stand in front of him and uncover my wound.

"You must be *Verrück!* crazy! You want a dressing for that little thing! Get out of here!"

"But it really and truly hurts" I stand my ground, argue.

Bored, he sticks a bit of plaster on my skin. After a week, he knows me well, and shouts from a distance, "You, shorty with the ulcer! Come here for a dressing!"

After that he starts to clean the ulcerated wound methodically and thoroughly. His intentions are good, but apart from pain, it has no positive results. It's better when he cauterizes it, even though that hurts like hell. To get the tissue to heal, he smears the edges of the wound with silver nitrate. Each touch of the cotton feels like a red-hot iron, so you can imagine what it's like when he runs a stick of hot nitrate across the wound. Sometimes it brings tears to my eyes. When it does, the *Pfleger* goes on cauterizing and says, "It's okay, Shorty, it'll pass. It hurts, but it'll pass."

For long hours after that, the wound burns horribly. Yes, the dressings are very painful; sometimes I don't get supper because of them, but it's a hundred times worse when I can't get in to have one. For the last three days, the Appels dragged on until late at night. And then, yesterday, there were no dressings because the *Pflegers* went on lice control to the blocks. Today, on the other hand, the *Blockführer* stopped me and I couldn't go. The old dressing had soaked through a long time ago. The bandage, which is paper, falls into shreds. The wound stinks hideously; my leg burns even when I'm resting at night. I have never removed the dressing, but this time I had to take the rotted bandage off. I removed the last piece of gauze and froze — bugs were crawling over the entire surface of the wound, which was about the size of two silver dollars. I wanted to run away, leave my disgusting, stinking leg behind. Actually, I couldn't see the wound at all. The whole of it was covered with fat, white grubs a few millimeters in size. I took them off with a scrap of paper. They fell on the floor, moved increasingly slowly; I think that they died immediately in the unfamiliar environment. I was astonished to see that they had cleaned the wound. It didn't, however, have any effect on its healing.

My legs bothered me more and more. I couldn't walk and was in too much pain at night to sleep. I lay tossing from side to side the whole night, falling asleep only toward morning, when I had to get up as the gong went off to begin a new day, a day even worse than the one that had gone before. I knew I couldn't last long, that I had to get myself into the hospital. Never mind the risk of a selection — I was going to die anyway. I had to go to hospital. That's why every day after the Appel I went with the sick Kommando, summoned to the doctor by the gong. The sick came running out of each Block, beaten, lame, covered with scabies. Because of my aching leg, I couldn't make it on time; it was always already full, and Bruno, the *Lagerältester*, kicked me away. He had too many weaklings and muzulmen there already, and, besides, tomorrow the Kommandos had to go out as normal — in their full contingents. I fought for myself, regardless, and, turned away one night, I reappeared the next. Bruno threw me out three times; the SS man on duty at the gong threw me out twice. Things were bad and getting worse. I was working now in the gardeners' Kommando that was known as the good one. The group leaders and cleverer gardeners stuffed themselves with cucumbers and tomatoes. Of the several-score prisoners chosen, as I had been, to work on the soil, only a few stole beets and stems of rhubarb. If one of them was caught, he got twenty-five lashes and was sent into the penal company, from which people rarely returned. On one occasion, a "thief" begged the Kapo and the SS man overseeing the Kommando on bended knee to let him stay with the gardeners. The Kapo made him squat, and placed six-inch nails under his knees. After three hours, they had worked themselves completely into the delinquent's flesh. So I contented myself with eating a few raw potatoes a day and, less often, beets or stalks of rhubarb.

We were levelling the ground for new plantings when one of the group leaders came up to us and shouted, "Hey! Which one of you is a gardener who knows how to plant seedlings — really knows?"

My palms were blistered from the spade; I kept falling over when I pushed the wheelbarrow; I had nothing to lose.

"I do, *Vorarbeiter!*"

A quick interrogation as to where I had worked, what I knew. I knew only one thing — to lie. I made up several gardening businesses, slung names of various localities around, and a minute later, carrying an enormous box of cabbages, wandered over to another part of the garden. I had once been a student at a polytechnic and, truth to tell, had been taught very little about planting. I knew how to distinguish between roots and leaves, and I knew that you had to shove them by one of their ends into the ground. The work was good, because you could kneel as you did it, and you could eat the seedlings. The little seedlings were very fragile and better for eating than the old stems. Cabbage was the tastiest of all, and one day I ate half a box of it.

After a few days of planting seedlings, my right knee, on which I kept kneeling, swelled, reddened, and hurt more and more. It wasn't that I couldn't kneel anymore; I couldn't even bend my leg. I examined it carefully and declared that it was an abscess, an ordinary boil, that everything would be all right in a couple of days. But I decided to try and exploit it — if they didn't want to take me into the hospital with a terrible ulcer, maybe they would with a bad knee. And again I drag myself to the sick *Raport* . . . The noncommissioned officer moves away from me in a decidedly nervous way, "It's erysipelas. Admit him at once! Get away from me! Off!"

Truth to tell, the doctor at the clinic screwed his face up with distaste declaring that it was an ordinary boil that could be cut without hospital care. However, an order was an order, and I wandered over to the surgical Block with a card made out: "Immediate surgery."

What a pleasure it was to find oneself in hospital! To be lying down next to a filthy colleague on a hard bed! To rest without being afraid, without fear, not having to wait for the gong, for the Block Elder, for the Kapo! The room, which stank with pus and creosol, seemed like the hallway to heaven. Rain patters against the window-panes; on the other side of the window people are getting soaked; far beyond the wires wagons are being pushed along the tracks. People are going to the gong and the Appel, and you are lying down and are as far, as far away from it as the imagination stretches. You can close your eyes and, in a half-sleep, dream about the times when we sped down roads together, lay in the sun, ran through the workshops of the polytechnic, always together, always happy. And later — it will be wonderful; when the guards have left the towers, we'll go back, ring the doorbell, everybody will be there, of course, waiting. . . .

But after a few days, the bed covered with a straw mattress as thin as a blanket begins to pinch. The dressings, which have not been changed for too long, stink. The wind coming in through windows opened for ventilation begins to blow through all the holes of the thin blanket. The tossing of the muzulman in bed next to you starts to bother you more and more. Pus drips from sodden bandages.

I was admitted on a Saturday. Saturday, Sunday, the only days of partial rest for the overworked staff. My boil, indifferent to holidays, burst. Three large craters opened up, pus flowed free. I squeezed it a little, gritted my teeth, and covered it with a piece of hard-won cigarette paper. On Monday, I hobbled over to the tiny clinic. They carefully and hygienically dressed my ulcer, but the knee — the doctor looked at my card.

"Idiots! What's there to cut? It burst all by itself you say? Splendid! There'll be less to deal with."

I became better and better off. I lay on the fourth ward where nurse Marian Wesołowski, whom I knew from my previous sicknesses, worked. Around noon, another nurse, the one from the clinic, came up to me. A short, stocky kid, he greeted me nicely, sat on the bed, and asked whether I would like some soup. Dear God, who wouldn't have wanted any old thing to eat, never mind soup! So he brought me a whole bowlful and, seeing how greedily I was eating, promised to give me something every day. I immediately tried to find out who he was, because I didn't remember the face. Józek Szyszczyński? No, I definitely don't know him. When he came on the following day, I set the matter straight even though the soup was wonderful. It turned out, of course, that he'd taken me for someone else, but "You're a muzulman and I brought it for you." He comes from near Skierniewic, which I know well, so we're practically neighbors.

I went to Józek for dressings. He was brutal, with no regard to pain, but very careful. I started to get better, revived, and began to worry. I went to Marian.

" I'm healing tragically fast, Marian."

"Ah, that's bad." The nurse was concerned. "They'll throw you back in the camp and you'll be finished off. You know what; go to the doctor, preferably to Zbożeń, because he's the head, say that you're willing to work, and you'll stay with us. We're short of *Pflegers* because a lot of them went over to the women's camp."

Zbożeń received me distrustfully, questioned me, and when I declared that I really did want to work no matter where, but preferably in the clinic, he told me to do a couple of dressings as a trial. I stood at the dressings station. As luck would have it, I got a sick man with a broken head. I washed it with hydrogen peroxide, put on a compress with the appropriate cream, and bandaged it correctly, like in the textbook. The second one had a boil on his buttock, the third, a nasty business in the crotch — normal clinic situations. Zbożeń watched in silence:

"All right. Where did you learn that?"

"Just from seeing it done. . . . I've read a bit."

"All right. What's your profession?"

"Automechanic," I replied carefully, admitting only to my position in the camp.

"All right. But if you're a chauffeur, I'm a porter," he spat out with fury.

But I stayed — and that was the most important thing. As a visible symbol of my position and power I stopped parading around in a shirt that was too short; I received wooden shoes and duck-cloth trousers.

That is how my nursing career started.

I O D I N E   A N D   P H E N O L

People died in the hospital. Their colleagues — doctors and nurses — bear part of the blame for that. The fault is theirs, even though it is a drop in the ocean compared to the crimes of the SS men which, rightly, weigh down this account. It is, however, a blame tragic in flavor. It is the fault of human pettiness and cowardliness.

Nothing in this account has been falsified: neither the characters nor the events. In this period, however, in contrast with this story, there was no washroom on the Block, and the sick had to go into the neighboring Block to wash.

I have trained myself to wake up a few minutes before the gong. I lie in total darkness curled up beneath the blanket, draw the warmth more tightly around me, and, half-asleep, half-awake, know I have to get up. At that moment, behind the black windowpanes against which white flakes of snow are beating horribly, the gong strikes increasingly loudly and quickly. The lamps in the neighboring Blocks go on like jack-o'-lanterns, and in the inky darkness the windowpane blazes yellow with the reflections of lanterns.

In the corridor a dull shuffle, shuffle, shuffle can be heard and then the sound of tap water. The sick are beginning to wash.

The stale smell of pus rises in the washroom. All the rooms, all the passageways, all the walls are permeated with this smell. The hospital's heavy air is filled to the brim with it. I stand in the washroom leaning against the wall, a persistent roar in my ears, as though sleep were a rushing river flowing out through me. Icy water trickles from the faucets. People crowd around them, pulling shirts off their backs, carefully rubbing water on face, head, neck, torso, extremities. There's nowhere to hang the shirts, so they hold them in their teeth. In this manner, they wash their bodies, except where there are bandages.

The crush grows heavier. They walked across the snow from the neighboring Block because they don't have a washroom there. They shake with cold, press their backs against each other to warm up.

Steam rises overhead; thick drops of water fall from the ceiling. The roaring in my head grows louder; my entire body feels painfully heavy. These nights, these nights . . . people crowd around, come nearer, nearer as if into my eyes. I no longer know what is sleep, what the persistent, nauseating smell of darkness, and what is people. Someone grabbed me, plastered me with something sticky and fell at my feet. Under me lay a man covered with wounds that looked like blue-brown stains in the dim light. Wet paper bandages covered with stinking discharge hung down in strips. His legs were violet, swollen like tree trunks. The left one was shattered to the bone. He raised his face twisted with pain:

"*Pfleger*, I'm not going to wash. I've got a bad leg."

"Fool, stop pretending. You use your leg to wash yourself?" someone at the faucet yelled back. Only then did I become fully conscious.

Rain mixed with snow and darkness falls relentlessly. Seen from above, the earth glistens like a wet road. The snow melts immediately. A penetrating damp draws in through the open windows.

The sick are very cold in bed under only one blanket. Their bodies shake; they have shiny blue lips and their faces are drawn from the cold.

Breakfast is given out — cold, stinking slops that pass for tea. Bowls of fluid wander from hand to hand, a few swigs each.

"A drink, a drink, for me   here, here . . . ," moan the feverish.

"You can't. Your legs will swell."

"Did you know, they're saying there'll be a transport from *KB* today, Jasiek?" Józek says, pouring ersatz coffee into bowls.

"Who and where?"

"Only Poles, apparently. A very bad transport."

"But not us? Not the hospital?"

"Precisely — nurses. But nothing's clear."

The floor — concrete, covered with water. A raw chill rises from it. Outside, the darkness is dispersing, and with it the persistent hospital smell. Sharp, fresh air pours in through the windows. But outside it's still darkness mixed with rain and snow. The lights on the wires glisten in the fog like enormous yolks. The darkness they guard begins to be peopled. It plucks people from everywhere, pulls them out of corners, chases them out of Blocks — black motionless cubes, illuminated windows shining here and there. You can't tell people apart, they swirl around in a mass, as though they had melted in snow and rain. They sway between the Blocks, come up to the light and fade into darkness. At last, the throng organizes itself more clearly and precisely, molds into quadrangles, moves restlessly for a little longer, and then freezes. The gong strikes yet again in the darkness, increasingly faster and clearer, until it vanishes into the sounds of an orchestra. The quadrangles of people sway and float out of the gate into the wintry wet darkness.

Time to eat the two pieces of bread left over from supper and go to the clinic.

The workday is starting.

Three hundred dressings a day. The clinic measures three-and-a-half by five meters. A table with creams, boxes of bandages, and instruments stands by one wall. Bandages, plaster, *sepso*, and instruments also lie under the table. Ten stools have been placed on the opposite side. At them, the doctors and nurses do the dressings. The operating table is under the window. Drops of damp drip from the windowsill.

The stench in the clinic gets worse. The pus of huge boils stinks; the heavy odor of artificial iodine acts like a disgusting, stifling narcotic.

One's back aches from bending over. Boils, tumors, furuncles, necrosis, frostbite. Everywhere — on limbs, on spine, on stomach, in armpits, between the legs. The old dressing into a barrel, smear the wound with cream, of course, bind it. The worst is necrosis. Here's the external part of the thigh: it runs through a whole gamut of colors from a vivid cold yellow through azure, green, violet all the way to black. I cut out the dead tissue, the sick man hisses with pain:

"Will it take long to heal? Because . . ."

"It'll take a while yet," I reply curtly.

"He'll soon have you cured," Józek offers from the stool.

Next. Next. The trash barrels are full of bandages; the pus in them smells. It's on the floor, on stools, on clothes.

The last dressing: a Jew with a fecal fistula. I help him lie down on the table, lift him carefully as though he were a leper. I cut the bandages off and expose the wound. Stench hits me right in the mouth. Someone in the corner wheezes, throws up violently.

In the middle of the stomach a spindle-shaped wound the size of a hand, and with inflamed edges, has opened. The epidermis is covered with boils. Rotted feces and the remains of food fill the whole wound and cover the stomach.

"The swine's still alive," one of the nurses said.

42

"He'll be dead in a couple of days. He's rotting all the way through," said another.

"Dering did it to him. He's sent more than one up the chimney."

"He made a career for himself doing that, and learned a bit about surgery. One muzulman less, one muzulman more, makes no difference," another concluded.

The sick man stares and moans out loud. I'm going to slap him in the face; I can't be more delicate than that. I wash the wound, clean the opening, which is as large as a dollar-piece, shunt the fecal hole straight into the intestine. Rinse, clean the edges, smear the skin with Vaseline. Then gauze, lignin, and bandage.

"Take him, I've had enough."

They look at me with pity and tolerance.

"He's for the gas anyway. Why kill yourself like this? How can you stand it?"

The gagging sickly smell of pus fills the clinic. My hands stink like they're not mine. Heaps of bloody bandages lie on the floor. Someone opened the window, and a wave of sharp, damp, fresh air blew in.

How can I stand it?

I look through the window. Rain mixed with snow falls relentlessly. A wind rises, blowing between the Blocks. Far beyond the camp, I can see people torn by the wind. They work hard, pushing wheelbarrows in front of them. They craw along like that, row after row. A wagon drives by pulled by people. The wheels get stuck in the mud. "Hey, get on with it!" they shout in chorus, and pull, lowering their heads way down to protect their faces from the wind and snow.

I can stand it.

Incisions now. Cutting through pus, boils; amputating frostbitten fingers. The operating table is in the center of the room; a big angry sterilizer gurgles and growls on the windowsill. Since the last time fish was fried in it, it "shoots" across your fingers because of a faulty insulator.

Everything is as normal. Dr. Kruczek comes in, nods his head, puts on a white coat, and says the time-honored words: "You, colleague, are going to do the dressings. Okay? Bring them in."

Everything is as usual: Józek brings in the sick man, Black gives the anesthetic, the doctor cuts, I dress the wound and take the still unconscious patient onto the ward. The test tube of ethyl chloride hisses, the drops soak noiselessly into the cotton wool, an over-whelming smell of anesthesia spreads through the clinic. Time and again the doctor whacks his lancet; pus sprays out mixed with blood. The tempo gets quicker, the line longer. A boil on the shoul-derblade, a tremendously swollen hand.

"On the table! Don't waste time! Hungarian anesthesia."

Black immediately presses the patient's lips with a towel; the doctor cuts once, twice; the sick man struggles, but it's all over. Lignin, gauze, bandage.

"Run to bed! Next!"

The food man sticks his head into the door of the clinic.

"Someone get the food; I've got too few people. Not even enough for twice."

"Black, you go, I'll do the anesthesia."

Next. Next. The tempo increases. There's no time to think. I can't keep up with the dressings.

"Faster, faster," the doctor hisses through his teeth. We've got to get through this stuff.

Józek throws a new patient deftly onto the table.

"Don't tie it. It's a waste of time."

"*Sepso! Sepso!*"

"Anesthesia! Faster, for God's sake!"

The sick man chokes under the mask, counts more and more slowly, more and more faintly.

"Eight . . . nine . . . nine . . ."

"Cut, he's ready."

"*Sepso*, damn you! *Sepso* first."

Józek splashes the patient with *sepso*, holding down the wound to be cut with his huge, rubber-gloved hands.

"He's not asleep. Careful."

"Quiet!"

Dr. Kruczek draws the lancet across an arm, blood spurts; the sick man screams with pain and tears off the mask, knocking the ether off the table with his feet.

"Damn it! That's a healthy arm! Hold him down!"

With my left hand I hold the patient down, squeeze the bottle of chloride in my left. Blood flows onto my clothes.

"Hold him," the doctor screams in rage, wildly gesticulating with his lancet. Józek chokes the sick man. Pours chloride straight onto his head. He's truly asleep now.

"Rub him with *sepso*, here, here!" The doctor himself rubs the area and cuts. Bright, clear blood spurts.

"He's healthy! Who put him down for an operation?" he yells furiously at me, throwing his lancet to the ground. I took off the mask; the sick man was regaining consciousness when the surgeon, still examining the patient, shouted happily, "It's here, it's here!" and taking the lancet off the ground shoved it into a huge purulence in the armpit. The patient leaped up with a scream, knocked the test tube of chloride out of my hand, and smashed the doctor in the face with his good hand. Józek grabbed him and pressed him to the table.

"Lie down, muzulman," he hissed through his teeth. "Jasiu tie him down, and apply the dressing."

On his way out of the room, the sick man raised his fist theatrically to the doctor, who was pale with fright:

"You . . . you . . . may you be damned . . . you treat people only with iodine." Józek burst out laughing.

"Don't complain, muzulman! A bit of iodine won't hurt you. But take care they don't rub you with phenol."

Rain mixed with snow falls outside the windows. Huge barrels of soup steam on the ward. From all the beds, poke voracious, pale, wasted faces with inflamed eyes. Carrying a bowlful of soup, I pass by their hard, jealous stares a second time. But I have to eat enough to have the strength to get through a whole day, carry a barrel of soup and tray of bread, take out the sick, and throw the dead out of bed. The barrels of soup are steaming, but I have to go out into the snow and rain to fetch medicine for tomorrow. A truck of medications from "Canada" is being unloaded at the pharmacy. These are the medicines brought in by Jews from all over Europe, and in the medicine there is gold and there is money. Kapos and Block Elders are standing around the truck. Guarding.

"Jasiu, we need medicine, and they won't give us any of these. Give me the suitcase and be careful."

"All right, I'm being careful."

Laden with both cases, Józek pushes the Block Elder and swears at him straight in the face:

"Get out of the way you bastard!"

The Block Elder grabs Józek by the throat; Józek starts scream-ing. A Kapo runs up, a fat nurse jumped off the truck, and a consider-able crowd gathers.

"They're trying to beat one of us!"

"Don't let him!"

"Shut your traps!"

Calmly and slowly I pull two enormous suitcases off the truck and stagger with them toward the Block. A worried Marian runs out of the door:

"What's going on?"

"They're beating Józek."

"For what?"

With a meaningful gesture, I point to the suitcases. He nods in an understanding manner and disappears into the crowd. After a while, pushing, pulling, and swearing, he yanks Józek out of the melée. Józek is dragging along packages from the pharmacy.

"Give me one," Marian says when they get to the Block. "They're too heavy for you."

"It's all right. But he wrote down my number. What'll happen?"

"Nothing. I'll get you out somehow."

"Take one from me, Marian, I don't think I'll be able to carry it up."

"Damn, they're heavy, but you chose well," he says weighing the case in his hand.

Rain mixed with snow falls outside the window. Inside, the sick are sitting on hastily arranged stools. They're wrapping themselves with their shirts, trembling with cold and terror. There are nineteen of them. They stare dumbly, extending their bandaged limbs.

"See Jasiek, another selection. Why?"

"As if you don't know. They announce such things here?"

"I'll go hide the cases, because the *Lagerarzt* will be here any minute to make the selection," Józek says and disappears through the doors of the clinic.

The feverish cleaning of the ward is finished. The floor has been swept and wiped with a wet rag. The sick are lying motionless on their backs, holding their arms stiffly by the sides of their bodies.

I look at those who are sitting — they know. They know the way to Twenty well, to the room where the doctor, Pańszczyk holds office hours and treats patients with phenol. The nurses hold the delinquent down more firmly by the arms, and *Herr Doktor*, professionally and matter-of-factly, pushes a long needle between the ribs and straight into the heart. A few drops of phenol solidifies the blood; death usually occurs instantly. Usually. Not always. Sometimes, out of haste or absentmindedness, the *Herr Doktor* forgets to draw phenol into the syringe; sometimes his hand jumps from fatigue and the needle doesn't reach the heart. At such times, instead of dying quickly and efficiently, the muzulman starts a wild uproar. The *Herr Doktor* then throws down the syringe and grabs a poker. This is a reliable, albeit primitive tool for breaking a skull to the quick. The nurses carry the corpse down to the cellar. In the evening, a truck will take it to Birkenau.

From below, the signal of the bell can be heard.

"*Achtung!*" shouts Doctor Grabczyński from the door, stiffening with expectation. Enter the *Lagerarzt*: tall, handsome, wearing a beautifully cut uniform, glowing with the shine of his box-calf boots, fragrant with a fashionable hair cream. He takes the cards of the sick from the doctor, looks down at them:

"Is this all?"

The Block was as quiet as church.

"These are the weakest . . . completely hopeless cases . . . but there are other difficult cases," the doctor stammered; he turned red and stopped with an expectant look at the other's lips.

The SS man looked at him coldly.

"Ye-e-s?"

He shook his head ironically and, placing the cards in his pocket, walked out.

"*Achtung!*"

The doors slammed, the doctor relaxed.

"Jasiek, the *Zuganger* will be here in a moment; look them over, will you? I am so tired. As for these — take them to twenty."

"Doctor, is it us . . . what's going to happen to us?" a man with an enormous boil on his leg asks the doctor from one of the stools.

"You'll go to a different Block, and then on a transport to Dachau."

"Not to the chimney? Is it true, doctor?"

"Of course, of course . . . leave me alone."

A couple of old Frenchmen sit to the side smiling ironically.

"*Monsieur*, a last cigarette if we may."

A long procession of people walks along a path worn through the snow, clacking their clogs. The wind raises their shirts and blows snow on their bare flesh. At the doors of Twenty, its *Pflegers* receive them.

"Jasiek," one of them whispers to me, "they're going to Birkenau."

"Gas?"

"Aha. Pańszczyk has too much work."

I return. Emaciated feverish people with wounds smelling of blood and pus walk into the Block in front of me. They wrap around themselves their long shirts, through which the wind blows.

These people are coming from the camp to the hospital. In place of those others. And like those others, they'll go to the gas.

In the meantime, the most important thing is to be busy. They're bathed, shaved, sprayed with paraffin against lice, looked over, written down, and sent to get dressings. We rub them with ichthammol and acid; we write down the treatments: this one for an incision, that one for an X ray, then everyone to bed. Two to a bed, naturally, but it is quite comfortable.

Off in a corner, Józek is rummaging through the suitcases. All the packages, boxes, factory-wrapped medicine are unsealed and carefully examined.

"Have you got anything?" I ask when I've finished the dressings. "We need to buy margarine."

"A thousand francs, some marks, three rings, a lady's watch, photographs, but just for decoration," he recites in a single breath.

"Hide them, the Block Elder's coming!"

At the door stands a tall, camel-like German. He's called Martin and had been a coworker of Governor Frank. He looks at the open cases for a moment and then shifts his gaze to us:

"Get out, you at the cases! Our Block has been assigned to help transport muzulmen to the gas. You'll go to the washrooms afterward to help load them. And you," he said to Józek, "I remember well. One transport of *Pflegers* has already gone to Mauthausen. I'll help you along as well. . . ." Józek shook his head as the man left.

"It's because of these cases, you know, but tough, one has to take risks."

"And if he sends you on a transport?"

"Is he God, or what? I'll manage. . . . But the medicines are good, aren't they?"

The medicines were good: Dutch vitamins and sulfamides sold for gold in the camp and made the difference between life and death for the sick.

We built a washroom between the first and second Blocks. We built it in the same way that we had glazed the windows of the *FKL* — we erected a building out of stolen materials and then the somewhat astonished and uneasy building managers confirmed the barracks' existence. We wash quite comfortably here. There's also room for the several hundred *muzulmen* who will shortly leave for Birkenau, the gas chamber. We stand in the doors of the washroom. Naked individuals squeeze by us. We grab them by the arm, checking the tattooed numbers, and count loudly in German. Trucks drive up, brakes squealing; people scramble onto them. SS screams mingle with the weeping and moaning of those who are leaving. Ghostly reflectors shine through the relentless snow.

There's a confusion at the last trucks.

"Take them back!" *Unterscharführer* Kler shouts from the door.

They throw a couple of people off the trucks, throw the snow-covered bodies into the washroom, and drag them out again immediately. We count monotonously in German.

The last truck growls; it is packed solid. The heap of bodies shakes, groans, and swears. Kler, who, as usual, is head of the transport, comes up to the door.

"How many?"

"Four-hundred and eighty-three," I reply clearly and without a moment's hesitation.

"He's made a mistake. Four-hundred and eighty-two," my companion says looking at the notebook.

I go pale. Kler's thin, dry face with its shifty, malicious little eyes flashes before me.

"If one's missing, you'll go," Kler says with a spiteful smile.

Just like Kazik, I automatically think, and his fat, jolly face comes to my mind. He went to Birkenau with the muzulmen to help unload. Went, unloaded, never came back. I wipe my eyes with my hand.

Kler pushes me toward the truck, asking the SS man who'd been counting on the other side of the door, "How many have you got?"

After a long delay, his answer penetrates my consciousness,

"Four-hundred and eighty-three."

"Off with you! You've got the luck of the devil," Kler says and gets into the truck.

The last truck carrying people to the gas vanishes through the gate into darkness.

I walk slowly back to the Block. The snow brushes softly against my hot cheeks and melts on my hands. The air is exceptionally clear and refreshing. Beyond the ring of lights along the wires, stretches a darkness that covers the free world. Marian catches me in the Block.

"You've got a letter. I've just brought it from the office."

I tear the envelope open impatiently. From my mother.

"My dearest son, I anxiously await your letters each day, and thank God that He is keeping you alive and well . . ."

"You owe me a cigarette for the letter," Marian says, looking over my shoulder.

Blue lights flicker across the room. The sick sleep pigeonholed in their beds. Heavy breathing can be heard; the air is steamy and stuffy.

The orderly slouches around with a bowl in his hand, going from bed to bed selling coffee for bread and scraps of margarine.

The lights are out in the nurses' room as well; only the night-lights are on. I lie fully dressed on the bed. I am unbelievably tired. Half-asleep, I hear whispers:

"Look, that swine is asleep! He has absolutely no feelings."

"Leave him alone; let the kid sleep if he can."

"Those from this morning have left. Just in their stripes and clogs."

"Where to?"

The whispers fade and draw nearer. People walk restlessly among the beds.

"Mauthausen. A penal transport. To be finished off in the quarries."

"And the ones from evening?"

"They're already in the washroom. They'll leave by morning."

"Oh, my God. What's going to happen? Is it the end?"

"More lists will come in the night. There'll be two transports: at midnight and at sometime before dawn."

"Is it certain?"

"Shut your trap! All the Poles are to be taken out as punishment. It's politics." The voices fade and mingle. I fall into heavy sleep. A noise on the ward wakes me at midnight. Józek is sitting beside me.

"I didn't want to wake you. You must be very tired. Did you load a lot for the gas?"

"Not many. Five hundred."

"Do you know that all the Polish *Pflegers* are to go?"

"I know. Did they take a lot from us?"

"Eight. And us? What do you think?"

"We're on the list of assisting personnel; maybe they won't take us. Nothing you can do about it anyway. Go to bed."

"And what about if they do take us, then what?"

"We'll go well rested to our death in the quarries."

"We have to think of something, Jasiek, I'm truly afraid."

"So take an aspirin. It'll help."

I pull the blanket firmly around me and sleep soundly until the gong.

Only a few of us get up at the gong. All of us assisting personnel, probably left behind through an oversight. We shake with cold and terror. Like those others . . .

"The washroom is overloaded with work, but there's going to be one more transport."

"When?"

"I don't know. Shall we go to work?"

"We must. The sick are waiting."

The Block Elder catches us at the door and gathers us together.

"*Los*, get in the truck. We're going to fetch fuel."

We rush down the stairs, but an SS man with a revolver in his hand is waiting in the corridor at the bottom.

"Freeze! If anyone moves, I'll shoot."

We stand in a line by the wall. Józek is white as chalk.

"So, it's us, too, Jasiek?"

I shrug.

"Now you get lucky, now you don't," I respond nastily.

Julek Oszacki, the office clerk, comes up to us, a thick folder under his arm. He takes down particulars.

"Number, last name, first name, Block, place of birth, age," he says in a montone, without lifting his eyes off the paper.

Finally, he comes up to me and says in the same calm, slow way:

"Be careful. Run . . ." pauses.

"Salski, Johann," I answer.

"They won't do anything to you."

"Sixty-six, forty-three," I say in one breath.

"Be sure to hide yourself well."

"Born in Warsaw," I go on.

"Good luck." He's already standing in front of the next one — by his side, an angry, sleepy, bored SS man with a pistol.

I squat down, tighten my bootlaces, and leap into a splendid hundred-meter sprint. I climb over the fence around the hospital yard. Uproar behind me, but I can't look back. Yard, doors, stairs, corridor. Furtively by the walls. At a bend in the corridor, I smack chest to chest into the *blockelder*. He's as surprised as I am. But I'm fighting for my life, so I'm quicker.

"Block Elder, the *SDG* sent me to the clinic for two dressings."

"Run!" he says and goes on his way.

I go among the sick on my ward. They immediately understand what it's about. I get into someone's bed, the clerk bandages my head, they cover me up to the eyes with a blanket. Turmoil beneath me. The *blockelder* is screaming; they search feverishly for the clerk; an SS man moves slowly and deliberately through the ward.

"He hasn't been here?"

"He went downstairs right after the gong," the sick reply.

Finally when everything has quieted down, I climb out of bed.

It grows light outside the window. The Blocks stand motionless in the violet light of dawn waiting for the Appel. Lantern light falls onto gray, drenched, people.

Along the empty street a transport moves in fives to wade through mud. Summer stripes flicker white, clogs clatter across stones.

The procession stretches the length of Blocks, bidden farewell by the silence of the camp. The gates clatter open. The transport vanishes into the gray-blue, fog-soaked, darkness leading to Mauthausen.

My mother's letter rustles in my pocket.

Life has to be fought for. I am going to fight.

THE HISTORY OF
A CERTAIN TABLE

Are you familiar with Strug?* I appropriated "The Adventures of a Certain Bullet" from him, changed "Bullet" to "Table," so that there wouldn't be an explosion, and here it is. This could be the story of a paving stone, or an SS man's whip. It's a story that connects people and facts, a story about the misery of the prisoners and the well-being of the prominents.

A rustling forest, woodcutters. A tree trunk rolls down the hill pushed by people dressed in funny, striped clothes. Never mind that the incline is too steep, the trunk too heavy. Sometimes a human fragment in striped duck cloth remains behind on a road in the mountain forest, or by the railroad wagons, or right at the sawmill. Somewhere in an office a number is struck off a list. And one person suffers no more in a German camp.

Planks and boards dry in tall piles. Again, people in stripes arrange and sort them. A rasp of mechanical lathes, boards, planks, misshapen parts of wooden construction spill out to infinity. A blade of the planing machine flows with blood; again a new patient with torn fingers arrives at the camp hospital. How? Why?

" . . . they beat you and drive you to work with the spade if everything isn't done. The shield was off . . . As long as it goes faster."

"But listen," the wounded's voice trembles with anxiety, "I'll be able to work again? Do something! The spade will finish me."

And after a few weeks, a man with a bandaged hand stands at the machine again, and again gets it in the face for bloodying a finished piece. And the finished staves, planks, and dowels pile up in the assembly hall at *DAW* Auschwitz in ammunitions boxes, beds, stools.

An ordinary, standard bed got itself into the warehouse.

A long column of five hundred prisoners stretched along the road and disappeared in a cloud of dust. Everybody, strong or weak,

*Novelist Andrzej Strug, pseudonym of Tadeusz Galecki, 1870–1937

old or young, carried a "front" or three "sides." They stumbled on potholes, lost wooden clogs, moaned from the blows of the *Kapos,* and walked, walked to a distant camp to leave a choking yoke of beds and return for the next. Three trips before noon and two after.

In the fourth dozen, stood wing A block 21. Four three-tiered beds put together form a "dozen," probably because in twelve places sleep twenty-four people. Block 21 A, the hospital Block, department of purulent surgery. Patients, placed in pairs for lack of space, moaned in their beds. People died — numbers. The *Lagerarzt* came to the Block, dragged the "interesting cases" out of bed for unnecessary operations, the "hopeless cases" for a quicker death in the gas chamber. The bed, stamped *"DAW* Auschwitz," stood on a floor licked clean with rags, alternately stinking now of carbolic acid, now of pus, oozing with weeks of unchanged dressings, then again of carbolic acid, creosol, or cuprex — the single, unfailing disinfectants. At first, it had stood shining with the whiteness of pine planks, later, glowing red from paint bought with sick people's margarine. Until, in the end, the lord of life and death, Martini, Block Elder of block 21, decided that it was too tight in that corner, and the entire twelve had to be thrown out.

The bed stood dismantled in the yard, until some organizer packed it onto a truck and took it to Birkenau, which was rapidly expanding, officially and unofficially. Officially, electrified fences were put up, the earth beneath the barracks was levelled, foundations were laid beneath the modern, brick crematoria. Unofficially, on the other hand, all kinds of useful, everyday things were brought to Birkenau, starting with watches and margarine and ending with fashionable, smuggled beds. And so, too, that bed, turned upside down, taken apart and put together again countless times came at last to *the Zigeuner,* the Gypsy camp. The *Lagerältester* of *KB,* mad Jackowski himself, gave a bribe to the warehouseman in charge of these beds. The *SDG* himself, *Rottenführer* Bara, the one who said of himself, "I am not a German, I am not a Pole, I am Bara the thief," watched to see that there would be no difficulty at the gate of the camp when the procession of laden orderlies brought in the stolen beds.

And, again, that same bed stood on the hospital Block. But it was a different Block: instead of shiny, excessively clean walls, wooden, spit bespattered shingles enclosed a muddy, clay, dirt hut. The bed stood in the nurses' quarters, because, understandably, there were only bunks for the sick. The lodgers changed quickly, as quickly as life in the Gypsy camp flowed. First, the Block Elder slept on it with his lover; then, when he went to the penal company, his place was taken by the head doctor, who, in turn, gave his place to the sick, beautiful Irene. He nursed her, breathed on her, examined her, took her temperature. But in spite of all the care, Irene died. Died despite glucose, physiological salts, and a thousand other injections and medicines, in spite of all the doctor's and friends' long, sleepless nights. The biggest cocaine dealer in Germany died.

The madly-in-love doctor couldn't save her, the *Pflegers* waiting for any sign of life couldn't, neither could a few visits by the *Lagerarzt*, *Hauptsturmführer* Mengele, who expressed his readiness to supply all necessary medications. The doctor smiled uncertainly and shrugged his shoulders. Anyway, how could *Hauptsturmführer* Mengele have known that the doctor had in his private cupboard medicines that he hadn't seen since the outbreak of war and would probably not see again? But even though everything was there for Irene, she died on a simple camp bed. And, in the end, even the bed vanished.

A secret, underground, dogged battle raged between "Perełka," Jurek Szymkowiak, a former sergeant with the French Foreign Legion and now *Raportschreiber KB*, and Frölich (the gray eminence of the hospital in old Auschwitz), who had recently arrived in the Gypsy camp. Both sides fought with all means at their disposal: intrigues, leaks, anonymous letters. Until it came to open warfare. Perełka at the head of an armed band of carrion eaters — blindly loyal nurses carrying out and loading corpses moved one evening into Frölich's cave. Broken doors shattered. Platters of wonderful canapés whistled through the air, landing on the Auschwitz eminence's stupified face. His specially invited girlfriends fled from the feast. Everything fell onto one spot with a crash. The happy victors left in the dark of night shouting loudly.

A few minutes later, Frölich tripped against a heap of broken dishes in the ruins of what had moments before been a beautiful room. In the corner stood the unhappy bed, leaning to the side and ripped almost in half. Frölich got up, looked at the room, rubbed the lump on his forehead, and powdered the bruise under his eye, then took the carefully hidden gold and stones out of the hiding place in the bed and threw the bed itself onto a pile of firewood.

But this is not the end of the story. A few days later, the clerk from another Block, Tadeusz Lach, was looking for a table. A table was absolutely necessary because typhus had broken out in the camp, and the crush in Tadeusz's Block had increased greatly. Every day, dozens, scores of people of various ages and sexes came. Everyone had to be written down, the numbers checked, the cards of the sick organized to the annoyance of the doctors. Tadeusz didn't find a table; no one wanted to either lend or sell him one; he had to relinquish his clerkly pride, take an ax in his hand, and make something he could call a table out of the bed. And so, Tadeusz, instead of strolling through the Block in amazing, immaculate, white, ironed trousers, sits long hours in the Block and pushes a procession of ghosts across the improvised table: old men with gray hair and misty eyes, women with infants at their breasts, young dark Gypsy dancers with hot, feverish bodies. All naked, all horribly filthy and lousy, all connected by one trivial thing: in their hands a crumpled card with a clinic seal, prisoner number, and the number — Block 23 — broken by the word *Fleck*.

A week later came the return wave, a lot more terrible.

"Today at twenty-two hours prepare the transport of the sick to which belong all those who came to the camp after . . ." And someone else says, ". . . the transport of Polish Gypsies from the eastern borders brought typhus into the camp; everybody is to be gassed, a thousand five hundred people, and the camp will be freed from the epidemic."

The one who says this says it without irony. But he knows, and we know, it's a lie. They can gas that thousand five hundred, they can gas ten thousand, but they won't eliminate the disease in the filthy, lousy camp. They can exterminate people, but they can't exterminate lice.

"All right, but why do they cover themselves in this stupid way? With this lousy fleck fever?"

"You idiot, appearances have to be kept up, for the reports. One hand washes the other . . ."

And again the procession of condemned moves in front of the clerk's table. Nurses bring tiny babies and lay them on the edge of the table; the weakened children lean against the edge and look fearfully at Tadek. He sits with pursed lips and silently records the numbers. Trucks leave for the crematorium. In the empty Block stands the rickety table with a big stain of blood — one of the SS had hurried the loading of the trucks.

Then the table wandered into the warehouse. The chief warehouse man, Władek, had pestered it out of Tadek. The storekeepers had crowded around the table, and behind them, the children — maybe they'll wheedle something to eat. They cut and count the portions on the table: thin pieces of white bread for the children, slightly bigger ones of black bread for the grownups, microscopic portions of butter and cold cuts. And in the evening, after the distribution of rations, come the traders. The table is shoved into a corner of the room. From one of its leaves, Władek pulls "saved" pieces of kielbasa, sticks of margarine. Pieces of gold, gems, go into the hidey-hole in the floor. A bottle of spirits remains on the table.

The last time I saw the table, its legs broken, was in the trash on the other side of the storeroom windows. It was only then that I put that together with a meeting on the previous day: I went to Władek in the warehouse, met his helper Zbyszek at the door; he was leaving, hugging Hanka who was straightening her skirt, and behind them in the corner stood a strangely overturned table.

A DAY AT HARMENZ

A Day at Harmenz is the account of an external Kommando working outside of the camp enclosure. There were many external Kommandos and they went by various names, but their days were like those of the grave-building Kommando of Harmenz. And although we went outside of the camp into the "real" world, nevertheless our real "world," the camp, dragged along behind us. The experiences have been collected into a single day in this account. People don't have last names, but the first names, other than those of the women, have remained unchanged. Only Becker was called something else. The real Becker worked in the Kommando, but didn't come from Poznań; he was a Jew from France and, out of hunger, ate raw frogs.

I

The shadows of the chestnut trees are green and soft. They sway gently over the ground, still moist after being newly turned over, and rise up in sea-green cupolas scented with the morning freshness. The trees form a high palisade along the road, their crowns dissolve into the hue of the sky. From the direction of the ponds comes the heavy, intoxicating smell of the marshes. The grass, green and velvety, is still silvered with dew, but the earth already steams in the sun. It will be a hot day.

But the shade under the chestnut trees is green and soft. I sit in the sand beneath its cover, and with a large adjustable wrench tighten up the fishplates along the railway tracks. The wrench is cool and fits comfortably in my hand. I strike it against the rails at even intervals. A firm metallic sound reverberates throughout all Harmenz and comes back from afar in an unfamiliar echo. Several Greeks have gathered around me. They stand resting on their spades. But the men from Salonica and the vineyards of Macedonia do not like the shade. They stand in the open, remove their shirts, and expose to the sun their unbelievably thin shoulders covered with scabs and sores. It is getting hot.

"Working hard today, aren't you? Good morning, Tadek. How would you like something to eat?"

"Good morning, Mrs Haneczka! No thanks. Actually, I am just banging so hard because of our new Kapo . . . Forgive me for not getting up, but you understand: there's a war on, *Bewegung, Arbeit . . .*"

Mrs Haneczka smiles.

"Of course I understand. You know, I wouldn't have recognized you if I hadn't known it was you. Do you remember when you used to hide in the bushes to eat the unpeeled potatoes I stole for you from the chicken house?"

"Eat them? My dear lady, I devoured them! Careful, here comes the SS"

Mrs Haneczka threw a handful of grain from her sieve to the chickens that came running from all directions. Then, as she looked around, she shrugged.

"Oh, it's only the chief. I can twist him around my little finger."

"Around such a tiny finger? You are a very brave woman."

I slammed the wrench hard against the rails, trying to beat out "La donna è mobile" in her honour.

"For heaven's sake, don't make so much noise! But seriously, how about something to eat? I'm on my way to the house, I could bring you something."

"Thank you most kindly, Mrs Haneczka, but I think you fed me quite enough when I was poor . . ."

". . . poor, but honest," she finished with a touch of irony.

"Well, helpless, at any rate," I retorted. "But speaking of helplessness, I had two fine pieces of soap for you, called by the most beautiful of all names, 'Warsaw,' and . . ."

". . . and, someone's stolen them, as usual?"

"Someone's stolen them, as usual. When I had nothing, I slept in peace. And now! No matter how well I wrap my packages and tie them with string and wire, someone always manages to get them. A few days ago they organized a jar of honey off me, and now the soap. But just wait till I catch the thief!"

Mrs. Haneczka laughed.

"I can imagine . . . Don't be such a child! As for the soap, you really needn't worry. I got two cakes today, from Ivan. Oh, I almost forgot, please give Ivan this little packet, it's a piece of lard," and she laid a small package at the foot of the tree. "See, here's the soap he gave me."

She unwrapped it; it looked strangely familiar. I went over and examined it more closely. On both of the large cakes was imprinted the cameo of King Sigismund and the word "Warsaw."

I handed the package back to her without a word.

"Yes, very fine soap," I said after a moment.

I looked across the field, towards the scattered groups of workers. In one group, right by the potatoes, I spotted Ivan. He was circling watchfully around his men like a sheepdog, calling out words I could not make out at that distance, and waving his tall wooden stick.

"Just wait till I catch the thief," I repeated, not realizing that I was talking to empty space. Mrs Haneczka had left. From the distance, she turned and called back:

"Dinner as usual, under the chestnuts!"

"Thank you!"

Again I began to strike the wrench against the rails and tighten up the loose bolts.

Mrs Haneczka was popular with the Greeks, since from time to time she brought them a few potatoes.

"Mrs Haneczka *gut, extra prima.* Is she your Madonna?"

"My Madonna?" I protested, inadvertently striking my finger with the wrench. "She's a friend, see? *Camarade, filos, compris Greco bandito?*"

"*Greco niks bandito, Greco gut man.* But why you not eat from her? *Patatas?*"

"I'm not hungry. I have enough to eat."

"*Nix gut, nix gut.*" The old porter from Salonica who knew twelve Southern languages shook his head. "We are hungry, always hungry, always, always . . ."

He stretched out his bony arms. Under the skin covered with scabs and sores, the muscles played with a strangely distinct movement, as though they were quite separate from the rest of him. A smile softened the outline of his tense face, but could not extinguish the permanent fever in his eyes.

"If you're hungry, ask her for food yourself. Let her give it to you. And now go on back to work, *laborando, laborando,* I'm getting tired of you."

"No, Tadek, I think you are wrong," spoke up an old, fat Jew, stepping out from behind. He rested his spade on the ground and, standing over me, continued: "You've been hungry too, so you should be able to understand us. What would it cost you to ask her for a bucket of potatoes?"

He drawled out the word "bucket" with relish.

"Get off my back, Becker — you and your philosophy — and stick to your digging, *comprise?* And let me tell you something: when your time comes to go to the gas, I'll help you along personally, and with great pleasure. D'you want to know why?"

"Why, in God's name?"

"Because of Poznań. Or isn't it true that you were a camp senior at the Jewish camp outside Poznań?"

"Well, what if it is?"

"And isn't it true that you killed your own people? And that you hanged them on the post for every bit of stolen margarine or bread?"

"I hanged thieves."

"Listen, Becker, they say your son is in Quarantine."

Becker's fingers tightened around the spade handle; his eyes began to appraise my body, my neck, my head.

"You better let go of that spade, and stop looking at me with such murderous eyes. Tell me, is it true that your own son has given orders to have you killed, because of Poznań?"

"It is true," he said darkly. "And it is also true that in Poznań I personally hanged my other son, and not by the arms, but by the neck. He stole bread."

"You swine!" I exploded.

But Becker, the old, melancholy, silver-haired Jew, had already calmed down. He looked down at me almost with pity and asked.

"How long have you been in the camp?"

"Oh, a few months."

"You know something, Tadek, I think you're a nice boy," he said unexpectedly, "but you haven't really known hunger, have you?"

"That depends on what you mean by hunger."

"Real hunger is when one man regards another man as something to eat. I have been hungry like that, you see." Since I said nothing but only banged the wrench against the rails form time to time, mechanically looking left and right to see if the Kapo was around, he continued: "Our camp, over there, was small . . . Right next to a road. Many people walked along that road, well-dressed men, women too. They passed on their way to church on Sundays, for instance. Or there were couples out for a stroll. And a little farther on was a village, just an ordinary village. There, people had everything, only half a mile from us. And we had turnips . . . good God, our people were ready to eat each other! So, you see, wasn't I to kill the cooks who bought vodka with our butter, and cigarettes with our bread? My son stole, so I killed him, too. I am a porter, I know life."

I looked at him with curiosity, as though I had never seen him before.

"And you, you never ate anything but your own ration?"

"That was different. I was a camp senior."

"Look out! *Laborando, laborando, presto!*" I yelled suddenly, for from around a bend in the road came an SS man on a bicycle. As he rode by, he eyed us closely. All backs bent down, all spades were lifted heavily in the air. I began to hammer furiously against the rails.

The SS man vanished beyond the trees. The spades stopped moving; the Greeks lapsed into their usual torpor.

"What time is it?"

"I don't know. It's a long time yet till dinner. But you know, Becker? I'll tell you this in parting: today there's going to be a selection in the camp. I sincerely hope that you, along with your scabs and sores, go straight to the chimney!"

"A selection? How do you know . . ."

"Upset you, didn't I? There's going to be one, that's all. Scared, eh? You know the story about the wolf . . ." I smiled spitefully at my own wit and walked away humming a popular camp tango called "Cremo." The Jew's empty eyes, suddenly void of all content, stared fixedly into space.

II

The railway tracks on which I was working criss-crossed the whole field. At one end I had taken them right up to a heap of burned bones which a truck had brought from the crematoria; the other end I had run to the pond, where the bones were to be finally deposited; in one spot I took them up to a mound of sand, which was to be spread level over the field to give a dry base to the marshy soil; elsewhere I laid them along an embankment used for collecting sand. The tracks ran this way and that, and wherever they intersected there was an enormous turntable, which had to be shifted from one spot to another.

A group of half-naked men surrounded the turntable, bent down and clutched it with their fingers.

"*Hooch!* Up!" I screamed, raising my hand like an orchestra conductor for better effect. The men tugged, once, and again. One of them fell heavily over the turntable, unable to stay on his feet. Kicked repeatedly by his comrades, he crawled out of the ring and, lifting his face smeared with sand and tears off the ground, groaned:

"*Zu schwer, zu schwer* . . . It's too heavy, comrade, too heavy . . ."
Then he thrust his bloody fist into his mouth and sucked greedily.

"Back to work, *auf!* Up with you! Now, once more! *Hooch!* Up!"

"Up!" repeated the men in an even chorus. They bent down as low as they could, arched their bony, fish-like backs, straining every muscle in their bodies. But the hands clinging to the turntable hung limp and helpless.

"Up!"

"Up!"

Suddenly a rain of blows fell across the ring of arched backs, bowed shoulders, and heads bent almost to the ground. A spade struck against skulls, slashed the skin through to the bone, slammed across bellies with a hollow groan. The men swarmed around the turntable. And all at once there was a terrible roar; the turntable moved, rose in the air and, swaying uncertainly above the men's heads, started forward, threatening to fall at any moment.

"You dogs!" shouted the Kapo after them "Can't you do anything without help from me!" Breathing heavily he rubbed his crimson, swollen face and ran an absent gaze over the group as if seeing them for the first time. Then he turned to me:

"You there, railway man! Hot today, isn't it?"

"It is, Kapo. That turntable should be put down by the third incubator, right? And what about the rails?"

"Run them right up to the ditch."

"But there's an embankment in the way."

"Then dig through it. The job must be finished by noon. And by evening make me four stretchers. Maybe some corpses will have to be carried back to camp. Hot today, eh?"

"Yes, but Kapo . . ."

"Listen, railway man, let me have a lemon."

"Send your boy over later. I haven't got one on me."

He nodded a few times and walked away, limping. He was going to the house for some food, but I knew he would get nothing there, as long as he kept on beating the prisoners. We set the turntable down. With a terrible effort we pulled the rails up to it, levered them into position, tightened up the bolts with our bare hands. Finally the hungry, feverish men lay down to rest, their bodies weak, blood-stained. The sun hung high in the sky, the heat was growing deadly.

"What time is it, comrade?"

"Ten," I answered without lifting my eyes from the rails.

"Lord, Lord, Still two hours till dinner. Is it true that there's to be a selection in the camp today, that we'll all go to the cremo?"

They already knew about the selection. Secretly, they dressed their wounds, trying to make them cleaner and fewer; they tore off their bandages, massaged their muscles, splashed themselves with water so as to be fresher and more agile for the evening. They fought for their existence fiercely and heroically. But some no longer cared. They moved only to avoid being whipped, devoured grass and sticky clay to keep from feeling too much hunger; they walked around in a daze, like living corpses.

"All of us . . . crematorium. But all Germans will be *kaput*. War *fini*, all Germans . . . crematorium. All: women, children. Understand?"

"I understand, *Greco gut*. Don't worry, there won't be any selection, *keine Angst*."

I dug across the embankment. The light, handy spade virtually worked by itself in my hands. The slabs of wet earth yielded easily and flew softly in the air. Work is not unpleasant when one has eaten a breakfast of smoked bacon with bread and garlic and washed it down with a tin of evaporated milk.

The *Kommandoführer*, a sickly little SS man, worn out from walking among the diggers, had seated himself in the meagre shade under the brick incubator, his shirt unbuttoned on his thin chest. He was an expert in lashing a whip. Only the day before I had felt it twice on my own back.

"What's new, plate layer?"

I swung my spade, slicing through the top layers of earth.

"Three hundred thousand Bolsheviks have fallen at Orzel."

"That's good news, no? What do you think?"

"Sure it's good news. Especially since the same number of Germans were killed too. And the Bolsheviks will be up here before the year is out, if things continue this way."

"You think so?" He smiled bitterly and repeated the ritual question: "How much longer to dinner?"

I took out my watch, an old piece of junk with funny Roman numbers. I was fond of it because it reminded me of a watch my father used to own. I bought it at the camp for a packet of figs.

"It's eleven."

The German got up from under the brick wall and took the watch from my hand.

"Give it to me. I like it."

"I can't, it's my own, from home."

"You can't? Ah, that's too bad." He swung his arm and hurled the watch against the brick wall. Then he seated himself calmly back in the shade and tucked his legs under him. "Hot today, isn't it?"

Without a word I picked up my broken watch and began to whistle. First a foxtrot, then an old tango, then the "Song of Warsaw" and all the Polish cavalry tunes, and finally the entire repertory of the political left.

But just when I got to the middle of the "International," I suddenly felt a tall shadow move over me. A heavy hand struck across my back. I turned my head and froze in terror. The Kapo's huge, bloated red face hovered over me, his spade swaying dangerously in mid-air. The stripes of his prison suit stood out sharply against the green of the distant trees. A small red triangle with the numbers 3277 dangled before my eyes, growing more and more enormous.

"What's that you're whistling?" he asked, looking straight into my eyes.

"It's a sort of international song, sir."

"Do you know the words?"

"Well . . . some . . . I've heard them a few times," I said cautiously.

"And have you heard this one?"

And in a hoarse voice he began singing the "Red Flag." He let his spade drop, his eyes glistened excitedly. Then he broke off suddenly, picked up the spade and shook his head, half with contempt, half with pity.

"If a real SS man'd heard you, you wouldn't be alive right now. But that one over there . . ."

The sickly German resting against the brick wall laughed good-naturedly:

"You call this hard labor? You should have been in the Caucasus, like me!"

"Yes, but sir, we've already filled one pond with human bones, and how many more were filled before, and how much was dumped into the Vistula, this neither you nor I know."

"Enough, you dirty dog!" and he rose from under the wall and looked around for his whip.

"Get your men and go on to dinner," said the Kapo quickly.

I dropped my spade and vanished around the corner of the incubator. In the distance I could still hear the Kapo's voice, hoarse and asthmatic:

"Yes, yes, the dirty dogs! They should be finished off, every last one of them. You're right, *Herr Kommandoführer*."

III

We leave by the road that runs through Harmenz. The tall chestnuts murmur, their shade seems even more green, but somehow drier. Like withered leaves. It is the shade of mid-day.

After emerging on to the road you have to pass a little house with green shutters. Awkward little hearts have been roughly cut out in their centres, and white ruffled curtains are half-drawn over the windows. Under the windows grow delicate, pale roses. A mass of funny little pink flowers peeks out of the window-boxes. On the steps of the veranda, shaded with dark-green ivy, a little girl is playing with a big, sulky dog. The dog, obviously bored, lets her pull him by the ears, and only from time to time shakes his heavy head to chase away the flies. The girl wears a little white dress, her arms are brown and suntanned. The dog is a black Dobermann Pinscher. The girl is the daughter of the *Unterscharführer*, the boss of Harmenz, and the little house with its little window-boxes and its ruffled curtains is his house.

Before you reach the road, you have to cross over several yards of soft, sticky mud mixed with sawdust and sprinkled with a disinfectant. This is to prevent us from bringing germs into Harmenz. I slip cautiously around the edge of the mess, and we emerge on to the road, where large cauldrons of soup have already been set up in a long row. A truck has brought them from the camp. Each Kommando has its own cauldrons marked with chalk. I walk around them. We made it on time — no one has yet stolen any of our food.

"These five are ours, good, take them away. The two rows over there belong to the women, hands off. Aha, here's one." I go on talking loudly, and at the same time drag over a cauldron that belongs to the next Kommando, leaving one of ours, only half the size, in its place. I quickly change the chalk marks.

"Take it away!" I boldly shout to the Greeks, who stand eyeing the procedure with total approval.

"Hey you, what d'you think you're doing switching those cauldrons? Wait, stop!" yell the men from the other Kommando that has just arrived for dinner, only a little too late.

"Who switched anything? You'd better watch your language, man!"

They start running towards us, but the Greeks quickly draw the cauldrons over the ground, groaning, swearing in their own tongue, *putare* and *porka*, urging each other on, until they disappear beyond the markers that separate the rest of the world from Harmenz. I follow behind. I can still hear the men at the cauldrons cursing me up and down, obviously taking a dim view of my entire family, as well as my ancestors. But it is okay: today was my turn, tomorrow will be theirs, first come, first served. Our Kommando patriotism never goes beyond the bounds of sport.

The soup gurgles in the cauldrons. The Greeks have set them down on the ground several paces apart and pant heavily, like fish cast upon the sand. With their fingers they eagerly collect the little trickles of sticky hot liquid oozing from under the loosely screwed-on covers. I know how it tastes, that mixture of dust, dirt and sweat from the palm. I carried the cauldrons myself not so long ago.

The Greeks stand around in silence and gaze expectantly into my eyes. With a solemn face I walk up to the middle cauldron, slowly turn the screw, for one endless half-second keep my hand on the cover and — raise it. The light in the dozen pair of eyes fades suddenly — nettle soup. A thin white fluid gurgles in the cauldron, yellow rings of margarine float on the surface. But everybody knows by its color that on the bottom there are whole, unchopped, stringy nettle stalks which look like rot and stink horribly, and that the soup is the same all the way down: water, water, water . . . For a moment the world goes dark before the men's eyes. I replace the cover. We carry the cauldrons down the slope without exchanging a word.

Walking in a wide arc, I cross the field to where Ivan's group is tearing up the surface of the meadow by the potato patch. A long row of men in camp stripes stands motionless along a high ridge of black earth. Once in a while a spade moves, someone bends over, freezes for a moment in that position, and then straightens up slowly, shifts the spade and remains for a long time in the half turn, the uncompleted gesture. After a while someone else stirs, swings the spade, and again falls into the same limp stupor. The men do not work with their hands but with their eyes. As soon as an SS man or the Kapo appears, the foreman scrambles heavily to his feet, the clatter of the spades grows a bit more lively. But whenever possible, the spades swing up and down empty. The limbs move like those of marionettes — absurd, angular.

I find Ivan inside a sheltered nook. With his pocket-knife he is carving designs in the bark of a thick piece of wood — squares, love knots, little hearts, Ukrainian patterns. An old, trusted Greek kneels beside him, stuffing something inside his bag. I just catch sight of a white feathered wing and the red beak of a goose before Ivan, seeing me come in, throws his coat over the bag. The lard has melted inside my pocket and there is an ugly stain on my trousers.

"From Mrs Haneczka," I say in a matter-of-fact tone.

"Didn't she send a message? I was supposed to get some eggs."

"She only asked me to thank you for the soap. She liked it very much."

"Good. I happened to buy it last night from a Greek Jew in Canada. Gave him three eggs for it."

Ivan unwraps the lard. It is squashed, soft and yellowish. The very sight of it makes me nauseous, perhaps because I ate too much smoked bacon this morning, and keep tasting it in my mouth.

"Ah, the bitch! Two such fine pieces of soap and this is all she sends? Didn't she give you any cake?" Ivan looks at me suspiciously.

"You're entirely right, Ivan, she didn't give you enough, that's a fact. I've seen the soap . . ."

"You have?" He fidgets uneasily. "Well, I must be going. It's time I gave my men a little shove."

"Yes, I saw it. She really has given you too little. You deserve more. Especially from me. And you'll get it, I promise you . . ."

We look hard into each other's eyes.

IV

There is a mass of tall reeds along one side of the ditch, while the other side is thick with raspberry bushes with pale, dusty leaves. Muddy water runs slowly along the bottom of the ditch, alive with all sorts of green, slimy creatures. Once in a while a black, wriggling eel comes up with the mud — the Greeks always eat it raw.

I stand straddled across the ditch and slowly work my spade over the bottom, at the same time trying to avoid wetting my shoes. The guard, a slow-witted fellow with a small mustache and several triangles on his arm to indicate long service, has walked up to the edge of the ditch and stands watching me in silence.

"And what's that you're making over here?" he asks finally.

"A dyke. And later we'll clean out the ditch, sir."

"Where did you get such a fine pair of shoes?"

I do, in fact, have good shoes — hand made, with a double sole and ingeniously punched holes, Hungarian style. My friends brought them from the loading ramp.

"I got them here at the camp, and this shirt, too," I explain, showing him my silk shirt which cost me a pound of tomatoes.

"So you get shoes like that? Just look at what I've got to wear," and he points to his worn-out, cracked boots with a patch on the right toe. I nod sympathetically.

"Listen, how about selling me yours?"

I throw him a look of utter amazement.

"But how can I sell you camp property? How can I?"

He rests his rifle against the bench, walks up closer and leans over the water in which he can see his own reflection. I reach down and splash it around with my spade.

"As long as nobody knows, it's all right. I'll give you bread, I've got some in my sack."

Last week alone I received sixteen loaves of bread from Warsaw. Besides, a pair of shoes like mine is good for at least a liter of vodka. Therefore I merely smile at him politely.

"Thank you, but we get such good rations in the camp that I'm not hungry. I have enough bread and lard. But if you, sir, have too much, why don't you give it to the Jews working over there by the embankment? The one, for example, that's carrying the turf," I say, pointing to the skinny little Jew with red, watery eyes. "He's a very decent fellow. Anyway, my shoes aren't all that good, the sole is coming off." I have, it is true, a crack in my sole. Sometimes I hide a few dollars there, sometimes a few marks, sometimes a letter. The guard bites his lip and gazes at me from under knitted brows.

"What did they lock you up for?" he asks.

"I was walking along the street — there was a round-up. They nabbed me, locked me up, brought me here. For no reason."

"That's what all of you say."

"No, sir, not all. A friend of mine was arrested for singing out of tune. You know, *falsch gesungen*."

The spade which I drag uninterruptedly over the bottom of the slimy ditch comes up against something hard. I tear at it. A piece of wire. I curse under my breath. The guard continues to stare at me, dumbfounded.

"*Was, falsch gesungen?*"

"Well, it's a long story. Once, during a church service in Warsaw, when everyone was singing hymns, my friend started singing the national anthem. But since he sang out of tune, they locked him up. And they said they wouldn't let him out until he learned to sing properly. They even beat him regularly, but it was no use. I'm sure he won't get out before the war is over, because he's quite unmusical. Once he even confused a German march with Chopin's 'funeral march!'"

The guard hissed through his teeth and walked back to his bench. He sat down, picked up his rifle and, playing absent-mindedly with the bolt, went through the motions of loading and firing. Then he suddenly raised his head, as if remembering something.

"You! Come over here! I'll let you have the bread if you go and give it to the Jews yourself," he said, reaching for his sack.

I smiled as politely as I could.

Along the other side of the ditch runs the line of sentries, and the guards have orders to fire on sight at any prisoner who crossed into the zone beyond it. For every head they get three day's furlough and five marks.

"Unfortunately, I'm not allowed to. But if you wish, sir, you may throw the bread over. I'll catch it, I really will."

I stand waiting, but all of a sudden the guard drops the sack to the ground, jumps to his feet, and salutes. The *Rottenführer* is passing along the road.

Janek — a young, charming native son of Warsaw, who understands nothing of the ways of the camp and probably never will — was working diligently at my side, shovelling the mud and the sand and piling it neatly alongside the ditch, almost directly at the guard's feet. The *Rottenführer* approached and looked at us in the way one looks at a pair of horses drawing a cart, or cattle grazing in the field. Janek threw him a broad, friendly, man-to-man smile.

"We're cleaning out the ditch, sir, it certainly is full of mud."

The *Rottenführer* started and eyed the speaking prisoner with utter astonishment.

"Come here!" he said.

Janek put down his spade, jumped over the ditch, and walked up to him. The *Rottenführer* raised his hand and slammed him across the face with all his strength. Janek staggered, clutched at the raspberry bushes, and slid down into the slime. The water gurgled and I began to choke with laughter.

"I don't give a damn what you might be doing in the ditch! You can do nothing for all I care. But when you're addressing an SS man, take off your cap and stand to attention," said the *Rottenführer* and walked off. I helped Janek scramble out of the mud.

"What did I get that for, what, in the name of heaven?" he asked in amazement, utterly confused.

"Next time, don't volunteer," I said, "and now go and wash."

Just as we were finishing cleaning out the ditch, the Kapo's boy arrived. I reached for my sack. I moved aside a loaf of bread, a piece of lard and an onion. I took out a lemon. The guard observed me in silence from across the ditch.

"Here boy, take this for your Kapo," I said.

"Okay, Tadek. And listen, how about something to eat? You know, something sweet. Or a few eggs. No, no, I'm not hungry. I ate at the house. Mrs Haneczka made me some scrambled eggs. What a woman! Except that she's always asking about Ivan. But you see, when the Kapo goes over there they never give him anything."

"If he stopped beating people, maybe they would."

"You tell him that."

"And what has he got you for? Don't you know how to organize things? If you're smart and keep your eyes open, you'll see that some of the men catch geese and then fry them in the barracks at night, while your Kapo has to eat soup. By the way, how did he enjoy the nettles?"

The boy listens attentively with a knowing smile on his face. He is young but quite clever. Though only sixteen, he has already served in the German army, and has done quite a lot of smuggling besides.

"Let me have it straight, Tadek. After all, we know each other well. Who are you putting me on to?"

I shrug my shoulders.

"Nobody. But you take a good look at the geese."

"Do you know that another disappeared yesterday, and the *Unterscharführer* whipped the Kapo and was so furious he also took his watch? Well, I'll be going, and I promise to keep my eyes open."

We walk back together, since it is time for dinner. Piercing whistles come from the direction of the cauldrons. The men drop their tools wherever they happen to be standing. Abandoned spades stick out on the embankment in rows. Exhausted prisoners from all over the field drag themselves slowly towards the cauldrons, trying to stretch out the blessed moment just before dinner, to relish the hunger which they will shortly satisfy. Ivan's group is last, for Ivan has stopped by the ditch and talks a long time to "my" guard. The guard points his hand, Ivan nods. But shouts and calls urge him away. As he walks by, he flings at me:

"Didn't get much accomplished, did you?"

"The day is still young," I retort.

He throws me a challenging sidelong glance.

V

Inside the empty incubator the Kapo's boy is setting out the dishes, wiping the benches and preparing the table for dinner. The Kommando clerk, a Greek linguist, huddles in one corner, trying to make himself as small and inconspicuous as possible. Through the wide-open doors we can see his face, the color of a boiled lobster, and his eyes, watery as frog-spawn. Outside, in a little courtyard encircled by a high ridge of earth, the prisoners are gathered. They have sat down in formation, exactly as they were standing, lined up five in a row, arranged in groups. Their legs are crossed, their bodies erect, their hands down along their thighs. While dinner is being served nobody is allowed to move a muscle. Afterwards, they will be permitted to lean back and rest against the knees of the man behind, but never, never to break formation. Over to the left, under the shade of the ridge, sit the SS guards. Relaxed, their revolvers lying across their knees, they take slices of bread from their sacks, carefully spread them with margarine and eat slowly, savouring each mouthful. Beside one of them squats Rubin, a Jew from Canada. They talk in whispers. It is strictly business, partly for Rubin, partly for the Kapo. The Kapo himself, huge and red-faced, stands over by the cauldron.

We run around with bowls in our hands, like highly skilled waiters. In complete silence we serve the soup, in complete silence we wrest the bowls out of hands that still try desperately to scrape up some food from the empty bottom, wanting to prolong the moment of eating, to take a last drop, to run a finger over the edge. Suddenly the Kapo plunges between the ranks — he has spotted a man licking his bowl. He pushes him over, kicks him time and again in the genitals, and then goes off, stepping over arms, knees, faces, taking care to avoid those who are still eating.

All eyes look eagerly into the Kapo's face. There are two more cauldrons — second helpings. Each day the Kapo relishes this particular moment. The many years spent at the camp entitle him to the absolute power he has over the men. With the end of his ladle he points out the chosen few who merit a second helping. He never makes a mistake. The second helping is for those who work better, for the stronger, the healthier. The sick, the weaklings, the emaciated, have no right to an extra bowl of water with nettles. Food must not be wasted on people who are about to go to the gas chamber.

The foremen, by virtue of their office, are entitled to two full bowls of soup with potatoes and meat scooped up from the bottom of the cauldron. Holding my bowl in my hand I glance around me, undecided. I can feel someone's intent stare fixed on me. In the first row sits Becker, his bulging, hungry eyes glued to the soup.

"Here, take it, maybe you'll choke on it."

Without a word he seizes the bowl from my hand and eats greedily.

"Be sure to set the plate down beside you for the Kapo's boy to collect; don't let the Kapo see it."

I give my second bowl to Andrzej. In return he will bring me apples. He works in the orchard.

"Rubin, what news did you hear from the guard?" I ask in an undertone as I walk past him to get in the shade.

"He says they've occupied Kiev," he whispers.

I stop, astonished. He waves me on impatiently. I walk to the shade, fold my coat under me so as not to soil my silk shirt, and stretch out comfortably. This is a time to rest, every man as best he can.

The Kapo, having eaten two bowls of soup, went to the incubator to doze off. Then his boy drew a slice of boiled meat out of his pocket, cut it up on bread, and proceeded to eat solemnly before the eyes of the hungry crowd, taking an occasional bite at an onion, crunching it like an apple. The men have stretched out in tight rows, one behind the other, and, covering their faces with their coats, have dropped off into a heavy but restless sleep.

Andrzej and I lie in the shade. A short distance away we can see girls with white kerchiefs on their heads — a women's Kommando has settled down near by. The girls wave, giggle, and try to attract our attention. A few of us wave back. At the edge of the courtyard, one girl is on her knees, holding a large, heavy beam extended above her head. Every minute or so, the SS man guarding the Kommando slackens the leash of his dog. The dog leaps up to the girl's face, barking furiously.

"A thief?" I wonder lazily, turning to Andrzej.

"No, they caught her in the corn with Petro. Petro ran away," he says.

"Can she hold it for five minutes?"

"She can. She's a strong girl."

She did not. Her arms sagged, the beam tumbled down, and she fell forward on the dirt, breaking into loud sobs. Andrzej turned away and looked at me.

"You haven't got a cigarette, have you? Too bad. Ah, life!" He wrapped his coat around his head, stretched out, and fell asleep. I too was getting ready to doze off when the Kapo's boy tugged at my sleeve.

"Kapo wants you. But watch your step, he's really mad."

The Kapo has just awakened, his eyes are red. He rubs them, staring fixedly into space.

"You!" He presses his finger to my chest. "Why did you give your soup away?"

"I've got other food."

"What did he give you in exchange?"

"Nothing."

He shakes his head in disbelief. His enormous jaws work, like those of a cow chewing the cud.

"Tomorrow you won't get any soup at all. It is for those who have nothing else to eat. Understand?"

"All right, Kapo."

"Why haven't you made the four stretchers, the way I told you? Did you forget?"

"I haven't had time. You saw what I was doing all morning."

"You'll make them this afternoon. And watch out, or you'll end up on one of them yourself. I can fix that, believe me."

"May I go now?"

Only then did he look directly into my face. He fixed on me the lifeless, vacant stare of a man torn out of profound contemplation.

"Why are you still here?" he asked.

VI

From beneath the chestnut trees growing along the road came a stifled cry. I collected my wrenches and screws, arranged the stretchers one on top of the other, and called:

"Janek, don't forget the box, and be a good boy!" and I rushed to the road.

There, on the ground, lay Becker, moaning and spitting blood. Ivan stood over him, blindly kicking his face, his back, his belly . . .

"Look what he's done! Gobbled up all of your dinner, the thieving swine!"

Mrs Haneczka's tin bowl with some mush still left on the bottom was lying in the dirt. Becker's face was smeared with mush all over.

"I shoved his ugly mug right in it," said Ivan, panting heavily. "There, he's all yours, I've got to go."

I turned to Becker. "Wash out the bowl and set it under the tree. And watch out for the Kapo. I've just finished making four stretchers. You know what that means, don't you?"

On the road Andrzej is teaching two Greek Jews to march. They do not know how. The Kapo has already broken two whips over their heads and warned them that they must learn, or else . . . Andrzej tied a stick to each of their legs and tries his best to explain: "You no good bastard, can't you understand what's left, what's right? *Links, links!*" The terrified Greeks, their eyes popping, march round and round in a circle shuffling their feet along the gravel. A huge cloud of dust rises in the air. By the ditch, next to the guard who wanted my shoes, several friends of mine are busily "arranging" the earth. They pat it down gently and smooth it over with the backs of their spades, like dough. As I walk past them on my way to the other end of the field, leaving deep tracks in the soft earth, they call loudly:

"Hey, Tadek, what's new?"

"Not much, they've taken Kiev!"

"Is that really true!"

"What a silly question!"

Shouting back and forth I pass them and continue on along the ditch. Suddenly I hear someone scream after me:

"Halt, halt, du Warschauer!"

Running behind me along the other side of the ditch is "my" guard, his rifle aimed. "Stop, stop!"

I stop. The guard fights his way through the raspberry bushes, loudly cocks his rifle.

"What's that you just said? About Kiev? So, now you're spreading political rumors! So, you've got a secret organization! Number, number, let's have your serial number!"

Shaking with fury and indignation he holds out a scrap of paper, nervously searches for a pencil. I feel an emptiness in the pit of my stomach, but I recover quickly.

"Excuse me, sir, but I think you misunderstood. Your Polish is not too good. I was speaking of the sticks* Andrzej tied to the feet of the Greeks, over there on the road. I was saying how funny they looked."

"That's right, that's exactly what he was saying." The men who have gathered around us nod in agreement.

The guard swings the butt of his rifle, as if trying to hit me from across the ditch.

"You, you! . . . I'm going to report you to the Political Department today! Come on, what's your number?"

"One hundred and nineteen, one hundred and . . ."

"Let's see your arm!"

"Here." I hold out my forearm with the number tattooed on it, feeling certain he cannot read it at that distance.

"Come closer!"

"That's *verboten.* You may report me if you like, but I'm not as stupid as 'White Vaska.'"

A few days ago White Vaska climbed up a birch tree growing along the sentry line to cut some twigs for a broom. In the camp, a broom like that may be exchanged for bread or soup. A guard took aim and fired, a bullet passed sideways through Vaska's chest and

---

* An untranslatable play on words. The Polish word for stick is pronounced almost the same as Kiev.

came out in the back between his shoulder blades. We carried the boy's body back to camp.

I walk away feeling angry. Around the bend of the road, Rubin catches up with me.

"See what you've done? Now what's going to happen?"

"Why should anything happen?"

"Ah, but you'll tell them you got it from me . . . Oy, what a fine thing you did! How could you've shouted so loud? You're out to ruin me, Tadek!"

"What are you scared of? Our people don't sing."

"Yes, I know it, and you know it, but *sicher ist sicher*. Better to be on the safe side. Listen, how about letting the guard have your shoes? I guarantee he'll co-operate. I'll try talking to him myself, see? For you I'll do it. He and I have done business before."

"Great, now I'll also have that to tell them about you, Rubin."

"Our future looks black, Tadek . . . Better let him have the shoes, and I'll settle the details with him later. He's not a bad guy."

"Only he's lived too long. I intend to keep my shoes, because I like them. But I have a watch. It isn't running, and the glass is broken, but then, what have I got you for? You're a clever man, Rubin. In fact, you can give him your own watch, it didn't cost you anything."

"Oy, Tadek. Tadek . . ."

Rubin stashes away my watch. In the distance I hear a shout:

"Hey, railwayman!"

I rush across the field. The Kapo's eyes glisten dangerously; there are traces of foam around the corners of his mouth. His hands, his enormous gorilla hands, sway back and forth, his fingers twitch nervously.

"What were you trading with Rubin?"

"But didn't you see, Kapo? You always see everything. I gave him my watch."

"Whaat?" Slowly his hands begin to move towards my throat.

Without making the slightest move (he is a wild beast, I suddenly thought), without shifting my eyes from his face, I burst out in one breath:

"I gave him my watch because the guard wants to report me to the Political Department for subversive activities."

The Kapo's hands relaxed slowly and dropped to his sides. His jaw hung loose, like an old dog's. He rocked the spade to and fro, undecided.

"Go back to work. And watch out or they'll be carrying you back to camp on one of those stretchers of yours . . ."

At that moment he suddenly stiffened to attention and tore his cap off his head. I threw myself to one side, struck in the rear by a bicycle. I removed my cap. The *Unterscharführer*, the boss of all Harmenz, hopped off the bicycle, his face red and excited.

"What's the matter with this crazy Kommando? Why are your men over there walking around with sticks tied to their feet? Why aren't they working?"

"They're learning how to march, sir."

"They can't march? Then kill them! Did you hear, by the way, that another goose has disappeared?"

"Why are you standing here like a stupid oaf?" snarled the Kapo, turning to me. "You heard the *Unterscharführer*! Go and tell Andrzej to take care of them. *Los!*"

I flew down the path.

"Finish them off, Andrzej! *Kapo's* orders!"

Andrzej seized a stick and struck out at random. The Greek covered his head with his arm, let out a howl, and fell. Andrzej laid the stick across the man's throat, stood up on the two ends, and began to rock. I walked away quickly.

In the distance I see that the Kapo and the SS man have gone over to talk to my guard. The Kapo gesticulates violently, shaking his spade; his cap is down over his eyes. Then they walk away and in turn Rubin approaches the guard. The guard rises from the bench, draws close to the ditch and finally steps on to the dyke. In a little while Rubin nods to me.

"Come and thank Mr Guard for not reporting you."

Rubin is no longer wearing my watch.

I thank the guard and return to work. The old Greek, Ivan's confidant, stops me along the way.

"*Camarade, camarade,* that SS man came from the main camp, didn't he?"

"Where else?"

"Then it's really true about the selection!" and the withered, silver-haired old merchant from Salonica throws his spade aside and lifts up his arms, as though in a trance:

"*Nous sommes des hommes misérables, O Dieu, Dieu!*"

His pale-blue eyes gaze up into the equally pale and blue sky.

VII

We hoist up the little cart. Filled to the brim with sand, it has gone off the rails right at the turntable. Four pairs of bony arms push it backwards and forwards, rock it. We put it in motion, raise the front wheels, set them back on to the rails. Now we work a wedge underneath, but just when the cart is almost back on the rails we suddenly let go and straighten up.

"*Antreten!*" I scream, and blow my whistle.

The cart falls back heavily, its wheels dig into the earth. Someone tosses the wedge to the side; we pour the sand from the cart straight over the turntable. After all, it can be cleared away tomorrow.

"*Antreten.*" Only after a moment or two do we realize it is much too early. The sun still stands high above our heads, quite a distance from the tree crowns which it usually reaches by *Antreten* time. It cannot be later than three o'clock. The men look puzzled and anxious. We line up, five in a row, close ranks, straighten our backs, tighten our belts.

The camp clerk counts us over and over.

The SS men and the Kommando guards arrive from the direction of the house and form a ring around us. We stand motionless. In the rear of the Kommando several men are carrying two stretchers with two corpses.

Along the road there is more activity than usual. The people of Harmenz walk to and fro, disturbed by our early departure. But to the seasoned camp inmates the situation seems clear — there will, indeed, be a selection.

Several times already we caught sight of Mrs Haneczka's bright kerchief in the vicinity, but then it disappeared. Now she is back. Her questioning eyes glide over our faces. Setting her basket down on the ground, she leans against the barn and looks around. I follow the direction of her gaze. She is looking anxiously at Ivan.

The Kapo and the sickly *Kommandoführer* have arrived right behind the SS men.

"Spread out in open order and put up your hands," says the Kapo.

Now we understand: we are to be searched. We unfasten our coats, open up our sacks. The guard is swift and efficient. He runs his hands over your body, reaches inside your sack. In addition to several onions, some old bacon and what is left of my bread, he finds apples, obviously from our orchard.

"Where'd you get these?"

I raise my head — it is "my" guard.

"From a parcel, sir."

He looks me in the eyes with an ironic smile.

"I ate the very same kind this morning."

They disbowel our pockets, pull out corn cobs, herbs, seeds, apples, chunks of sunflower; now and then there is an abrupt scream: someone is being beaten up.

Suddenly the *Unterscharführer* pushed his way into the middle of the ranks and dragged aside Ivan's old Greek who was clutching a large, well-stuffed sack.

"Open it!" he snapped.

With trembling hands the Greek untied the rope. The *Unterscharführer* looked inside and called to the *kapo*:

"Look Kapo, here's our goose!"

And he drew out of the sack a big bird with enormous, widespread wings. The Kapo's boy, who had also rushed over, shouted triumphantly:

"Here it is, here it is, didn't I tell you?"

The Kapo raised his whip, ready to strike.

"Don't," said the SS man, stopping him. He drew a revolver out of his holster and, waving the weapon eloquently, turned to face the Greek.

"Where did you get it? If you won't answer I'll shoot you."

The Greek was silent. The SS man raised the revolver. I glanced at Ivan. His face was absolutely white. Our eyes met. He tightened his lips and stepped forward. He walked up to the SS man, took off his cap, and said:

"I gave it to him."

All eyes were fixed on Ivan. The *Unterscharführer* slowly raised the whip and struck him across the face, once, twice, three times. Then he began to strike his head. The whip hissed. Deep, bloody gashes stood out on Ivan's face, but he did not fall. He stood erect, hat in hand, his arms straight against his sides. He made no attempt to avoid the blows, but only swayed imperceptibly on his feet.

The *Unterscharführer* let his hand drop.

"Take his serial number and make up a report. Kommando — dismissed!"

We marched off at an even, military pace, leaving behind a heap of sunflower heads, weeds, rags, and crushed apples, and on top a large, red-beaked goose with tremendous wide-spread wings. In the rear of the Kommando walked Ivan, supported by no one. Behind him, on stretchers, we carried two corpses covered with branches.

As we passed Mrs Haneczka, I turned to look at her. She stood pale and straight, her hands pressed over her breast. Her lips quivered nervously. She raised her head and looked at me. Then I saw that her large black eyes were filled with tears.

After roll-call we were driven into the barracks. We lay on the bunks, peered through the cracks in the walls, and waited for the selection to come to an end.

"I feel as if this damn selection were somehow my fault. What a curious power words have . . . Here in Auschwitz even evil words seem to materialize."

"Take it easy," said Kazik. "Instead, let me have something to go with this sausage."

"Don't you have any tomatoes?"

"You must be kidding!"

I pushed aside the sandwiches he had made.

"I can't eat."

Outside, the selection was almost finished. The SS doctor, having taken the serial numbers and noted the total of the men selected, went on to the next barracks. Kazik was getting ready to leave.

"I'm off to try and find some cigarettes. But you know, Tadek, you're really a sucker. If anyone'd eaten up my mush, I'd have made mincemeat of him."

At that moment, a large grey head emerged from below, and a pair of blinking, guilty eyes gazed up at us over the edge of the bunk. It was Becker, his face exhausted and somehow even older-looking.

"Tadek, I want to ask a favour of you."

"Go ahead," I said, leaning down to him.

"Tadek, I'm going to the cremo."

I leaned over still more and peered into his eyes — they were calm and empty.

"Tadek, I've been so hungry for such a long time. Give me something to eat. Just this last time."

"Do you know this Jew?" asked Kazik, tapping my knee.

"It's Becker," I answered in a whisper. "Okay, Jew, come on up and eat. And when you've had enough, take the rest with you to the cremo. Climb up. I don't sleep here anyway, so I don't mind your lice."

"Tadek," Kazik pulled at my arm, "come with me. I've got a wonderful apple cake at my place, straight from home."

As he scrambled down, he nudged me.

"Look," he whispered.

I looked at Becker. His eyes were half-closed and, like a blind man, he was vainly groping with his hand for the board to pull himself on to the bunk.

THIS WAY FOR
THE GAS, LADIES
AND GENTLEMEN

We say that prisoners leave in a delicate, gray smoke through the crematorium chimney, and that Jews from other countries whose transports are unloaded from the ramp every day float out in black smoke. A group of prisoners known as Canada in camp jargon works here. The work of these people was hard, physically exhausting, and psychologically not to be endured by the occasional actor. The work continues without a break for several hours, several days, several years. Lasts without a break through four and a half million burned people. However, those who loaded them into the gas weren't bad people. They were Jews whose families were also burned.

They weren't bad people, they were simply accustomed.

All of us walk around naked. The delousing is finally over, and our striped suits are back from the tanks of Cyclone B solution, an efficient killer of lice in clothing and of men in gas chambers. Only the inmates in the blocks cut off from ours by the "Spanish goats"* still have nothing to wear. But all the same, all of us walk around naked: the heat is unbearable. The camp has been sealed off tight. Not a single prisoner, not one solitary louse, can sneak through the gate. The labor Kommandos have stopped working. All day, thousands of naked men shuffle up and down the roads, cluster around the squares, or lie against the walls and on top of the roofs. We have been sleeping on plain boards, since our mattresses and blankets are still being disinfected. From the rear Blocks we have a view of the FKL — *Frauenkonzentrationslager;* there too the delousing is in full swing. Twenty-eight thousand women have been stripped naked and driven out of the barracks. Now they swarm around the large yard between the Blocks.

The heat rises, the hours are endless. We are without even our usual diversion: the wide roads leading to the crematoria are empty.

* Crossed wooden beams wrapped in barbed wire.

For several days now, no new transports have come in. Part of Canada has been liquidated and detailed to a labor Kommando — one of the very toughest — at Harmenz. For there exists in the camp a special brand of justice based on envy: when the rich and mighty fall, their friends see to it that they fall to the very bottom. And Canada, our Canada, which smells not of maple forests but of French perfume, has amassed great fortunes in diamonds and currency from all over Europe.

Several of us sit on the top bunk, our legs dangling over the edge. We slice the neat loaves of crisp, crunchy bread. It is a bit coarse to the taste, the kind that stays fresh for days. Sent all the way from Warsaw — only a week ago my mother held this white loaf in her hands — dear Lord, dear Lord . . .

We unwrap the bacon, the onion, we open a can of evaporated milk. Henri, the fat Frenchman, dreams aloud of the French wine brought by the transports from Strasbourg, Paris, Marseille . . . Sweat streams down his body.

"Listen, *mon ami*, next time we go up on the loading ramp, I'll bring you real champagne. You haven't tried it before, eh?"

"No. But you'll never be able to smuggle it through the gate, so stop teasing. Why not try and organize some shoes for me instead — you know, the perforated kind, with a double sole, and what about that shirt you promised me long ago?"

"Patience, patience. When the new transports come, I'll bring all you want. We'll be going on the ramp again!"

"And what if there aren't any more cremo transports?" I say spitefully. "Can't you see how much easier life is becoming around here: no limit on packages, no more beatings? You even write letters home . . . One hears all kind of talk, and, dammit, they'll run out of people!"

"Stop talking nonsense." Henri's serious fat face moves rhythmically, his mouth is full of sardines. We have been friends for a long time, but I do not even know his last name. "Stop talking nonsense," he repeats, swallowing with effort. "They can't run out of people, or we'll starve to death in this blasted camp. All of us live on what they bring."

"All? We have our packages . . ."

"Sure, you and your friend, and ten other friends of yours. Some of you Poles get packages. But what about us, and the Jews, and the Russkis? And what if we had no food, no organization from the transports, do you think you'd be eating those packages of yours in peace? We wouldn't let you!"

"You would, you'd starve to death like the Greeks. Around here, whoever has grub, has power."

"Anyway, you have enough, we have enough, so why argue?"

Right, why argue? They have enough, I have enough, we eat together and we sleep on the same bunks. Henry slices the bread, he makes a tomato salad. It tastes good with the commissary mustard.

Below us, naked, sweat-drenched men crowd the narrow barracks aisles or lie packed in eights and tens in the lower bunks. Their nude, withered bodies stink of sweat and excrement; their cheeks are hollow. Directly beneath me, in the bottom bunk, lies a rabbi. He has covered his head with a piece of rag torn off a blanket and reads from a Hebrew prayer book (there is no shortage of this type of literature at the camp), wailing loudly, monotonously.

"Can't somebody shut him up? He's been raving as if he'd caught God himself by the feet."

"I don't feel like moving. Let him rave. They'll take him to the oven that much sooner."

"Religion is the opium of the people," Henri, who is a Communist and a *rentier,* says sententiously. "If they didn't believe in God and eternal life, they'd have smashed the crematoria long ago."

"Why haven't you done it then?"

The question is rhetorical; the Frenchman ignores it.

"Idiot," he says simply, and stuffs a tomato in his mouth.

Just as we finish our snack, there is a sudden commotion at the door. The Muzulmen scurry in fright to the safety of their bunks, a messenger runs into the Block Elder's shack. The Elder, his face solemn, steps out at once.

"Canada! *Antreten!* But fast! There's a transport coming!"

"Great God!" yells Henri, jumping off the bunk. He swallows the rest of his tomato, snatches his coat, screams *"Raus"* at the men below, and in a flash is at the door. We can hear a scramble in the other bunks. Canada is leaving for the ramp.

"Henri, the shoes!" I call after him.

"Keine Angst!" he shouts back, already outside.

I proceed to put away the food. I tie a piece of rope around the suitcase where the onions and the tomatoes from my father's garden in Warsaw mingle with Portuguese sardines, bacon from Lublin (that's from my brother), and authentic sweetmeats from Salonica. I tie it all up, pull on my trousers, and slide off the bunk.

"*Platz!*" I yell, pushing my way through the Greeks. They step aside. At the door I bump into Henri.

"*Was ist los?*"

"Want to come with us on the ramp?"

"Sure, why not?"

"Come along then, grab your coat! We're short of a few men. I've already told the Kapo," and he shoves me out of the barracks door.

We line up. Someone has marked down our numbers, someone up ahead yells, "March, march," and now we are running towards the gate, accompanied by the shouts of a multilingual throng that is already being pushed back to the barracks. Not everybody is lucky enough to be going on the ramp . . . We have almost reached the gate. *Links, zwei, drei, vier! Mützen ab!* Erect, arms stretched stiffly along our hips, we march past the gate briskly, smartly, almost gracefully. A sleepy SS man with a large pad in his hand checks us off, waving us ahead in groups of five.

"*Hundert!*" he calls after we have all passed.

"*Stimmt!*" comes a hoarse answer from out front.

We march fast, almost at a run. There are guards all around, young men with automatics. We pass camp II B, then some deserted barracks and a clump of unfamiliar green — apple and pear trees. We cross the circle of watchtowers and, running, burst on to the highway. We have arrived. Just a few more yards. There, surrounded by trees, is the ramp.

A cheerful little station, very much like any other provincial railway stop: a small square framed by tall chestnuts and paved with yellow gravel. Not far off, beside the road, squats a tiny wooden shed, uglier and more flimsy then the ugliest and flimsiest railway shack; farther along lie stacks of old rails, heaps of wooden beams, barracks parts, bricks, paving stones. This is where they load freight for Birkenau: supplies for the construction of the camp, and people for the gas chambers. Trucks drive around, load up lumber, cement, people — a regular daily routine.

And now the guards are being posted along the rails, across the beams, in the green shade of the Silesian chestnuts, to form a tight circle around the ramp. They wipe the sweat from their faces and sip out of their canteens. It is unbearably hot; the sun stands motionless at its zenith.

"Fall out!"

We sit down in the narrow streaks of shade along the stacked rails. The hungry Greeks (several of them managed to come along, God only knows how) rummage underneath the rails. One of them finds some pieces of mildewed bread, another a few half-rotten sardines. They eat.

"*Schweinedreck*," spits a young, tall guard with corn-coloured hair and dreamy blue eyes. "For God's sake, any minute you'll have so much food to stuff down your guts, you'll bust!" He adjusts his gun, wipes his face with a handkerchief.

"Hey you, fatso!" His boot lightly touches Henri's shoulder, "*Pass mal auf*, want a drink?"

"Sure, but I haven't got any marks," replies the Frenchman with a professional air.

"*Schade*, too bad."

"Come, come, *Herr Posten*, isn't my word good enough any more? Haven't we done business before? How much?"

"One hundred. *Gemacht?*"

"*Gemacht.*"

We drink the water, lukewarm and tasteless. It will be paid for by the people who have not yet arrived.

"Now you be careful," says Henri, turning to me. He tosses away the empty bottle. It strikes the rails and bursts into tiny fragments. "Don't take any money, they might be checking. Anyway, who the hell needs money? You've got enough to eat. Don't take suits, either, or they'll think you're planning to escape. Just get a shirt, silk only, with a collar. And a vest. And if you find something to drink, don't bother calling me. I know how to shift for myself, but you watch your step or they'll let you have it."

"Do they beat you up here?"

"Naturally. You've got to have eyes in your ass. *Arschaugen.*"

Around us sit the Greeks, their jaws working greedily, like huge human insects. They munch on stale lumps of bread. They are restless, wondering what will happen next. The sight of the large beams and the stacks of rails has them worried. They dislike carrying heavy loads.

"*Was wir arbeiten?*" they ask.

"*Niks. Transport kommen, alles Krematorium, compris?*"

"*Alles verstehen*," they answer in crematorium Esperanto. All is well — they will not have to move the heavy rails or carry the beams.

In the meantime, the ramp has become increasingly alive with activity, increasingly noisy. The crews are being divided into those who will open and unload the arriving cattle cars and those who will be posted by the wooden steps. They receive instructions on how to proceed most efficiently. Motor cycles drive up, delivering SS officers, bemedalled, glittering with brass, beefy men with highly polished boots and shiny, brutal faces. Some have brought their briefcases, others hold thin, flexible whips. This gives them an air of military readiness and agility. They walk in and out of the commissary — for the miserable little shack by the road serves as their commissary, where in the summertime they drink mineral water, *Studentenquelle,* and where in winter they can warm up with a glass of hot wine. They greet each other in the state-approved way, raising an arm Roman fashion, then shake hands cordially, exchange warm smiles, discuss mail from home, their children, their families. Some stroll majestically on the ramp. The silver squares on their collars glitter, the gravel crunches under their boots, their bamboo whips snap impatiently.

We lie against the rails in the narrow streaks of shade, breathe unevenly, occasionally exchange a few words in our various tongues, and gaze listlessly at the majestic men in green uniforms, at the close, yet unattainable, green trees, and at the steeple of a distant church from which a belated "Angelus" has just sounded.

"The transport is coming," somebody says. We spring to our feet, all eyes turn in one direction. Around the bend, one after another, the cattle cars begin rolling in. The train backs into the station, a conductor leans out, waves his hand, blows a whistle. The locomotive whistles back with a shrieking noise, puffs, the train rolls slowly alongside the ramp. In the tiny barred windows appear pale, wilted, exhausted human faces, terror-stricken women with tangled hair, unshaven men. They gaze at the station in silence. And then, suddenly, there is a stir inside the cars and a pounding against the wooden boards.

"Water! Air!" — weary, desperate cries.

Heads push through the windows, mouths gasp frantically for air. They draw a few breaths, then disappear; others come in their place, then also disappear. The cries and moans grow louder.

A man in a green uniform covered with more glitter than any of the others jerks his head impatiently, his lips twist in annoyance. He inhales deeply, then with a rapid gesture throws his cigarette away and signals to the guard. The guard removes the automatic from his shoulder, aims, sends a series of shots along the train. All is quiet now. Meanwhile, the trucks have arrived, steps are being drawn up, and the Canada men stand ready at their posts by the train doors. The SS officer with the briefcase raises his hand.

"Whoever takes gold, or anything at all besides food, will be shot for stealing Reich property. Understand? *Verstanden?*"

"*Jawohl!*" we answer eagerly

"*Also los!* Begin!"

The bolts crack, the doors fall open. A wave of fresh air rushes inside the train. People . . . inhumanly crammed, buried under incredible heaps of luggage, suitcases, trunks, packages, crates, bundles of every description (everything that had been their past and was to start their future). Monstrously squeezed together, they have fainted from heat, suffocated, crushed one another. Now they push towards the opened doors, breathing like fish cast out on the sand.

"Attention! Out, and take your luggage with you! Take out everything. Pile all your stuff near the exits. Yes, your coats too. It is summer. March to the left. Understand?"

"Sir, what's going to happen to us?" They jump from the train on to the gravel, anxious, worn-out.

"Where are you people from?"

"Sosnowiec-Będzin. Sir, what's going to happen to us?" They repeat the question stubbornly, gazing into our tired eyes.

"I don't know, I don't understand Polish."

It is the camp law: people going to their death must be deceived to the very end. This is the only permissible form of charity. The heat is tremendous. The sun hangs directly over our heads, the white, hot sky quivers, the air vibrates, an occasional breeze feels like a sizzling blast from a furnace. Our lips are parched, the mouth fills with the salty taste of blood, the body is weak and heavy from lying in the sun. Water!

A huge, multicolored wave of people loaded down with luggage pours from the train like a blind, mad river trying to find a new bed. But before they have a chance to recover, before they can draw a breath of fresh air and look at the sky, bundles are snatched from their hands, coats ripped off their backs, their purses and umbrellas taken away.

89

"But please, sir, it's for the sun, I cannot . . ."

"*Verboten!*" one of us barks through clenched teeth. There is an SS man standing behind your back, calm, efficient, watchful.

"*Meine Herrschaften,* this way, ladies and gentlemen, try not to throw your things around, please. Show some goodwill," he says courteously, his restless hands playing with the slender whip.

"Of course, of course," they answer as they pass, and now they walk alongside the train somewhat more cheerfully. A woman reaches down quickly to pick up her handbag. The whip flies, the woman screams, stumbles, and falls under the feet of the surging crowd. Behind her, a child cries in a thin little voice "Mamele!" — a very small girl with tangled black curls.

The heaps grow. Suitcases, bundles, blankets, coats, handbags that open as they fall, spilling coins, gold, watches; mountains of bread pile up at the exits, heaps of marmalade, jams, masses of meat, sausages; sugar spills on the gravel. Trucks, loaded with people, start up with a deafening roar and drive off amidst the wailing and screaming of the women separated from their children, and the stupefied silence of the men left behind. They are the ones who had been ordered to step to the right — the healthy and the young who will go to the camp. In the end, they too will not escape death, but first they must work.

Trucks leave and return, without interruption, as on a monstrous conveyor belt. A Red Cross van drives back and forth, back and forth, incessantly: it transports the gas that will kill these people. The enormous cross on the hood, red as blood, seems to dissolve in the sun.

The Canada men at the trucks cannot stop for a single moment, even to catch their breath. They shove the people up the steps, pack them in tightly, sixty per truck, more or less. Nearby stands a young, cleanshaven "gentleman," an SS officer with a notebook in his hand. For each departing truck he enters a mark; sixteen gone means one thousand people, more or less. The gentleman is calm, precise. No truck can leave without a signal from him, or a mark in his notebook: *Ordnung muss sein.* The marks swell into thousands, the thousands into whole transports, which afterwards we shall simply call "from Salonica," "from Strasbourg," "from Rotterdam." This one will be called "Sosnowiec-Będzin." The new prisoners from Sosnowiec-Będzin will receive serial numbers 131–2 — thousand, of course, though afterwards we shall simply say 131–2, for short.

The transports swell into weeks, months, years. When the war is over, they will count up the marks in their notebooks — all four and a half million of them. The bloodiest battle of the war, the greatest victory of the strong, united Germany. *Ein Reich, ein Volk, ein Führer* — and four crematoria.

The train has been emptied. A thin, pock-marked SS man peers inside, shakes his head in disgust and motions to our group, pointing his finger at the door.

"*Rein.* Clean it up!"

We climb inside. In the corners amid human excrement and abandoned wrist-watches lie squashed, trampled infants, naked little monsters with enormous heads and bloated bellies. We carry them out like chickens, holding several in each hand.

"Don't take them to the trucks, pass them on to the women," says the SS man, lighting a cigarette. His cigarette lighter is not working properly; he examines it carefully.

"Take them, for God's sake!" I explode as the women run from me in horror, covering their eyes.

The name of God sounds strangely pointless, since the women and the infants will go on the trucks, every one of them, without exception. We all know what this means, and we look at each other with hate and horror.

"What, you don't want to take them?" asks the pockmarked SS man with a note of surprise and reproach in his voice, and reaches for his revolver.

"You mustn't shoot, I'll carry them." A tall, gray-haired woman takes the little corpses out of my hands and for an instant gazes straight into my eyes.

"My poor boy," she whispers and smiles at me. Then she walks away, staggering along the path. I lean against the side of the train. I am terribly tired. Someone pulls at my sleeve.

"*En avant*, to the rails, come on!"

I look up, but the face swims before my eyes, dissolves, huge and transparent, melts into the motionless trees and the sea of people . . . I blink rapidly: Henri.

"Listen, Henri, are we good people?"

"That's stupid. Why do you ask?"

"You see, my friend, you see, I don't know why, but I am furious, simply furious with these people — furious because I must be here because of them. I feel no pity. I am not sorry they're going to the gas chamber. Damn them all! I could throw myself at them, beat them with my fists. It must be pathological, I just can't understand . . ."

"Ah, on the contrary, it is natural, predictable, calculated. The ramp exhausts you, you rebel — and the easiest way to relieve your hate is to turn against someone weaker. Why, I'd even call it healthy. It's simple logic, *compris?*" He props himself up comfortably against the heap of rails. "Look at the Greeks, they know how to make the best of it! They stuff their bellies with anything they find. One of them has just devoured a full jar of marmalade."

"Pigs! Tomorrow half of them will die of the shits."

"Pigs? You've been hungry."

"Pigs!" I repeat furiously. I close my eyes. The air is filled with ghastly cries, the earth trembles beneath me, I can feel sticky moisture on my eyelids. My throat is completely dry.

The morbid procession streams on and on — trucks growl like mad dogs. I shut my eyes tight, but I can still see corpses dragged from the train, trampled infants, cripples piled on top of the dead, wave after wave . . . freight cars roll in, the heaps of clothing, suitcases and bundles grow, people climb out, look at the sun, take a few breaths, beg for water, get into the trucks, drive away. And again freight cars roll in, again people . . . The scenes become confused in my mind — I am not sure if all of this is actually happening, or if I am dreaming. There is a humming inside my head; I feel that I must vomit.

Henri tugs at my arm.

"Don't sleep, we're off to load up the loot."

All the people are gone. In the distance, the last few trucks roll along the road in clouds of dust, the train has left, several SS officers promenade up and down the ramp. The silver glitters on their collars. Their boots shine, their red, beefy faces shine. Among them there is a woman — only now I realize she has been here all along — withered, flat-chested, bony, her thin, colorless hair pulled back and tied in a "Nordic" knot; her hands are in the pockets of her wide skirt. With a rat-like, resolute smile glued on her thin lips she sniffs around the corners of the ramp. She detests feminine beauty with the hatred of a woman who is herself repulsive, and knows it. Yes, I have seen her many times before and I know her well: she is the Kommandant of the FKL She has come to look over the new crop of women, for some of them, instead of going on the trucks, will go on foot — to the concentration camp. There our boys, the barbers from Zauna, will shave their heads and will have a good laugh at their "outside world" modesty.

We proceed to load the loot. We lift huge trunks, heave them on to the trucks. There they are arranged in stacks, packed tightly. Occasionally somebody slashes one open with a knife, for pleasure or in search of vodka and perfume. One of the crates falls open; suits, shirts, books drop out on the ground . . . I pick up a small, heavy package. I unwrap it — gold, about two handfuls, bracelets, rings, brooches, diamonds . . .

"Gib hier," an SS man says calmly, holding up his briefcase already full of gold and colorful foreign currency. He locks the case, hands it to an officer, takes another, an empty one, and stands by the next truck, waiting. The gold will go to the Reich.

It is hot, terribly hot. Our throats are dry, each word hurts. Anything for a sip of water! Faster, faster, so that it is over, so that we may rest. At last we are done, all the trucks have gone. Now we swiftly clean up the remaining dirt: there must be "no trace left of the Schweinerei." But just as the last truck disappears behind the trees and we walk, finally, to rest in the shade, a shrill whistle sounds around the bend. Slowly, terribly slowly, a train rolls in, the engine whistles back with a deafening shriek. Again weary, pale faces at the windows, flat as though cut out of paper, with huge, feverishly burning eyes. Already trucks are pulling up, already the composed gentleman with the notebook is at his post, and the SS men emerge from the commissary carrying briefcases for the gold and money. We unseal the train doors.

It is impossible to control oneself any longer. Brutally we tear suitcases from their hands, impatiently pull off their coats. Go on, go on, vanish! They go, they vanish. Men, women, children. Some of them know.

Here is a woman — she walks quickly, but tries to appear calm. A small child with a pink cherub's face runs after her and, unable to keep up, stretches out his little arms and cries: "Mama! Mama!"

"Pick up your child, woman!"

"It's not mine, sir, not mine!" she shouts hysterically and runs on, covering her face with her hands. She wants to hide, she wants to reach those who will not ride the trucks, those who will go on foot, those who will stay alive. She is young, healthy, good-looking, she wants to live.

But the child runs after her, wailing loudly: "Mama, mama, don't leave me!"

"It's not mine, not mine, no!"

Andrzej, a sailor from Sevastopol, grabs hold of her. His eyes are glassy from vodka and the heat. With one powerful blow he knocks her off her feet, then, as she falls, takes her by the hair and pulls her up again. His face twitches with rage.

"Ah, you bloody Jewess! So you're running from your own child! I'll show you, you whore!" His huge hand chokes her, he lifts her in the air and heaves her on to the truck like a heavy sack of grain.

"Here! And take this with you, bitch!" and he throws the child at her feet.

"*Gut gemacht,* good work. That's the way to deal with degenerate mothers," says the SS man standing at the foot of the truck. "*Gut, gut, Russki.*"

"Shut your mouth," growls Andrzej through clenched teeth, and walks away. From under a pile of rags he pulls out a canteen, unscrews the cork, takes a few deep swallows, passes it to me. The strong vodka burns the throat. My head swims, my legs are shaky, again I feel like throwing up.

And suddenly, above the teeming crowd pushing forward like a river driven by an unseen power, a girl appears. She descends lightly from the train, hops on to the gravel, looks around inquiringly, as if somewhat surprised. Her soft, blonde hair has fallen on her shoulders in a torrent, she throws it back impatiently. With a natural gesture she runs her hands down her blouse, casually straightens her skirt. She stands like this for an instant, gazing at the crowd, then turns and with a gliding look examines our faces, as though searching for someone. Unknowingly, I continue to stare at her, until our eyes meet.

"Listen, tell me, where are they taking us?"

I look at her without saying a word. Here, standing before me, is a girl, a girl with enchanting blonde hair, with beautiful breasts, wearing a little cotton blouse, a girl with a wise, mature look in her eyes. Here she stands, gazing straight into my face, waiting. And over there is the gas chamber: communal death, disgusting and ugly. And over in the other direction is the concentration camp: the shaved head, the heavy Soviet trousers in sweltering heat, the sickening, stale odor of dirty, damp female bodies, the animal hunger, the inhuman labor, and later the same gas chamber, only an even more hideous, more terrible death . . .

Why did she bring it? I think to myself, noticing a lovely gold watch on her delicate wrist. They'll take it away from her anyway.

"Listen, tell me," she repeats.

I remain silent. Her lips tighten.

"I know," she says with a shade of proud contempt in her voice, tossing her head. She walks off resolutely in the direction of the trucks. Someone tries to stop her; she boldly pushes him aside and runs up the steps. In the distance I can only catch a glimpse of her blonde hair flying in the breeze.

I go back inside the train; I carry out dead infants; I unload luggage. I touch corpses, but I cannot overcome the mounting, uncontrollable terror. I try to escape from the corpses, but they are everywhere: lined up on the gravel, on the cement edge of the ramp, inside the cattle cars. Babies, hideous naked women, men twisted by convulsions. I run off as far as I can go, but immediately a whip slashes across my back. Out of the corner of my eye I see an SS man, swearing profusely. I stagger forward and run, lose myself in the Canada group. Now, at last, I can once more rest against the stack of rails. The sun has leaned low over the horizon and illuminates the ramp with a reddish glow; the shadows of the trees have become elongated, ghost-like. In the silence that settles over nature at this time of day, the human cries seem to rise all the way to the sky.

Only from this distance does one have a full view of the inferno on the teeming ramp. I see a pair of human beings who have fallen to the ground locked in a last desperate embrace. The man has dug his fingers into the woman's flesh and has caught her clothing with his teeth. She screams hysterically, swears, cries, until at last a large boot comes down over her throat and she is silent. They are pulled apart and dragged like cattle to the truck. I see four Canada men lugging a corpse: a huge, swollen female corpse. Cursing, dripping wet from the strain, they kick out of their way some stray children who have been running all over the ramp, howling like dogs. The men pick them up by the collars, heads, arms, and toss them inside the trucks, on top of the heaps. The four men have trouble lifting the fat corpse on to the car, they call others for help, and all together they hoist up the mound of meat. Big, swollen, puffed-up corpses are being collected from all over the ramp; on top of them are piled the invalids, the smothered, the sick, the unconscious. The heap seethes, howls, groans. The driver starts the motor, the truck begins rolling.

"*Halt! Halt!*" an SS man yells after them. "Stop, damn you!"

They are dragging to the truck an old man wearing tails and a band around his arm. His head knocks against the gravel and pavement; he moans and wails in an uninterrupted monotone: "*Ich will mit dem Herrn Kommandanten sprechen* — I wish to speak with the commandant . . ." With senile stubbornness he keeps repeating these words all the way. Thrown on the truck, trampled by others, choked, he still wails: "*Ich will mit dem . . .*"

"Look here, old man!" a young SS man calls, laughing jovially. "In half an hour you'll be talking with the top Kommandant! Only don't forget to greet him with a *Heil Hitler!*"

Several other men are carrying a small girl with only one leg. They hold her by the arms and the one leg. Tears are running down her face and she whispers faintly: "Sir, it hurts, it hurts . . ." They throw her on the truck on top of the corpses. She will burn alive along with them.

The evening has come, cool and clear. The stars are out. We lie against the rails. It is incredibly quiet. Anemic bulbs hang from the top of the high lamp-posts; beyond the circle of light stretches an impenetrable darkness. Just one step, and a man could vanish for ever. But the guards are watching, their automatics ready.

"Did you get the shoes?" asks Henri.

"No."

"Why?"

"My God, man, I am finished, absolutely finished!"

"So soon? After only two transports? Just look at me, I . . . since Christmas, at least a million people have passed through my hands. The worst of all are the transports from around Paris — one is always bumping into friends."

"And what do you say to them?"

"That first they will have a bath, and later we'll meet at the camp. What would you say?"

I do not answer. We drink coffee with vodka; somebody opens a tin of cocoa and mixes it with sugar. We scoop it up by the handful, the cocoa sticks to the lips. Again coffee, again vodka.

"Henri, what are we waiting for?"

"There'll be another transport."

"I'm not going to unload it! I can't take any more."

"So, it's got you down? Canada is nice, eh?" Henri grins indulgently and disappears into the darkness. In a moment he is back again.

"All right. Just sit here quietly and don't let an SS man see you. I'll try to find you your shoes."

"Just leave me alone. Never mind the shoes." I want to sleep. It is very late.

Another whistle, another transport. Freight cars emerge out of the darkness, pass under the lamp-posts, and again vanish in the night. The ramp is small, but the circle of lights is smaller. The unloading will have to be done gradually. Somewhere the trucks are growling. They back up against the steps, black, ghostlike, their searchlights flash across the trees. *Wasser! Luft!* The same all over again, like a late showing of the same film: a volley of shots, the train falls silent. Only this time a little girl pushes herself halfway through the small window and, losing her balance, falls out on to the gravel. Stunned, she lies still for a moment, then stands up and begins walking around in a circle, faster and faster, waving her rigid arms in the air, breathing loudly and spasmodically, whining in a faint voice. Her mind has given way in the inferno inside the train. The whining is hard on the nerves: an SS man approaches calmly, his heavy boot strikes between her shoulders. She falls. Holding her down with his foot, he draws his revolver, fires once, then again. She remains face down, kicking the gravel with her feet, until she stiffens. They proceed to unseal the train.

I am back on the ramp, standing by the doors. A warm, sickening smell gushes from inside. The mountain of people filling the car almost halfway up to the ceiling is motionless, horribly tangled, but still steaming.

"*Ausladen!*" comes the command. An SS man steps out from the darkness. Across his chest hangs a portable searchlight. He throws a stream of light inside.

"Why are you standing about like sheep? Start unloading!" His whip flies and falls across our backs. I seize a corpse by the hand; the fingers close tightly around mine. I pull back with a shriek and stagger away. My heart pounds, jumps up to my throat. I can no longer control the nausea. Hunched under the train I begin to vomit. Then, like a drunk, I weave over to the stack of rails.

I lie against the cool, kind metal and dream about returning to the camp, about my bunk, on which there is no mattress, about sleep among comrades who are not going to the gas tonight. Suddenly I see

97

the camp as a haven of peace. It is true, others may be dying, but one is somehow still alive, one has enough food, enough strength to work . . .

The lights on the ramp flicker with a spectral glow, the wave of people — feverish, agitated, stupefied people — flows on and on, endlessly. They think that now they will have to face a new life in the camp, and they prepare themselves emotionally for the hard struggle ahead. They do not know that in just a few moments they will die, that the gold, money, and diamonds which they have so prudently hidden in their clothing and on their bodies are now useless to them. Experienced professionals will probe into every recess of their flesh, will pull the gold from under the tongue and the diamonds from the uterus and the colon. They will rip out gold teeth. In tightly sealed crates they will ship them to Berlin.

The SS men's black figures move about, dignified, businesslike. The gentleman with the notebook puts down his final marks, rounds out the figures: fifteen thousand.

Many, very many, trucks have been driven to the crematoria today.

It is almost over. The dead are being cleared off the ramp and piled into the last truck. The Canada men, weighed down under a load of bread, marmalade and sugar, and smelling of perfume and fresh linen, line up to go. For several days the entire camp will live off this transport. For several days the entire camp will talk about "Sosnowiec-Będzin." That was a good, rich transport.

The stars are already beginning to pale as we walk back to the camp. The sky grows translucent and opens high above our heads — it is getting light.

Great columns of smoke rise from the crematoria and merge up above into a huge black river which very slowly floats across the sky over Birkenau and disappears beyond the forests in the direction of Trzebinia. The "Sosnowiec-Będzin" transport is already burning.

We pass a heavily armed SS detachment on its way to change guard. The men march briskly, in step, shoulder to shoulder, one mass, one will.

"*Und morgen die ganze Welt . . .*" they sing at the top of their lungs.

"*Rechts ran!* To the right march!" snaps a command from up front. We move out of their way.

FIRE FREEZES *

*T*he Gypsy camp was the most interesting section of Auschwitz; it was almost a "family" camp. The Gypsies, originally treated as "internees" (allowed to keep money, gold, belongings, etc.), began in a short time to die of typhus at a fantastic rate. Many Polish doctors and nurses fell at the same time. The greatest wealth, the most licentious orgies, the most blatant thievery could be seen there. The female dancers, actresses, fortune-tellers, and prostitutes enjoyed a great popularity both with the prisoners and the SS.

The abnormal conditions of camp life led in the Gypsy camp to madness, fights, and tragic surprises. Just such a surprise in the life of Auschwitz was the entire Gypsy camp, and just such a surprise was the end of the Gypsy camp: in July 1944, the whole camp went to the gas.

I

A sudden banging at the door woke me at midnight. A mighty thumping, legs kicking against the door. Then amid the curses and inarticulate echoes, the chief's voice rumbled across the Egyptian darkness.

"Open up! Open up! It's the chief."

Below me swirled breathless whispering.

"Jerzy, what's going to happen?"

" I'm scared Stefan!"

"Quiet!" Jerzy ordered in a penetrating whisper. "You're naked, Ellen! Where are your pajamas?"

"I don't know. Somewhere in the bed."

"Oh, hell, they could find them. Get out of bed, girls, and follow me. Give me your hand. Open the door, Stefan, only do it slowly. Nobody has been here, and we don't know anything. Understand? Jan, pretend to be sleepy."

Footsteps rustled in the darkness. The sound of a door opening. Silence. A beating started at the window.

"Open up! *Kontrole, verdammt,*" yelled the chief and swore in German.

*The title of this story is taken from the famous eighteenth century Polish Christmas carol, *Bóg się rodzi,* God is Born, lyrics by Franciszek Karpinski.

"Coming, chief, I'm opening up. We were asleep and I didn't hear anything," Stefan shouted in the darkness, and unbarred the door with a clatter.

A thin beam of torchlight splashed from the threshold, ran quickly across the room, and stopped at the bed. In the doorway, stood a short, frozen SS man, and behind him Janek, the kitchen Kapo. Ah! He'd had an argument with us yesterday and had sent the chief on control. But it wasn't the chief's job to catch Klara, who had been studiously avoiding him lately, red-handed.

Frozen steam blasted through the open door and rolled along the floor.

"Close the door behind you, chief," said Jerzy, wrapping himself up tightly in his blanket. "Thank God, it's the end of December."

"Shut your trap!" the chief growled through clenched teeth. "Where's Klara?"

He drew an arc with his hand, and the light from the torch ran through all the corners of the room.

I yawned loudly in my bed, and, inhaling sleepily, lay back on the pillow.

"Turn on the light, Stefan" Jerzy said. "The chief will probably want to search. But she's not here."

"Where is she?"

"How would I know who she's sleeping with?" Jerzy answered the question with a question. "Janek, have you got a cigarette? You woke me out of a dream."

Silently, Janek gave him a cigarette and touched it with a lighter.

"You're not allowed to smoke in the barracks," Jerzy said sententiously, and inhaled deeply.

Meanwhile, the chief looked around the room, throwing evil glances, now under the table, now under the bed; he opened the doors of the stove without thinking, and immediately slammed them in anger; finally, he pulled at the door and walked into the vegetable storeroom, looking into bins of turnips and carrots, and scattering, in disbelief, the beets lying to the side.

"She has to be here," he said to himself, "where have they hidden her?"

He looked at the door to the bread storeroom and reached into his pocket for the key.

Then he changed his mind. "Idiot. I've got the key, myself."

On his way out he again poked around the room and drew out of a corner a half-empty flask of vodka.

"What's this for?"

"What do you mean, chief? It's Christmas Eve today. Perhaps you'll have one with us?" Stefan suggested, pouring the vodka into tumblers.

They clinked glasses.

"*Prosit!*"

"I'm not pouring you one, Janek, because you probably don't like vodka."

"We'll take a look-see. I'm going to the kitchen, chief."

"We'll go together. *Gute Nacht!*"

Stefan turned off the light and pulled back the curtain.

"They really have gone to the kitchen," he reported in a whisper.

Jerzy took a key out of the grate and opened the bread store-room.

"Come on, girls, we can go back to sleep."

"Have you gone mad?" I protested from bed, "let them go back to their block; they might check there as well."

"What do you think, Jerzy," Stefan asked in concern.

"Jan is right, we got away with it this time, but they are mad-men: you drink with them, steal with them, but they're ready to shove you in the bunker, or worse, for any stupid thing, for any stupid girl," reflected Jerzy.

The terrified and frozen girls emerged from the storeroom. Their eyes had grown accustomed to the darkness. Ellen was not badly built . . . !

"Ellen, what a lovely body you have," said Stefan appreciatively, smacking his lips.

"Stefan! How can you say that in front of me," yelled Klara with indignation.

"She's naked, and you're not."

"Jerzy, my pajamas?" whispered Ellen, her teeth chattering.

"I would have forgotten." Jerzy took the silk out from under his shirt.

Ellen came back in.

"Jerzy, remember about the eggs, they'd do for *Eiercognac.*"

"Shut the door, its as cold as hell and she's got eggs on the brain," the boy said ill-humoredly. "Hide the key, Stefan, because if they see that we've got a duplicate for the storeroom, it will be bad. The gallows — carved in granite."

"Wood, surely," I murmured from the upper bunk.

"All the same we should think about Christmas Eve."

Adam threw the key into the ash can and shuffled into the depths of the hut. The sounds of glass and of someone drinking out of a bottle came from the darkness.

"I've already thought about Christmas," he said, scrambling into bed, and he began to sing in a voice broken by hiccups, "Fire freezes, glow dies down . . ."

"It's not freezing," he suddenly said in anger, pointing to the window that had started to redden with the bloody glow of the fire from the crematorium.

II

"She got a craving for eggs, dammit!" grumbled Jerzy, standing in front of the wires. "What weather!"

A penetrating, milky fog hung over the whole camp. The damp wires drowned in it as though drowning in cream. Somewhere at their end stood a tower with a guard; you could see only the posts and, up high, some kind of dark stain against the milky syrup. From afar came the singing of the guard and the stamping of feet against the floor of the tower.

In the neighboring stretch of camp, "D," it was still quiet and empty. Here and there scrunched-up people slipped by and seeped into the fog.

"I'm bringing the coffee," I said, burying my ears in the collar of my jacket.

"And they're still asleep over there!" Jerzy snarled and, picking a stone up off the ground, smashed it against the door on the other side of the wire.

Finally, a sleepy *Nachtwache* came out of the barracks.

"*Nachtwache*, two eggs! At once! If you've got them!"

"And the bread? I need some now."

"Catch it, louse!"

The bread traced a broad arc over the wire. The *Nachtwache* catches it with skill, like a goalie. Then he disappears and brings out a pot full of eggs.

"How shall we do the eggs? Throw them? One at a time, perhaps?"

"Of course, not! They'll break! Give them to me through the wire."

Jerzy crossed the "neutral" zone, tripped with a curse on the stop sign with the death's-head on it, and carefully put his hand through the wire.

"Be careful, its electrified," I warned him in a friendly fashion.

"You idiot, you'd think I'd come from the moon!"

Slowly and carefully he started to slip the canteen with the eggs through the double barbed wire. The edge of the metal dish suddenly scraped against the electrified wire. Jerzy made a few funny, angular, gestures; his hands grabbed the wire; and he froze in a painful spasm.

"Stop, stop!" I shouted and started to tear him off the wire by his clothes. I ripped him off and dragged him to the side. He wasn't moving. I looked around — Gypsies were walking to the kitchen carrying urns of coffee on poles.

"Eh! *Zigeuner*, one of you come here!" I shouted, waving my hand emphatically.

A few of them ran up, throwing the poles on the ground and smacking their hands against their sides for warmth.

"*Tragen, magazin*, carry, to the warehouse," I said, pointing to the motionless body.

It was long after the first gong that, thanks to artificial respiration, Jerzy opened his eyes and shook his head in disbelief.

"My head hurts like I've drunk too much vodka."

"But without eggs," I said. "Lie here awhile, and I'll go to the warehouse."

I went by the vegetable bins and into the warehouse.

Stefan was sitting on the counter, swinging his legs. He bent his red drunkard's face toward me and muttered confidentially, "How about Ellen? Did you see her breasts?"

"Get out of here, Stefan, you've been drunk since morning, you swine."

"Jasiek, try to understand. Either it's Christmas Eve, or it isn't. You know, I forgot" — he felt in his pocket — "Biański was here, he brought a letter from my wife, that wonderful woman. Read!"

But forgetting that he hadn't given me the letter, he took a drag from the bottle.

"Do you want a drink? I know, I know, you don't drink, but to Christmas Eve and to Biański's health. An SS man, but a decent one!"

"*Herr* chief," he announced to the arriving SS man, "I am reporting obediently: two prisoners at work! You'll join us, chief?" and he handed him half a tumbler of spirits.

III

"We'll arrange everything by noon?" The chief's small, red face twists itself into a question mark. "You know, at my place, Christmas Eve begins at three; my wife'll be mad if I'm late."

"No problem, we'll manage."

"What about the kielbasa? Will we come out even?" He hits his hand tellingly against his briefcase. Piles of bread for distribution are ranged on the shelves, and even more have been saved. Barrels of marmalade and cartons of margarine. Portions of kielbasa lie in boxes. We stop counting.

"They didn't give us five hundred portions."

"The main warehouse again?"

"From Camp D."

Two helpers, Gypsies, look greedily at the kielbasa; we know them.

"Put it to the side. I'll take care of them," says the chief through clenched teeth and takes the briefcase off the table. Just at that moment, Stefan crawled out of some corner, observed by nobody.

"I'll go curse them out," he said, and walked, reeling, out of the warehouse. He walked drunkenly across the wide camp road and, crawling under the wire, started to shout to the warehouse workers who were just unloading bread in Lager D.

"You! You greedy pig, the chief says that you gave us too little kielbasa!"

Those on the cart shouted back in chorus, "You stole it yourself and ate it, you filthy swine!"

"Give the kielbasa back, Stefan!"

"Right!" Stefan threatened them with his fist. "You're not going to get a single can of condensed milk from us!"

That last argument won. One of the warehouse workers leaped out of the cart and came up to the wire.

"Don't yell, Stefan " he said in a conciliatory way. "We haven't got any kielbasa left today, how could we have? It's Christmas Eve, isn't it? We want to have a drink, too, but we'll give it to you after the holidays? Okay?"

"You stole prisoners' rations for vodka, you thieves," Stefan muttered darkly, and walked away from the wire.

So we cut the rations of kielbasa in half and in that way achieve not only fairness but also extras.

"We'll give that one for the children, too, and the children's one is better; we'll take it for ourselves. Into the briefcase, chief."

Several whole rings disappear into his briefcase, the rest we distribute among the barrels that had been brought before time from the barracks.

"They're ready, chief! Now the margarine. Give us the cartons! Unwrap the paper, Ewald!"

With a loud thud the sticks of margarine drop onto the table and flatten out lightly. Just what we're after. The little machine, a cube, ideally suited to the sticks, cuts them into portions, leaving small shavings on the side. A few grams from a stick, up to twenty kilos from the cuttings for the whole camp of several hundred thousand people.

The chief sat down at the table, dully watching the growing pile of shavings.

"Stick it together and cut it, and leave the whole sticks with us; they'll come in handy, won't they? *Leben und leben lassen . . . Achtung!*"

We all stiffened and threw down the tools we were holding in our hands. In the silence that had suddenly descended, a small Gypsy moved uncertainly, not knowing what to do with the block of margarine that he was holding in his hands.

"At attention, monkey," he hissed through his teeth.

The camp doctor stood in the doorway, framed in silver. He waved away with his hand the greeting of the chief, who had frozen into the appropriate position, and he cast his eye over the warehouse:

"What's that?"

The chief turned as white as a sheet. His lips trembled; he wanted to say something, but I forestalled him:

"*Herr Haupsturmführer,*" I began, "these are the remains of the margarine, which we are cutting into portions. That machine" — I pointed out the metal gadget — "isn't exactly suited to the size of the portions, you understand, sir, it's hard to do."

"Yes," he said, uncertainly, "what do you do with the rest?"

"It's taken to the kitchen for soup. A prisoner always gets what's due to him."

The doctor rubbed his chin thoughtfully.

"Isn't it possible," he said, turning to me, "to cut the sticks into nine portions, instead of ten, and to stick the rest together and cut it again into nines?"

"Yes, but the hygeine!" I cried triumphantly, sure of my facts. "In truth, we wash our hands and the tables before we cut, but who can guarantee the cleanliness of these bits? That's why we put them in the soup, where the cooking disinfects them."

The doctor looked at me in amazement.

"You're right," he said, "Let's go to the kitchen."

I picked up the box of shavings, throwing a mean glance at Ewald, who had not gotten rid of the evidence in time. The Gypsy was still holding the carton of margarine in his hands. His eyes were fixed on the ground. A light shudder went across his shoulders.

In the kitchen, they look at me with surprise. On the table, lie pieces of meat to be cooked, and open cartons of margarine. Fire roars beneath the cauldrons; the soup, which is being stirred incessantly by the cooks, steams and bubbles. From somewhere amid the shining pans and the clouds of billowing steam, a sweaty Janek emerges wiping his hands on his apron.

"*Kapo*, I've brought you some margarine for the soup. At the chief's request. You know, it's from shavings. As usual."

Janek looks at me, blinking his eyes. I can sense the tall, still figure of the doctor behind me.

"As usual," the *Kapo* says at last and, without missing a beat, throws the margarine into the cauldrons, dividing it with a spoon. When he's finished, he gives me the empty carton.

"It'll come in handy tomorrow," he added in German.

The *Lagerarzt* left without a word. Janek nodded his head in his direction.

"You know where he's gone? To make a selection in the women's Lager. Damn it! Even on Christmas Eve. I've got a little Jewish girl there in the hospital. *Dowiedzenia, Panna Genia, kup se wózek, kup se wózek do jezdzenia,*" he sang softly.

"You fool, it won't be so bad."

"When he selects? Have you ever heard of Mengele letting a single female through? He'll send them all to the gas. So what," he said, punching me in the arm, "what's gone is gone. Shall we have a drink? We're quits, aren't we? The margarine for the inspection . . ."

We squeezed hands.

IV

Trager stand in a row beneath the window of the warehouse. Their caps in their hands, Gypsies stand in the snow. As is fitting, they stand as straight as ramrods. The Block Elder, a slender young man in an elegant black jacket buttoned up to the chin, whose turn it was to be on duty at the distribution of provisions, walks in a circle between the two rows, adjusting postures with the end of his cane. Sometimes, he shoves his cane in between heads and nudges a lowered chin, sometimes, he pokes a bent back or flattens fingers bent against the cold. "So you still don't know what *at attention* means? You want something to eat?" The black, flaming eyes of the Gypsies look at him in silent hatred. The double row is standing as still as a wall. With a spring in his step, the Block man walks up to the window and, taking off his cap, reports to the chief the camp's "readiness" to receive food.

"*Block Eins!*"

The wall of people moves and breaks, four Gypsies jump out, grab a *Trager* off the floor and run up to the window. We throw loaves of bread for the adults and pieces of bread for the children straight into the Trager. They read from a notebook what is owing and to whom. After the distribution, I lean out of the window.

"You can check it right here, by the window. Complaints will be of no use later. And now *hau ab*, off to the Block!"

The Gypsies grab the *Trager* and disappear behind the coal of the warehouse. Others jump forward to take their place.

It's nearly twelve and I am neither washed, nor dressed, nor have I even finished work. The chief, restless and angry, walks from one corner to another, shoving his hands deep into his pockets. He stops by Stefan, who, having just returned from outside, had brought a couple of bottles, and placing them in a corner, had sat down quietly next to them.

"Stefan, where's Klara?" he asked. "I've got to go home earlier today. It's Christmas Eve, you understand."

His eyes were glistening like those of a cowed dog.

"Klara is mine, even though her breasts are not as beautiful as Ellen's. Mine!" Stefan answered, drunkenly picking up by the neck the bottle of vodka, which he poured in a stream onto his head.

I snatched the bottle out of his hand and turned to the SS man who was livid with rage: "*Total betrunken.* Completely drunk. Take no notice of him, chief. Lie still, animal." I rammed him down with my knee because he was trying to crawl up. Out of the corner of my eye, as I struggled with Stefan, I noticed Ewald throwing two loaves of bread out of this window. Someone's hands grabbed them from the other side. "You thief! How can you? You don't have enough, heh? I'll teach you, you'll see," I added. "And now get back to the Block and bring Klara to my room, but don't let anyone know you're doing it, understand?"

"Okay, Jan," he answered quietly, and looked around with frightened, large, childlike eyes. A stick of margarine was poking out of his pocket. It was good that the chief hadn't see it. He'd have created hell; he was very sensitive to such pointless theft.

But the chief didn't even turn around. He stood in front of Stefan for a moment and then went into our room. Stefan was muttering something in the corner.

I looked at the Appelplatz. Dirty, bedraggled Gypsies were wandering along the roads. They were crawling around the garbage cans, loitering in front the kitchen, and, driven away from there by the cooks, they came up to the wire. Barefoot children were shuffling through the snow. Crowds of them dispersing in front of an SS man walking down the middle of the road.

I came out onto the threshold.

"Chief, let me in, chief."

The SS man turned and, waving his hand from afar, approached. I invited him in.

"So, Jan, you're not finished yet? It's Christmas Eve."

I gestured toward the door with my head.

"The chief and Klara," I said in a low voice.

"Oh, that swine. He's not worth a spit!" Biański responded contemptuously. "I brought Stefan a letter from home this morning. You'll be bored over the holidays. And sad?"

"Of course we will."

"Don't you worry. The war will be over soon and the devil'll take all this," he consoled. "Would you like me to send a letter home for you?"

I thought for a moment.

"A letter's a letter, but maybe you'd send a package? I'll pay well."

"A package is more difficult, because there's a customs control at the border. You can't avoid it."

"But if I gave you one?"

"I'd send it."

"Okay, when should I have it ready?"

"Today. I'm on duty the whole evening. A rotten Christmas Eve," he sighed. "But what can you do? People have gone mad. *So, so. Alles kaputt . . .*"

I walked over to the corner, dragged out Stefan's bottle, took a ring of kielbasa off the shelf, and gave it all to the SS man.

"Hide it, it'll come in handy in the evening."

"I'll drink while I'm at the guardpost; it's damn boring," Biański said, delighted. He looked out the window.

"I'm off, because a bread truck is on its way to you. I don't want them to see me here. Get the package ready." He nodded his head, and walked off quickly.

With a dull groan of its motor, the truck stopped in front of the warehouse door. I leaned out of the window.

"One moment, *Herr Unterscharführer*," I shouted to the black-uniformed SS man who was jumping out of the cab, "we'll be right there to unload." The truck was immediately surrounded by curious and hungry Gypsy children, greedily eyeing the piles of bread heaped in the back.

In the meantime Stefan had crawled out of his corner, chased off the little Gypsies with a loud *"hau ab!"* clambered onto the truck, and was starting to throw the loaves into the dirty, trodden snow instead of into Ewald's barrel.

The *Unterscharführer* threatened him with his fist.

"Get off the truck!" he shouted, grabbing his revolver.

In response, Stefan threw a couple of loaves right down at his feet and kept walking around the bread-laden truck.

"Jan!" he shouted, "I wish you could see how beautiful everything looks from above! Our Lager isn't just any old thing! Wherever you look, there's barbed wire and roofs, and snow on the roofs. When we win, we'll turn the whole world into a huge camp!"

With vulgar curses, the SS man clambered up to him and threw him down with a massive blow to the back of his neck, and when, on hearing the noise, I ran out of the warehouse, he screamed at me, "I'll lock you all up in the bunker! I'll fix you, *ihr Slavine!* Where's the chief?"

The chief wasn't in the warehouse. For obvious reasons, he was in our room with Klara. So Stefan went up to the door and, beating out a march with his fists, shouted, "Chief, chief, enough, *Herr Unter-scharführer* wants to make trouble for you, chief!"

It had an effect. The chief came out of the hut, red in the face and sweaty, zipping up his trousers. He was panting with rage.

"What the devil is going on here?"

The conveyer pointed to the loaves of bread lying in the mud and waved his hand in Stefan's direction.

"So what?" the chief spat out with contempt. "You've never seen bread? They'll eat it, anyway. Look at those swine creeping around it."

A couple of thin, ragged children were circling around by the truck, waiting for their chance. Adults were watching them from a distance, shouting something in Romany.

"Get out of here!" I shouted, and chased off the children.

"I'm going to go to the front soon, anyway," the chief added. The *Unterscharführer* nodded his head sympathetically.

Diplomatically, I pushed a packet of cigarettes over to him.

"Do you smoke?" The question was purely rhetorical.

He put the packet into his greasy trousers.

"I didn't know it was so jolly here," he said placatingly, "every-body's completely drunk."

"Perhaps you'd like something to drink? To Christmas Eve. Come on in."

After a few glasses of rum, the chief disappeared again through the doors to the obvious room, and the conveyer drove off, seen out by Stefan who, with his arm around his neck, said in good-bye, "Kiss me, darling, kiss me."

V

I handed Baiński a jar of formalin.

"This is it."

The SS man smiled helplessly, "How am I supposed to send it?"

"In the normal way. As a sample of no value. A specimen for testing. Do you know what's inside?" I shook the jar. "A child's liver." Biański's eyes widened incredulously. "What do you mean?"

"It's quite simple, chief. A worthless sample: contents — a human liver for testing, for a doctor. And inside? — you know. This is for you," I pulled a gold Longine watch out of my pocket. The SS man tried it on his wrist and smiled happily.

110

"All right, I'll send it for you. What a clever idea! But where did you get this?"

He looked around the room, as if he expected to see a ravaged corpse.

"Don't worry," I said, laughing out loud, "it's off a dead man, anyway. The selection was huge."

We clinked glasses and wished each other Happy Christmas.

The freshly washed floor smells damp. It is clean and cosy. A tiny Christmas tree decorated with cotton wool in imitation of snow stands on a table spread with a white cloth. *Opłatek* — Christmas wafer — on a little plate under the tree. From home. On another plate — holiday cookies. A few bottles of some fruit vodka, doughnuts sent from the kitchen.

The iron stove blows heat. It is very warm. Steam glistens on the whitewashed planks of the ceiling. The fragrance of rum and spirits rises in the room. Cigarette smoke hangs in delicate, blue, streams above the christmas tree and along the window.

I lie on the bed, tired and exhausted. I can still feel in my muscles the weight of thousands of loaves of bread and the rough cartons of margarine. Margarine, kielbasa, bread, vodka, girls, money. I have to send home again . . . gold, gold . . .steaming, fresh corpses by the crematorium, but they had been alive, too? Ah, its Weksler, a good doctor, a good man, a good man, a good . . . his face is motionless, he's looking me straight in the eye without amazement. A lancet glistens in his supple, narrow palm. A lancet? No, it's the liver of a dissected child.

"Why isn't he surprised?" I think lazily. "What if I were to ask him for a banana?" The pale face dissolves into the room. Only the shining, wise eyes are left.

"How many do you want? How many? Two? Twenty? Two hundred! Two hundred!"

The bruised, dried bodies turn along with the narrow, pale face; the doctor's eyes are underneath, they shine like diamonds in the liver . . .

"How many do you want? How many? How many!"

"How should I know how many? Probably about three liters, heh, Klara?" Stefan's voice comes from a distance.

I shook my head. Stefan was standing in the middle of the room holding his hand around the girl's neck.

"I must have drunk three liters, Jasiu. Either it's Christmas Eve, or it isn't, and you're asleep! Hey, musicians, play, dammit!"

The shrill squeak of the Gypsy choir burst through the open door. Two young Gypsy women tied together at the shoulders with colorful scarves started to dance at the threshold, shaking their bracelet-covered hands above their heads. I rose up and banged the door in their faces.

"You've got some ideas! Making women dance to the tune of 'Bóg sie rodzi,' God is Born!"

"Don't get mad, Jasiu, a bit of cultural entertainment won't hurt. Anyway, I'm celebrating Christmas Eve amongst my family today, so there have to be carols." He took photographs out of his wallet and placed them on the table.

"See, Klara, this is my wife, a very beloved woman. I got a letter from her today. A wife like that is quite something! And this is my little boy — see how he's grown."

"And this is your lover," Klara said, pointing to herself.

"And this is the crematorium, through which we'll go to freedom in the form of smoke out of the chimney," finished Stefan, nodding his head toward the window. "Klara, the family celebration is over. Come and nap for an hour, and then we'll go drink, drink until morning."

The girl started to unbutton her blouse. I went outside.

Evening was descending on Birkenau. The wind whistled between Blocks packed with people and buzzing like beehives. The long rows of Blocks divided by wire and long lines of lamps were falling into darkness. It seemed as though their light was circling silently above the wires and falling to the ground in drops.

In Lager D a huge christmas tree glistened with many colored lights, and quadrangles of motionless people were fading into the gathering dusk. For them, the Appel is still going on. A whipping post has been erected on the main street. The dark forms of officers stand without moving, as if they, too, were made of dusk.

Above the camp hung a black and starless night, but above the birch wood, there in the direction of the crematorium, the clouds were red with the glow of Christmas Eve. It was the Christmas Eve of those who were burning.

I move along the empty street of the camp at a slow pace, in the direction of the hospital Blocks.

I am going to my Christmas Eve.

VI

Packed tight with people, the Block is abuzz. Between the filthy bunks set close together on the dirt floor, shuffle the naked, emaciated sick. Out of countless bunks, lean the countless faces of sick women. Bruised, dark eyes burn in deep sockets. Dry, wrinkled breasts hang like empty sacks. Legs are as thin as sticks. Rough, cracked skin covered with pimples, scabs, and dotted with bug bites glistens in the dim light.

Children, small grotesques with distended bellies, crawl along the large brick stove that runs the length of the barracks. The *Pfleger* walks from bunk to bunk distributing food. He does so methodically, slowly, beating around the face those who want to take a double portion, or who take a piece of bread when they think he's not looking.

He climbs onto some bunk from which come a child's cry and a woman's curses and starts to restore order with his fists.

"Imagine," he says to me, pointing to a dark Gypsy woman leaning out of her bunk and looking at us resentfully, "that cow wanted to eat her child's portion. So tell me, these are humans?"

From a neighboring bunk comes a murmur of Gypsy voices:

"*Pfleger! Pfleger!* She's going to suffocate the child! She's a witch!"

"Let her try." The *Pfleger* threatens, and turning to me, adds with a shrug of his shoulders, "I can't stand over her. If she wants to, she'll suffocate him, and God himself won't be able to do anything about it. They're waiting with Christmas Eve for you," he adds, as though he's suddenly remembered.

Christmas Eve?

The green doors of the delivery room open. I push aside the blanket that serves as a curtain.

"Oh, what a lot of you!" I am genuinely pleased.

Dr. Kulesz is here, and Loda; all the nurses from the block, and even prominents like Italiana, the Gypsy Block Elder, and her sister with the funny name, Kican. Hans, an Estonian from Spain, is here. With difficulty, I squeeze behind their chairs to an empty place at the table that is spread with a white cloth. The hay under the cloth rustles when I lean my hands on the table. Loda lights the candle and turns off the lamp. The surgical instruments in the glass cabinets sparkle like ice. The glass anesthesia table stands behind Italiana — sandwiches, bowls of salads, and deep, steaming, bowls of *barszcz* are piled on it now.

"Ah, so this is why they came for beets yesterday," I think to myself.

The white Christmas wafer rustles between our fingers. I kiss the air next to someone's face.

"How good and dear you all are now, no one's whoring around, no one's stealing."

We recite the traditional greetings. "For the last time in the camp . . . let's hope that next year it'll be at home . . . let the war end as quickly as . . ." It really is just like at home. Doctor Kulesz could be any one of our fathers or uncles. He sits behind the table — old, outdated, without the slightest clue about organizing.

Tears well up in his eyes when he writes out a *Totenmeldung* for a child. He shares a Christmas wafer with me and his voice breaks.

"Colleague, dear colleague . . ."

I know he is honest, of course; he'll go to heaven, if there is a heaven. And that child he cries over will die all the sooner, because it needs that little piece of butter we have taken away from it. But if I hadn't stolen it, honest Kulesz would die of hunger tomorrow, and Loda would have nothing to eat. . . . It would have been better not to have come. It must be more cheerful there in the kitchen, the boys drinking, squeezing the girls.

How many of these things I stole, I think, looking at the sandwiches, at the mounds of salads, at the steaming *barszcz*. But if I hadn't stolen them, someone else would have done, and they would all have nothing. Someone else would have sold it or drunk it away, like Stefan. So I'm better than Stefan? Isn't it all the same?

The steaming *barszcz* and dumplings are fragrant with the smell of Christmas Eve at home.

"Jasiu, don't be sad, this must be the last time," Loda says quietly, placing her hand on my hand.

"It must be the last time," I reply, smiling at her.

Hans cuts the cake ceremoniously, giving everyone a piece. We start to sing carols. The difficult words sound strange on the Gypsy women's lips. The cigarette tastes strange. Home, and those who wait, recede into mist.

"And after that, we'll be together?" Loda looks at me, her large eyes glistening with tears.

"Together," I say, and think about the roads that, coming from two different directions, meet in the birch wood above which the clouds are always red.

*   *   *

Outside, it's total night. Stars shine high in the clear sky. The lights along the wires glisten with a ghastly pallor.

Jerzy crawls on all fours along the completely empty street, and behind him strides a small Gypsy vigorously beating on a drum hanging from a leather belt. A drunken Ellen prances around him, her shirt unbuttoned.

"Fire freezes!" Jerzy screams, and bangs on the door of our Block with his head.

Dull pistol shots fall in the darkness, and right afterward we can hear terrified human screams from one of the Blocks.

Biański, a smoking pistol in his hand, comes reeling into the circle of shaky light.

"*Was ist los,* chief?" I shout to him, "Was that you shooting?"

"Either it's Christmas Eve or it isn't," he shouts back to me. "The vodka was good! Look, Jan," he says, pointing to the wall of the Block with his hand. "That's how high the third level of bunks is; this is the second, and here" — he traces a vertical line — "the aisle. That means — the head will be a bit to the left."

He aims and fires. The wooden plank splits, and a sudden cry goes up inside the barracks.

The SS man bares his teeth.

"I hit the target, right? *Prosit.*" He looks at the Block from under his brow. "Yes, this is the third, this is the second, now we'll bang at the bottom one, just to be fair. Either it's Christmas Eve, or it isn't."

He raises his pistol and, spreading his legs, takes long and careful aim.

AUSCHWITZ, OUR
HOME, A LETTER

*In March 1944, a nursing course was conducted in Old Auschwitz, which had
as its aim the readying of a professional force of assistants for work in the camp
hospitals. But a description of this course is not the subject of these letters, which
had once been sent to the Women's Camp and are now taken from memory. Maybe
the atmosphere of the Old, Good, Auschwitz is such as was seen by a thinking man
and an "accustomed" one, to whom the techniques of the camp, the crematoria and
the orchestra, X ray and gallows, duplicity and betrayal, are no longer alien.*

I

So here I am, a student at the Auschwitz hospital. From the vast
population of Birkenau, only ten of us were selected and sent here to
be trained as medical orderlies, almost doctors. We shall be expected to know every bone in the human body, all about the circula-
tory system, what a peritoneum is, how to cure staphylococcus and
streptococcus, how to take out an appendix, and the various symp-
toms of emphysema.

We shall be entrusted with a lofty mission: to nurse back to
health our fellow inmates who may have the "misfortune" to become
ill, suffer from severe apathy, or feel depressed about life in general.
It will be up to us — the chosen ten out of Birkenau's twenty thousand — to lower the camp's mortality rate and to raise the prisoners'
morale. Or, in short, that is what we were told by the SS doctor
upon our departure from Birkenau. He then asked each of us our age
and occupation, and when I answered "student" he raised his eye-
brows in surprise.

"And what was it you studied?"

"The history of literature," I answered modestly.

He nodded his head with distaste; got into his car and drove
away.

Afterwards we marched to Auschwitz along a very beautiful
road, observing some very interesting scenery en route. Then we
were assigned guest quarters at one of the Auschwitz hospital

Blocks, and as soon as this dreary procedure was over, Staszek (you know, the one who once gave me a pair of brown trousers) and I took off for the camp; I in search of someone who might deliver this letter to you, and Staszek to the kitchens and the supply rooms to round up some food for supper — a loaf of white bread, a piece of lard and at least one sausage, since there are five of us living together.

I was, naturally, entirely unsuccessful, my serial number being over one million, whereas this place swarms with very "old numbers" who look down their noses at million-plus fellows like me. But Staszek promised to take care of my letter through his own contacts, provided it was not too heavy. "It must be a bore to write to a girl every day," he told me.

So, as soon as I learn all the bones in the human body and find out what a peritoneum is, I shall let you know how to cure your skin rash and what the woman in the bunk next to yours ought to take for her fever. But I know that even if I discovered the remedy for *ulcus duodeni*, I would still be unable to get you the ordinary Wilkinson's itch ointment, because there just is none to be had at the camp. We simply used to douse our patients with mint tea, at the same time uttering certain very effective magic words, which, unfortunately, I cannot repeat.

As for lowering the camp's mortality rate: some time ago one of the "bigwigs" in our Block fell ill; he felt terrible, had a high fever, and spoke more and more of dying. Finally one day he called me over. I sat down on the edge of the bed.

"Wouldn't you say I was fairly well known at the camp, eh?" he asked, looking anxiously into my eyes.

"There isn't one man around who wouldn't know you . . . and always remember you," I answered innocently.

"Look over there," he said, pointing at the window.

Tall flames were shooting up in the sky beyond the forest.

"Well, you see, I want to be put away separately. Not with all the others. Not on a heap. You understand?"

"Don't worry," I told him affectionately. "I'll even see to it that you get your own sheet. And I can put in a good word for you with the morgue boys."

He squeezed my hand in silence. But nothing came of it. He got well, and later sent me a piece of lard from the main camp. I use it to shine my shoes, for it happens to be made of fish oil. And so you have an example of my contribution to the lowering of the camp's mortality rate. But enough of camp talk for one day.

For almost a month now I have not had a letter from home . . .

II

What delightful days: no Appels, no duties to perform. The entire camp stands at attention, but we, the lucky spectators from another planet, lean out of the window and gaze at the world. The people smile at us, we smile at the people, they call us "Comrades from Birkenau," with a touch of pity . . . our lot being so miserable . . . and a touch of guilt . . . theirs being so fortunate. The view from the window is almost pastoral . . . not one cremo in sight. These people over here are crazy about Auschwitz. "Auschwitz, our home . . ." they say with pride.

And, in truth, they have good reason to be proud. I want you to imagine what this place is like: take the dreary Pawiak, add Serbia*, multiply them by twenty-eight and plant these prisons so close together that only tiny spaces are left between them; then encircle the whole thing with a double row of barbed wire and build a concrete wall on three sides; put in paved roads in place of the mud and plant a few anemic trees. Now lock inside fifteen thousand people who have all spent years in concentration camps, who have all suffered unbelievably and survived even the most terrible seasons, but now wear freshly pressed trousers and sway from side to side as they walk. After you had done all this you would understand why they look down with contempt and pity on their colleagues from Birkenau — where the barracks are made of wood, where there are no sidewalks, and where, in place of the bath-houses with hot running water, there are four crematoria.

From the orderlies' quarters, which have very white, rustic-looking walls, a cement floor, and many rows of triple-deck bunks, there is an excellent view of a "free-world" road. Here sometimes a man will pass; sometimes a car will drive by; sometimes a horse-drawn cart; and sometimes — a lonely bicycle, probably a laborer returning home after a day's work.

* Two Warsaw prisons.

118

In the far distance (you have no idea what a vast expanse can fit between the frames of one small window; after the war, if I survive, I would like to live in a tall building with windows facing open fields), there are some houses, and beyond them a dark-blue forest. There the earth is black and it must be damp. As in one of Staff's* sonnets — "A Walk in Springtime," remember?

Another window looks out on a birch-lined path — the *Birkenweg* — In the evening, after the roll-call, we stroll along this path, dignified and solemn, and greet friends in passing with a discreet bow. At one of the crossings stands a road marker and a sculpture showing two men seated on a bench, whispering to each other, while a third leans over their shoulders and listens. This means: beware . . . every one of your conversations is overheard, interpreted and reported to the proper authorities. In Auschwitz one man knows all there is to know about another: when he was a muzulman, how much he stole and through whom, the number of people he has strangled, and the number of people he has ruined. And they grin knowingly if you happen to utter a word of praise about anyone else.

Well then, imagine a Pawiak, multiplied many times, and surrounded with a double row of barbed wire. Not at all like Birkenau, with its watch-towers that really look like storks perched on their high, long legs, with searchlights at only every third post, and but a single row of barbed wire.

No, it is quite different here: there are searchlights at every other post, watch-towers on solid cement bases, a double-thick fence, plus a high concrete wall.

So we stroll along the *Birkenweg*, clean-shaven, fresh, carefree. Other prisoners stand about in small groups, linger in front of Block 10 where behind bars and tightly boarded-up windows there are girls — experimental guinea-pigs; but mostly they gather around the "educational" section, not because it houses a concert hall, a library, and a museum, but because up on the first floor there is the Puff. But I shall tell you about that in my next letter.

You know, it feels very strange to be writing to you, you whose face I have not seen for so long. At times I can barely remember what you look like — your image fades from my memory despite my efforts to recall it. And yet my dreams about you are incredibly

*A Polish lyrical poet.

vivid; they have an almost physical reality. A dream, you see, is not necessarily visual. It may be an emotional experience in which there is depth and where one feels the weight of an object and the warmth of a body . . .

It is hard for me to imagine you on a prison bunk, with your hair shaved off after typhus. I see you still as I saw you the last time at the Pawiak prison: a tall, willowy young woman with sad eyes and a gentle smile. Later, at the Gestapo headquarters, you sat with your head bent low, so I could see nothing but your black hair that has now been shaven off.

And this is what has remained most vivid in my memory: this picture of you, even though I can no longer clearly recall your face. And that is why I write you such long letters — they are our evening talks, like the ones we used to have on Staryszewska Street. And that is why my letters are not sad. I have kept my spirit and I know that you have not lost yours either. Despite everything. Despite your hidden face at the Gestapo headquarters, despite the typhoid fever, despite the pneumonia — and despite the shaved head.

But the people here . . . you see, they have lived through and survived all the incredible horrors of the concentration camp, the concentration camp of the early years, about which one hears so many fantastic stories. At one time they weighed sixty pounds or less, they were beaten, selected for the gas chamber — you can understand, then, why today they wear ridiculous tight jackets, walk with a characteristic sway, and have nothing but praise of Auschwitz.

We stroll along the *Birkenweg*, elegant, dressed in our civilian suits; but alas — our serial numbers are so high! And around us are nothing but one-hundred-and-three thousand, one-hundred-and-nineteen thousand . . . What a pity we did not get here a little sooner! A man in prison stripes approaches us: his number is twenty-seven thousand — it almost makes your head swim! A young fellow with the glassy stare of a masturbator and the walk of a hunted animal.

"Where're you from, comrades?"

"From Birkenau, friend."

"From Birkenau?" He examines us with a frown. "And looking so well? Awful, awful . . . How do you stand it over there?"

Witek, my skinny, tall friend and an excellent musician, pulls down his shirt cuffs.

"Unfortunately we had some trouble getting a piano, but otherwise we managed," he retorts.

The "old number" looks at us as though he were looking through dense fog.

"Because . . . around here we're afraid of Birkenau . . ."

III

Again the start of our training has been postponed, as we are awaiting the arrival of orderlies from neighbouring camps: from Janin, Jaworzyn and Buna, and from some more distant camps that are nevertheless part of Auschwitz. Meanwhile, we have had to listen to several lofty speeches made by our chief, black, dried-up little Adolf, who has recently come from Dachau and exudes *Kameradschaft*. By training orderlies, he expects to improve the camp's health, and by teaching us all about the nervous system, to reduce the mortality rate. Adolf is extremely pleasant and really out of another world. But, being a German, he fails to distinguish between reality and illusion, and is inclined to take words at their face value, as if they always represented the truth. He says *Kameraden* and thinks "We really are *Kameraden*." He says "reduce the suffering" and thinks such a thing is possible. Above the gates leading to the camp, these words are inscribed on metal scrolls: "Work makes you free." I suppose they believe it, the SS men and the German prisoners — those raised on Luther, Fichte, Hegel, Nietzsche.

And so, for the time being we have no school. I roam around the camp, sightseeing and making psychological notes for myself. In fact, three of us roam together — Staszek, Witek and I. Staszek usually hangs around the kitchens and the supply rooms, searching for men whom he has helped in the past and who he now expects will help him. And, sure enough, towards evening the procession begins. Odd, suspicious-looking characters come and go, their clean-shaven faces smiling compassionately. From the pockets of their tightly fitted jackets they pull out a piece of margarine, some white hospital bread, a slice of sausage, or a few cigarettes. They set these down on the lower bunk and disappear, as in a silent film. We divide the loot, add to it what we have received in our packages from home, and cook a meal on our stove with the colorful Majolica tiles.

Witek spends his time in a tireless search for a piano. There is one large black crate in the music room, which is located in the same block as the Puff, but playing during work hours is forbidden, and after the roll-call the piano is monopolized by the musicians who give symphony concerts every Sunday. Some day I must go to hear them.

Across from the music room we have spotted a door with "Library" written on it, but we have heard through reliable sources that it is for the *Reichsdeutsch* only, and contains nothing but mystery stories. I have not been able to verify this, for the room is always locked up as tight as a coffin.

Next door to the library is the Political Office, and beyond it, to complete the "cultural section," the museum. It houses photographs confiscated from the prisoners' letters. Nothing more. And what a pity — for it would have been interesting to have on exhibit that half-cooked human liver, a tiny nibble of which cost a Greek friend of mine twenty-five lashes across his rear-end.

But the most important place of all is one flight up. The Puff. Its windows are left slightly open at all times, even in winter. And from the windows — after Appel — peek out pretty little heads of various shades of colour, with delicate shoulders, as white and fresh as snow, emerging from their frilly blue, pink and sea-green robes (the green is my favourite color). Altogether there are, I am told, fifteen little heads, not counting the old Madame with the tremendous legendary breasts, who watches over the little heads, the white shoulders, etc. . . . The Madame does not lean out of the window, but like watchful Cerberus, officiates at the entrance to the Puff.

The Puff is for ever surrounded by a crowd of the most important citizens of the camp. For every Juliet there are at least a thousand Romeos. Hence the crowd, and the competition. The Romeos stand along the windows of the barracks across the street; they shout, wave, invite. The *Lagerältester* and the Camp Kapo are there, and so are the doctors from the hospital and the Kapos from the Kommandos. It is not unusual for a Juliet to have a steady admirer, and, along with promises of undying love and a blissful life together after the war, along with reproaches and bickering, one is apt to hear exchanges of a more basic nature, concerning such particulars as soap, perfume, silk panties, or cigarettes.

But there is a great deal of loyalty among the men: they do not compete unfairly. The girls at the windows are tender and desirable, but, like goldfish in an aquarium, unattainable.

This is how the Puff looks from the outside. To get inside you need a slip of paper issued by the clerical office as a reward for good conduct and diligent work. As guests from Birkenau, we were offered priority in this regard also, but we declined the favour; let the criminals use the facilities intended for them. Forgive me, therefore, but my report must be of necessity only second-hand, although it relies on such excellent witnesses as, for example, old *Pfleger* M from our barracks, whose serial number is almost three times lower than the last two figures in mine. One of the original founding fathers, you know! Which is why he rocks from side to side like a duck when he walks, and wears wide, carefully pressed trousers secured in front with safety pins. In the evening he returns to the barracks excited and happy. His system is to go to the clerical office when the numbers of the "elect" are being called, waiting to see if there will be an absentee. When this happens, he shouts *hier*, snatches the pass and races over to the Madame. He slips several packets of cigarettes in her hand, undergoes a few treatments of a hygienic nature, and, all sprayed and fresh, leaps upstairs. The Juliets stroll along the narrow hallway, their fluffy robes carelessly wrapped around them. In passing, one of them may ask *Pfleger* M indifferently:

"What number have you got?"

"Eight," he answers, glancing at his slip to make sure.

"Ah, it's not for me, it's for Irma, the little blonde over there," she will mutter and walks back to the window, her hips swaying softly.

Then *Pfleger* M goes to room No. 8. Before he enters, he must read a notice on the door saying that such and such is strictly forbidden, under severe penalty, that only such and such (a detailed list follows) is allowed, but only for so many minutes. He sighs at the sight of a spy-hole, which is occasionally used for peeping by the other girls, occasionally by the Madame, or the Puff's *Kommandoführer*, or the camp Kommandant himself. He drops a packet of cigarettes on the table, and . . . oh, at the same time he notices two packets of English cigarettes on top of the dresser. Then he does what he has come for and departs . . . absent-mindedly slipping the English cigarettes into his pocket. Once more he undergoes a disinfecting treatment, and later, pleased with himself and cheerful, he relates his adventure to us blow by blow.

But once in a while all the precautions fail . . . only recently the Puff again became contaminated. The place was locked up, the customers, traced through their numbers, were called in and subjected to a radical treatment. But, because of the flourishing black-market in passes, in most cases the wrong men underwent the cure. Ha, such is life. The Puff girls also used to make trips inside the camp. Dressed in men's suits, they would climb down a ladder in the middle of the night to join a drinking brawl or an orgy of some kind. But an SS guard from a near-by sector did not like it, and that was the end of that.

There is another place where women may be found: Block 10, the experimental block. The women in Block 10 are being artificially inseminated, injected with typhoid and malaria germs, or operated on. I once caught a glimpse of the man who heads the project: a man in a green hunting outfit and a gay little Tyrolian hat decorated with many brightly shining sports emblems, a man with the face of a kindly satyr. A university professor, I am told.

The women are kept behind barred and boarded-up windows, but still the place is often broken into and the women are inseminated, not at all artificially. This must make the old professor very angry indeed.

But you must not misunderstand — these men are not maniacs or perverts. Every man in the camp, as soon as he has had enough food and sleep, talks about women. Every man in the camp dreams about women. Every man in the camp tries to get hold of a woman. One *Lagerältester* wound up in a penal transport for repeatedly climbing through the window into the Puff. A nineteen-year-old SS man once caught the orchestra conductor, a stout, respectable gentleman, and several dentists inside an ambulance in unambiguous positions with the female patients who had come to have their teeth pulled. With a club which he happened to have in his hand, the young SS man administered due punishment across the most readily available parts of their anatomy. An episode of this sort is no discredit to anyone: you are unlucky if you are caught, that is all.

The woman obsession in the camp increases steadily. No wonder the Puff girls are treated like normal women with whom one talks of love and family. No wonder the men are so eager to visit the FKL in Birkenau. And stop to think, this is true not only of Auschwitz, it is true also of hundreds of "great" concentration camps, hundreds of *Oflags* and *Stalags* . . .

Do you know what I am thinking about as I write to you?

It is late evening. Separated by a large cabinet from the rest of the huge sick-ward full of heavily breathing patients, I sit alone by a dark window which reflects my face, the green lampshade, and the white sheet of paper on the table. Franz, a young boy from Vienna, took a liking to me the very first evening he arrived — so now I am sitting at his table, under his lamp, and am writing this letter to you on his paper. But I shall not write about the subjects we were discussing today at the camp: German literature, wine, romantic philosophy, problems of materialism.

Do you know what I am thinking about?

I am thinking about Staryszewska Street. I look at the dark window, at my face reflected in the glass, and outside I see the blackness occasionally broken by the sudden flash of the watch-tower searchlight that silhouettes fragments of objects in the dark. I look into the night and I think of Staryszewska Street. I remember the sky, pale and luminous, and the bombed-out house across the street. I think of how much I longed for your body during those days, and I often smile to myself imagining the consternation after my arrest when they must have found in my room, next to my books and my poems, your perfume and your robe, heavy and red like the brocades in Velazquez's paintings.

I think of how very mature you were; what devotion and — forgive me if I say it now — selflessness you brought to our love, how graciously you used to walk into my life which offered you nothing but a single room without plumbing, evenings with cold tea, a few wilting flowers, a dog that was always playfully gnawing at your shoes, and a paraffin lamp.

I think about these things and smile condescendingly when people speak to me of morality, of law, of tradition, of obligation . . . Or when they discard all tenderness and sentiment and, shaking their fists, proclaim this the age of toughness. I smile and I think that one human being must always be discovering another — through love. And that this is the most important thing on earth, and the most lasting.

And I think about my cell at the Pawiak prison. During the first week I felt I would not be able to endure a day without a book, without the circle of light under the paraffin lamp in the evening, without a sheet of paper, without you . . .

And indeed, habit is a powerful force: will you believe it, I paced up and down the cell and composed poems to the rhythm of my steps. One of them I wrote down in a cellmate's copy of the Bible, but the rest — and they were poems conceived in the style of Horace — I no longer remember.

125

IV

Today is Sunday. In the morning we made another little sight-seeing tour, took a look at the exterior of the women's experimental block (they push out their heads between the bars, just like the rabbits my father used to keep; do you remember — gray ones with one floppy ear?), and then we toured the S.K. Block (in its courtyard is the famous Black Wall where mass executions used to be carried out; today such business is handled more quietly and discreetly — in the crematoria). We saw some civilians: two frightened women in fur coats and a man with tired, worried eyes. Led by an SS man, they were being taken to the city jail which is temporarily located in the S.K. Block. The women gazed with horror at the prisoners in stripes and at the massive camp installations: the two-storey barracks, the double row of barbed wire, the concrete wall beyond it, the solid watch-towers. And they did not even know that the wall extends two yards into the ground, to prevent us from digging our way out! We smiled to cheer them up: after all, in a few weeks they will be released. Unless, of course, it is proved that they did indeed dabble in black marketeering. In that case they will go to the cremo. But they are really quite amusing, these civilians. They react to the camp as a wild boar reacts to firearms. Understanding nothing of how it functions, they look upon it as something inexplicable, almost abnormal, something beyond human endurance. Remember the horror you felt when they arrested you?

Today, having become totally familiar with the inexplicable and the abnormal; having learned to live on intimate terms with the crematoria, the itch and the tuberculosis; having understood the true meaning of wind, rain and sun, of bread and turnip soup, of work to survive, of slavery and power; having, so to say, daily broken bread with the beast — I look at these civilians with a certain indulgence, the way a scientist regards a layman, or the initiated an outsider.

Try to grasp the essence of this pattern of daily events, discarding your sense of horror and loathing and contempt, and find for it all a philosophic formula. For the gas chambers and the gold stolen from the victims, for the Appel and for the Puff, for the frightened civilians and for the "old numbers."

If I had said to you as we danced together in my room in the light of the paraffin lamp: listen, take a million people, or two million, or three, kill them in such a way that no one knows about it, not even they themselves, enslave several hundred thousand more, destroy their mutual loyalty, pit man against man, and . . . surely you would have thought me mad. Except that I would probably not have said these things to you, even if I had known what I know today. I would not have wanted to spoil our mood.

But this is how it is done: first just one ordinary barn, brightly whitewashed — and here they proceed to asphyxiate people. Later, four large buildings, accommodating twenty thousand at a time without any trouble. No hocus-pocus, no poison, no hypnosis. Only several men directing traffic to keep operations running smoothly, and the thousands flow along like water from an open tap. All this happens just beyond the anemic trees of the dusty little wood. Ordinary trucks bring people, return, then bring some more. No hocus-pocus, no poison, no hypnosis.

Why is it that nobody cries out, nobody spits in their faces, nobody jumps at their throats? We doff our caps to the SS men returning from the little wood; if our name is called we obediently go with them to die, and — we do nothing. We starve, we are drenched by rain, we are torn from our families. What is this mystery? This strange power of one man over another? This insane passivity that cannot be overcome? Our only strength is our great number — the gas chambers cannot accommodate all of us.

Or here is another way: the spade handle across the throat — that takes care of about a hundred people daily. Or, first nettle soup and dry bread and a number tattooed on your arm, and then a young, beefy SS man comes around with a dirty slip of paper in his hand, and then you are put in one of those trucks . . . Do you know when was the last time that the "Aryans" were selected for the gas chamber? April 4th. And do you remember when we arrived at the camp? April 29th. Do you realize what would have happened — and you with pneumonia — if we had arrived just a few months earlier?

The women who share your bunk must find my words rather surprising. "You told us he was so cheerful. And what about this letter? It's so full of gloom!" And probably they are a little bit shocked. But I think that we should speak about all the things that are happening around us. We are not evoking evil irresponsibly or in vain, for we have now become a part of it . . .

Once again it is late evening after a day full of curious happenings.

In the afternoon we went to see a boxing match in the huge *Waschraum* barracks used in the old days as the starting point for transports going to the gas chamber. We were led up to the front, although the hall was packed to capacity. The large waiting-room had been turned into a boxing ring. Floodlights overhead, a real referee (an Olympic referee from Poland, in fact), boxing stars of international fame, but only Aryans — Jews are not allowed to participate. And the very same people who knock out dozens of teeth every day, or who themselves have no teeth left inside their mouths, were now enthusiastically cheering Czortek, or Walter from Hamburg, or a young boy trained at the camp who has apparently developed into a first-class fighter. The memory of No. 77, who once fought and mercilessly defeated the Germans in the ring, revenging there what the other prisoners had to endure in the field, is still very much alive. The hall was thick with cigarette smoke and the fighters knocked each other around to their hearts' content. A bit unprofessionally perhaps, but with considerable perseverance.

"Just take a look at old Walter!" cried Staszek. "At the Kommando he can strike down a muzulman with one blow whenever the spirit moves him! And up here — it's already the third round and nothing happens! He's really getting a beating! Too many spectators I reckon, don't you think?"

The spectators indeed seemed to be in their seventh heaven, and there were we, seated, sure enough, in the front row, as befitted important guests.

Right after the boxing match I took in another show — I went to hear a concert. Over in Birkenau you could probably never imagine what feats of culture we are exposed to up here, just a few kilometers away from the smoldering chimneys. Just think — an orchestra playing the overture to *Tancred*, then something by Berlioz, then some Finnish dances by one of those composers with many "a"s in his name. Warsaw would not be ashamed of such music! But let me describe the whole thing from the beginning: I walked out of the boxing match, exhilarated and pleased, and immediately made way to the Puff block. The concert hall, located directly below the Puff, was crowded and noisy. People stood against the walls; the musicians, scattered throughout the room, were tuning their instruments. Over by the window — a raised platform. The kitchen Kapo (who is the orchestra conductor) mounted it; whereupon the potato peelers and cart pushers (I forgot to tell you that the orchestra members spend their days peeling potatoes and pushing carts) began to play. I sank into an empty chair between the clarinet and the bassoon and became lost in the music. Imagine — a thirty-piece orchestra in one ordinary room! Do you know what a volume of sound that can produce? The Kapo-conductor waved his arms with restraint, trying not to strike the wall, and clearly shook his fist at anyone who happened to hit a sour note, as if to warn him: "You'll pay for it in the potato field!" The players at the far end of the room (one at the drums, the other with the viola) tried to improvise as best they could. But almost all the instruments seemed drowned out by the bassoon, maybe because I was seated right by it. An audience of fifteen (there was no room for more) listened with the air of connoisseurs and rewarded the musicians with a little scattered applause . . . Somebody once called our camp *Betrugslager* — a fraud and a mockery. A little strip of lawn at the edge of the barracks, a yard resembling a village square, a sign reading "bath," are enough to fool millions of people, to deceive them until death. A mere boxing match, a green hedge along the wall, two deutsche marks per month for the more diligent prisoners, mustard in the canteen, a weekly delousing inspection, and the *Tancred* overture suffice to deceive the world — and us. People on the outside know that, of course, life over here is terrible; but after all, perhaps it is not really so bad if there is a symphony orchestra, and boxing, and green little lawns, and blankets on the bunks . . . But a bread ration that is not sufficient to keep you alive — is a mockery.

Work, during which you are not allowed to speak up, to sit down, to rest, is a mockery. And every half empty shovelful of earth that we toss on to the embankment is a mockery.

Look carefully at everything around you, and conserve your strength. For a day may come when it will be up to us to give an account of the fraud and mockery to the living — to speak up for the dead.

Not long ago, the labour Kommandos used to march in formation when returning to camp. The band played and the passing columns kept step with its beat. One day the D.A.W. Kommando and many of the others — some ten thousand men — were ordered to stop and stood waiting at the gate. At that moment several trucks full of naked women rolled in from the FKL The women stretched out their arms and pleaded:

"Save us! We are going to the gas chambers! Save us!"

And they rode slowly past us — the ten thousand silent men — and then disappeared from sight. Not one of us made a move, not one of us lifted a hand.

V

Our medical training has now been in progress for some time, but I have written little to you about it, because the attic where we work is very cold. We sit on organized stools and have a tremendously good time, particularly when we can fool around with the large models of the human body. The more serious students try to learn what this is all about, but Witek and I spend most of our time hurling sponges at one another or dueling with rulers, which brings Black Adolf close to despair. He waves his arms above our heads and talks about *Kameradschaft* and about the camp in general. We retreat quietly into a corner; Witek pulls a photograph of his wife out of his pocket, and asks in a muffled tone:

"I wonder how many men he's murdered over in Dachau? Otherwise, why would he be carrying on in this way? . . . How would you like to strangle him? . . ."

"Uhm . . . a good-looking woman, your wife. How did you ever get her?"

"One day we went for a walk in Pruszkow*. You know how it is — everything fresh and green, narrow winding paths, woods all around. We were walking along, happy and relaxed, when all at once an SS dog jumped out of the bushes and came straight at us."

"Liar! That was Pruszkow, not Auschwitz."

"An SS dog, I mean it — because the house near by had been taken over by the SS And the cur came straight at my girl! Well, what was I to do? I shot a few slugs into his hide, I grabbed the girl and said: 'Come on, Irene, we'd better get out of here!' But she did not budge an inch — just stood there, stupefied, and stared at the revolver. 'Where did you get that!' I barely managed to drag her away, I could already hear voices approaching. We ran straight across the fields, like two scared rabbits. It took me some time before I was able to convince Irene that this piece of iron was indispensable in my work."

Meanwhile another doctor had begun to lecture about the esophagus and other such things found inside the human body, but Witek went on, unruffled:

* A wooded suburb of Warsaw.

"Once I had a fight with a friend of mine. It's got to be him or me, I thought to myself. And the same idea, I felt certain, had occurred to him. I tailed him for about three days, but always taking care that there was nobody behind me. Finally I cornered him one evening over on Chmielna Street and I let him have it, except that I missed the right spot. The next day I went around — his arm was all bandaged up and he stared at me grimly. 'I've fallen down,' he said."

"And so what did you do?" I asked, finding the story rather timely.

"Nothing, because immediately after that I was locked up."

Whether his friend had anything to do with it or not is difficult to say, but Witek nevertheless refused to let fate get the better of him. At the Pawiak prison he became washroom attendant — a kind of helper to Kronschmidt who, together with one Ukrainian, used to amuse himself torturing Jews. You remember the cellars of Pawiak; the metal floors they had down there. Well, the Jews, naked, their bodies steaming after a hot bath, were forced to crawl over them, back and forth, back and forth. And have you ever seen the soles of military boots, studded with heavy nails? Well, Kronschmidt, wearing such boots, would climb on top of a naked man and make him crawl while he rode on his back. The Aryans were not treated quite as badly, although I too crawled on the floor, but in a different section, and nobody climbed on top of me; and it was not an ordinary occurrence but rather punishment for misbehavior. In addition, we had physical training: one hour every two days. First running around the yard, then falling to the ground and push-ups. Good, healthy exercise!

My record — seventy-six push-ups, and terrible pain in the arms until the next time. But the best exercise of all was the group game "Air raid, take cover!" Two rows of prisoners, chests pressed against backs, hold a ladder on their shoulders, supporting it with one hand. At the call "Air raid, take cover!" they fall to the ground, still holding the ladder on their shoulders. Whoever lets go, dies under the blows of the club. And then an SS man starts walking back and forth on the rungs of the ladder lying across your body. Then you must stand up and, without changing formation, fall down again.

You see, the inexplicable actually happens: you do miles of somersaults; spend hours simply rolling on the ground; you do hundreds of squat-jumps; you stand motionless for endless days and nights; you sit for a full month inside a cement coffin — the bunker; you hang from a post or a wooden pole extended between two chairs; you jump like a frog and crawl like a snake; drink bucketfuls of water until you suffocate; you are beaten with a thousand different whips and clubs, by a thousand different men. I listen avidly to tales about prisons — unknown provincial prisons like Małkini, Suwałki, Radom, Puławy, Lublin — about the monstrously perfected techniques for torturing man, and I find it impossible to believe that all this just sprang suddenly out of somebody's head, like Athena out of Zeus's. I find it impossible to comprehend this sudden frenzy of murder, this morning tide of unleashed atavism . . .

And another thing: death. I was told about a camp where transports of new prisoners arrived each day, dozens of people at a time. But the camp had only a certain quantity of daily food rations — I cannot recall how much, maybe enough for two, maybe three thousand — and *Herr Kommandant* disliked to see the prisoners starve. Each man, he felt, must receive his allotted portion. And always the camp had a few dozen men too many. So every evening a ballot, using cards or matches, was held in every Block, and the following morning the losers did not go to work. At noon they were led out behind the barbed-wire fence and shot.

And in the midst of the mounting tide of atavism stand men from a different world, men who conspire in order to end conspiracies among people, men who steal so that there will be no more stealing in the world, men who kill so that people will cease to murder one another.

Witek, you see, was such a man — a man from a different world — so he became the right-hand man to Kronschmidt, the most notorious killer at the Pawiak prison. But now he sat next to me, listening to what is inside the human body and how to cure whatever ails it with home-made remedies. Later there was a small row in the classroom. The doctor turned to Staszek, the fellow who is so good at organizing, and asked him to repeat everything he had been taught about the liver. Staszek repeated, but incorrectly.

"What you have just said is very stupid, and furthermore you might stand up when you answer," said the doctor.

"I'll sit if I want to," retorted Staszek, his face reddening. "And furthermore, you don't have to insult me, *Herr Doktor*."

"Quiet, you're in a classroom!"

"Naturally you want me to keep quiet, or I might say too much about some of your activities at the camp . . ."

Whereupon all of us started banging against the stools, scream-ing "yes! yes!" and the doctor flew out of the door. Adolf arrived, thundered for a few minutes about *Kameradschaft,* and we were sent back to our barracks — right in the middle of the digestive system. Staszek immediately rushed out in search of his friends, just in case the doctor should try to make trouble for him. But I am convinced he will not, because Staszek has powerful backing. One thing we have learned well about anatomy: at the camp you are not likely to trip if you stand on the shoulders of men who have influence. As for the doctor, many of his camp activities are common knowledge. It seems that he learned surgery experimenting with the sick. Who knows how many patients he has slashed to bits in the name of sci-entific research, and how many through sheer ignorance. No doubt quite a few, for the hospital is always crowded and the mortuary always full.

As you read this letter you must be thinking that I have completely forgotten the world we left behind. I go on and on about the camp, about its various aspects, trying to unravel their deeper significance, as though there were to be no future for us except right here . . .

But I do remember our room. The little Thermos bottle you once bought for me. It did not fit inside my pocket, so — to your dismay — it ended up under the bed. Or the round-up of civilians at Żoliborz, the course of which you kept reporting to me all through the day on the telephone — that the Germans were dragging people out of the trolley buses but you had got off at the previous stop; that the entire Block was surrounded, but you managed to escape across the fields, all the way to the Vistula. Or what you used to say to me when I complained about the war, about the inhuman-ity of man, and worried that we should grow up to be a generation of illiterates:

"Think of those who are in concentration camps. We are merely wasting time, while they suffer agonies."

Much of what I once said was naïve, immature. And it seems to me now that perhaps we were not really wasting time. Despite the madness of war, we lived for a world that would be different. For a better world to come when all this is over. And perhaps even our being here is a step towards that world. Do you really think that, without the hope that such a world is possible, that the rights of man will be restored again, we could stand the concentration camp even for one day? It is that very hope that makes people go without a murmur to the gas chambers, keeps them from risking a revolt, paralyses them into numb inactivity. It is hope that breaks down family ties, makes mothers renounce their children, or wives sell their bodies for bread, or husbands kill. It is hope that compels man to hold on to one more day of life, because that day may be the day of liberation. Ah, and not even the hope for a different, better world, but simply for life, a life of peace and rest. Never before in the history of mankind has hope been stronger than man, but never also has it done so much harm as it has in this war, in this concentration camp. We were never taught how to give up hope, and this is why today we perish in gas chambers.

Observe in what an original world we are living: how many men can you find in Europe who have never killed, or whom somebody does not wish to kill?

But still we continue to long for a world in which there is love between men, peace, and serene deliverance from our baser instincts. This, I suppose, is the nature of youth.

P.S. And yet, first of all, I should like to slaughter one or two men, just to throw off the concentration camp mentality, the effects of continual subservience, the effects of helplessly watching others being beaten and murdered, the effects of all this horror. I suspect, though, that I will be marked for life. I do not know whether we shall survive, but I like to think that one day we shall have the courage to tell the world the whole truth and call it by its proper name.

VI

For some days now we have had regular entertainment at midday: a column of men marches out of the *für Deutsche* Block and, loudly singing *Morgen Nach Heimat*, tramps round and round the camp, with the *Lagerältester* in the lead, marking time with his cane.

These men are the criminals, or army "volunteers." Those who are guilty of petty crimes will be shipped to the front lines. But the fellow who butchered his wife and mother-in-law and then let the canary out of its cage so that the poor little creature should not be unhappy in captivity, is the lucky one — he will remain in the camp. Meanwhile, however, all of them are here. One happy family!

They are being taught the art of marching and are watched for any signs that they may be developing a sense of social responsibility. As a matter of fact, they have exhibited a considerable amount of "social" initiative and have already managed to break into the supply rooms, to steal some packages, destroy the canteen and demolish the Puff (so it is closed again, to everyone's sorrow). "Why in hell," they say — and very wisely — "should we go and fight and risk our necks for the SS? . . . And who is going to polish our boots out there? We're quite satisfied to stay right here! Our glorious Fatherland? It will fall to pieces without any assistance from us . . . and out there, who will polish our boots, and how are we going to get pretty young boys?"

So the gang marches along the road singing "Tomorrow we march home." Notorious thugs, one and all: Seppel, the terror of the *Dachdecker*, who mercilessly forces you to work in rain, snow and freezing weather and shoves you off the roof if you hammer a nail in crookedly; Arno Böhm, number eight, an old-time Block Elder, Kapo and Camp Kapo, who used to kill men for selling tea in the black market and administered twenty-five lashes for every minute you were late and every word you uttered after the evening gong; he is also the man who always wrote short but touching letters, filled with love and nostalgia, to his old parents in Frankfurt. We recognize all of them: that one beat the prisoners at the D.A.W.; this one was the terror of Buna; the one next to him, the weakling, used to steal regularly and was therefore sent to the camp and put in charge of some miserable Kommando. There they go — one after the other — well-known homosexuals, alcoholics, dope addicts, sadists; and way in the back marches Kurt — well dressed, looking carefully around. He is not in step with the others, and he is not singing. After all, I thought to myself, it was he who managed to find you for me and who then carried our letters. So I raced downstairs and said to him: "Kurt, I am sure you must be hungry. Why don't you come up — you enlisted criminal?" and I pointed at our windows. And indeed he showed up at our place in the evening, just in time for the dinner which we had cooked on our big tile stove. Kurt is very nice (it sounds odd, but I cannot think of a better word) and really knows how to tell stories. He once wanted to be a musician, but his father, a prosperous storekeeper, threw him out of the house. Kurt went to Berlin. There he met a girl, the daughter of another storekeeper, lived with her, did some writing for the sports magazines, spent a month in jail after a row with a *Stahlhelm*, and afterwards never went back to see the girl. He managed to acquire a sports car and he smuggled currency. He saw the girl once on the street, but he did not have the nerve to speak to her. Then he took trips to Yugoslavia and Austria until he was caught and put in jail. And since he already had a record (that unfortunate first month), after the jail it was the concentration camp for him and the waiting for the war to end.

It is late evening — way past Appel. Several of us sit around the table, telling stories. Everybody here tells stories — on the way to work, returning to the camp, working in the fields and in the trucks, in the bunks at night, standing at Appel. Stories from books and stories from life. And almost always about the world outside the barbed-wire fence. But somehow today we cannot get away from camp tales, maybe because Kurt is about to leave.

"Actually, people on the outside knew very little about the camp. Sure, we had heard about the pointless work, paving roads, for example, only to tear them up again, or the endless spreading of gravel. And, of course, about how terrible it all is. Various tales were circulated. But, to tell the truth, we weren't particularly interested in all this. We were certain of only one thing — once you got in, you didn't get out."

"If you'd been here two years ago, the wind would have blown your ashes out of the chimney long ago," interrupted Staszek (the one who is such an expert at organizing).

I shrugged. "Maybe it would have, and maybe not. It hasn't blown yours out, so it might not have blown mine out either. You know, back in Pawiak we once had a fellow from Auschwitz."

"Sent back for a trial, I suppose."

"Exactly. so we started asking him questions, but he wouldn't talk, oh no. All he'd say was: 'Come and you'll see for yourself. Why should I waste my breath? It would be like talking to children.'"

"Were you afraid of the camp?"

"Yes, I was afraid. We left Pawiak in the morning, and were driven to the station in trucks. It's not good — the sun is behind our backs, we thought. That means the West station. Auschwitz. They loaded us quickly into the freight trains, sixty in each car, in alphabetical order. It wasn't even too crowded."

"Were you allowed to bring some of your things?"

"Yes, I was. I took a blanket and a robe given to me by my girl, and two sheets."

"You were a fool. You should have left them for your friends. Didn't you know they'd take everything away?

"I suppose so, but . . . And then we pulled all the nails out of one wall, tore the planks away, and started to climb out! But up on the roof they had a machine gun and promptly cut down the first three men. The fourth foolishly stuck his head out of the car and got a bullet right in the back of the neck. Immediately the train was stopped and we squeezed ourselves against the corners of the car. There were screams, curses — total hell! 'Didn't I tell you not to do it?' 'Cowards!' 'They'll kill us all!' and swearing, but what swearing!"

"Not worse than in the woman's section?"

"No, not worse, but very strong stuff, believe me. And there I sat, under the heap of people, at the very bottom. And I thought to myself: Good, when they start shooting I won't be the first to get it. And it was good. They did shoot. They fired a series of bullets right into the heap, killed two, wounded one in the abdomen, and *los, aus*, without our belongings! Well, I thought, that's it. Now they'll finish us all off. I was a little sad about leaving the robe, since I had a Bible hidden in the pocket, and anyway, you see, it was from my girl."

"Didn't you say the blanket too was from your girl?"

"It was. I also regretted leaving the blanket. But I couldn't take anything because they threw me down the steps. You have no idea how tremendous the world looks when you fall out of a closed, packed freight car! The sky is so high . . ."

". . . and blue . . ."

"Exactly, blue, and the trees smell wonderful. The forest — you want to take it in your hand! The SS men surrounded us on all sides, holding their automatics. They took four men aside and herded the rest of us into another car. Now we travelled one hundred and twenty of us in one car, plus three dead and one wounded. We nearly suffocated. It was so hot that water ran from the ceiling, literally. Not one tiny window, nothing, the whole car was boarded up. We shouted for air and water, but when they started shooting, we shut up instantly. Then we all collapsed on the floor and lay panting, like slaughtered cattle. I took off first one shirt, then the other. Sweat streamed down my body. My nose bled continuously. My ears hummed. I longed for Auschwitz, because it would mean air. Finally the doors were thrown open alongside a ramp, and my strength returned completely with the first whiff of fresh air. It was an April night — starlit, cool. I did not feel the cold, although the shirt I had put on was soaking wet. Someone behind me reached forward and embraced me. Through the thick, heavy darkness I could see in the distance the gleaming lights of the concentration camp. And above them flickered a nervous, reddish flame. The darkness rose up under it so that it seemed as though the flame were burning on top of a gigantic mountain. "The crematorium" — passed a whisper through the crowd."

"How you can talk! It's evident that you're a poet . . ." said Witek approvingly.

"We walked to the camp carrying the dead. Behind I could hear heavy breathing and I imagined that perhaps my girl was walking behind me. From time to time there came the hollow thud of a falling blow. Just before we reached the gate somebody struck my thigh with a bayonet. It didn't hurt, only my leg became very warm. Blood was streaming down my thigh and leg. After a few steps my muscles became stiff and I began to limp. The SS man escorting us struck a few other men who were up front and said as we were entering the camp:

"Here you will have a good long rest."

"That was on Thursday night. On Monday I joined a labor Kommando in Budy, several kilometres outside the camp, to carry telegraph poles. My leg hurt like the devil. It was quite a rest!"

"Big deal," said Witek, "the Jews travel in much worse conditions, you know. So what do you have to brag about?"

Opinions were divided as to modes of travel and as to the Jews.

"Jews . . . you know what the Jews are like!" said Staszek. "Wait and see, they'll manage to run a business in any camp! Whether it's the cremo or the ghetto, every one of them will sell his own mother for a bowl of turnips! One morning our labor Kommando was waiting to leave for work, and right next to us stood the *Sonder.* Immediately I saw Moise, a former bookkeeper. He's from Mława, I'm from Mława, you know how it is. We had palled around together and done business together — mutual confidence and trust. 'What's the trouble, Moise?' I said. 'You seem out of sorts.' 'I've got some new pictures of my family.' 'That's good! Why should it upset you?' 'Good? Hell! I've sent my own father to the oven!' 'Impossible!' 'Possible, because I have. He came with a transport, and saw me in front of the gas chamber. I was lining up the people. He threw his arms around me, and began kissing me and asking, what's going to happen. He told me he was hungry because they'd been riding for two days without any food. But right away the *Kommandoführer* yells at me to not stand around, to get back to work. What was I to do? 'Go on, Father,' I said, 'wash yourself in the bath-house and then we'll talk. Can't you see I'm busy now?' So my father went on to the gas chamber. And later I found the pictures in his coat pocket. Now tell me, what's so good about my having the pictures?"

We laughed. "Anyway, it's lucky they don't gas Aryans any longer. Anything but that!"

"In the old days they did," said one of the Auschwitz old-timers who always seemed to join our group. I've been in this Block a long time and I remember a lot of things. You wouldn't believe how many people have passed through my hands, straight to the gas chamber — friends, school-mates, acquaintances from my home town! By now I have even forgotten their faces. An anonymous mass — that's all. But one episode I will undoubtedly remember for the rest of my life. At the time I was an ambulance orderly. I can't say I was any too gentle when it came to dressing wounds — there was no time for fooling around, you know. You scraped a little at the arm, the back, or whatever — then cotton, bandages, and out! Next! You didn't even bother to look at the face. Nor did anyone bother to thank you; there was nothing to thank you for. But once, after I had dressed a phlegmon wound, all of a sudden a man said to me, pausing at the door: "*Spasibo*, thank you, *Herr Pfleger!*" The poor devil was so pale, so weak, he could barely hold himself up on his swollen legs. Later I went to visit him and took him some soup. He had the phlegmon on his right buttock, then his entire thigh became covered with running sores. He suffered horribly. He wept and spoke of his mother. "Stop it," I would say to him. "All of us have mothers, and we're not crying." I tried to console him as best I could, but he lamented that he would never go home again. But what was I able to give him? A bowl of soup, a piece of bread once in a while . . . I did my best to protect little Toleczka from being selected for the gas, but finally they found him and took down his name. One day I went to see him. He was feverish. "It doesn't matter that I'm going to the gas chamber," he said to me. "That's how it has to be, I reckon. But when the war is over and you get out . . . " "I don't know whether I'll survive, Toleczka," I interrupted. "You will survive," he went on stubbornly, "and you will go to see my mother. There will be no borders after the war, I know, and there will be no countries, no concentration camps, and people will never kill one another. *Wied' eto poslednij boj,*" he repeated firmly. "It is our last fight, you understand?" "I understand," I told him. "You will go to my mother and tell her I died. Died so that there would be no more borders. Or wars. Or concentration camps. You will tell her?" "I'll tell her." "Memorize this: my mother lives in Dalniewostoczny county, the city of Chabrowsk, Tolstoy Street, number 24. Now repeat it." I repeated it. I went to see Block Elder Szary who still might have been able to save Toleczka. He struck me across the mouth and threw me out of his shack. Toleczka went to the gas chamber. Several months later Szary was taken out in a transport. At the moment of his departure he pleaded for a cigarette. I tipped the men not to give him any. And they didn't. Perhaps I did a wrong thing, for he was on his way to Mauthausen to be killed. But I memorized Toleczka's mother's address: Dalniewostoczny County, the city of Chabrowsk, Tolstoy Street . . ."

We were silent. Kurt, who understood nothing of what was said, wondered what was going on. Witek explained:

"We're talking about the camp and wondering whether there will be a better world some day. How about you, have you something to say about it?"

Kurt looked at us with a smile and then spoke slowly, so we should all understand:

"I have only a short tale to tell. I was in Mauthausen. Two prisoners had escaped and were caught on Christmas Eve itself. The entire camp stood at Appel to watch them hang. The Christmas tree was lighted. then the *Lagerführer* stepped forward, turned to the prisoners and barked a command:

"*Haftlinge, Mützen ab!*"

"We took our caps off. And then, for the traditional Christmas message, the *Lagerführer* spoke these words:

"Those who behave like swine will be treated like swine. *Haftlinge, Mützen auf!*"

"Dismissed!"

"We broke up and lighted our cigarettes. We were silent. Everyone began thinking of his own problems."

VII

If the barrack walls were suddenly to fall away, many thousands of people, packed together, squeezed tightly in their bunks, would remain suspended in mid-air. Such a sight would be more gruesome than the medieval paintings of the Last Judgment. For one of the ugliest sights to a man is that of another man sleeping on his tiny portion of the bunk, of the space which he must occupy, because he has a body — a body that has been exploited to the utmost: with a number tattooed on it to save on dog tags, with just enough sleep at night to work during the day, and just enough time to eat. And just enough food so it will not die wastefully. As for actual living, there is only one place for it — a piece of the bunk. The rest belongs to the camp, the Fatherland. But not even this small space, nor the shirt you wear, nor the spade you work with are your own. If you get sick, everything is taken away from you: your clothes, your cap, your organized scarf, your handkerchief. If you die — your gold teeth, already recorded in the camp inventory, are extracted. Your body is burned and your ashes are used to fertilize the fields or fill in the ponds. Although in fact so much fat and bone is wasted in the burning, so much flesh, so much heat! But elsewhere they make soap out of people, and lampshades out of human skin, and jewellery out of the bones.

We work beneath the earth and above it, under a roof and in the rain, with the spade, the pickaxe and the crowbar. We carry huge sacks of cement, lay bricks, put down rails, spread gravel, trample the earth . . . We are laying the foundation for some new, monstrous civilization. Only now do I realize what price was paid for building the ancient civilizations. The Egyptian pyramids, the temples, and Greek statues — what a hideous crime they were! How much blood must have poured on to the Roman roads, the bulwarks, and the city walls. Antiquity — the tremendous concentration camp where the slave was branded on the forehead by his master, and crucified for trying to escape! Antiquity — the conspiracy of free men against slaves!

You know how much I used to like Plato. Today I realize he lied. For the things of this world are not a reflection of the ideal, but a product of human sweat, blood and hard labour. It is we who built the pyramids, hewed the marble for the temples and the rocks for the imperial roads, we who pulled the oars in the galleys and dragged wooden ploughs, while they wrote dialogues and dramas, rationalized their intrigues by appeals in the name of the Fatherland, made wars over boundaries and democracies. We were filthy and died real deaths. They were "esthetic" and carried on subtle debates.

There can be no beauty if it is paid for by human injustice, nor truth that passes over injustice in silence, nor moral virtue that condones it.

What does ancient history say about us? It knows the crafty slave from Terence and Plautus, it knows the people's tribunes, the brothers Gracchi, and the name of one slave — Spartacus.

They are the ones who have made history, yet the murderer — Scipio — the lawmakers — Cicero or Demosthenes — are the men remembered today. We rave over the extermination of the Etruscans, the destruction of Carthage, over treason, deceit, plunder. Roman law! Yes, today too there is a law!

If the Germans win the war, what will the world know about us? They will erect huge buildings, highways, factories, soaring monuments. Our hands will be placed under every brick, and our backs will carry the steel rails and the slabs of concrete. They will kill off our families, our sick, our aged. They will murder our children.

And we shall be forgotten, drowned out by the voices of the poets, the jurists, the philosophers, the priests. They will produce their own beauty, virtue and truth. They will produce religion.

Where Auschwitz stands today, three years ago there were villages and farms. There were rich meadows, shaded country lanes, apple orchards. There were people, no better nor worse than any other people.

And then we arrived. We drove the people out, demolished their houses, levelled the earth, kneaded it into mud. We built barracks, fences, crematoria. We brought scurvy, phlegmon and lice.

Now we work in mines and factories, and the fruit of our labor brings enormous profits to somebody.

The story of the building of Auschwitz is an interesting one. A German Company built our camp — the barracks, halls, shacks, bunks, chimneys. When the bill was presented, it turned out to be so fantastic that it stunned not only the Auschwitz officials but Berlin itself. Gentlemen — they said — it is not possible, you are making much too much profit, there must be a mistake! Regrettably — replied the Company — here are the bills. Well yes — said Berlin — but we simply cannot . . . In that case, half — suggested the patriotic Company. Thirty per cent — haggled Berlin manfully, and that is what was finally agreed upon. Since then all the bills are cut accordingly. But the Company is not worried; like all German companies, it is increasing its capital. It has done fantastic business at Auschwitz and is now waiting calmly for the war to end. The same goes for the companies in plumbing, in well-drilling, in electrical appliances; for the producers of brick, cement, metal and lumber, the makers of barracks parts and striped prison suits. The same thing is true of the huge automobile company, and of the scrap demolition outfit. And of the owners of the coalmines in Mysłowice, Gliwice, Janin and Jaworzna. Those of us who survive will one day demand compensation for our work. Not in money, or goods, but in hard, relentless labor.

When the patients finally fall asleep, I have time to talk with you. In the darkness, I can see your face, and although my words are full of bitterness and hatred that must be foreign to you, I know you listen carefully.

Your fate has now become a part of my own. Except that your hands are not suited to the pickaxe and your body not accustomed to scurvy. We are bound together by our love and by the love of those who have stayed behind, those who live for us and who constitute our world. The faces of our parents, friends, the shapes of objects we left behind   these are the things we share. And even if nothing is left to us but our bodies on the hospital bunk, we shall still have our memories and our feelings.

VIII

You cannot imagine how very happy I am!

First of all — the tall electrician. I go to him every morning with Kurt (because he is Kurt's contact), bringing along my letters to you. The electrician, a fantastically old serial number, just a bit over one thousand, loads up on sausage, sugar and lingerie, and slides a stack of letters somewhere in his shoe. The electrician is bald and has no particular sympathy for our love. The electrician frowns upon every letter I bring. The electrician declares when I want to give him some cigarettes:

"Look pal, here in Auschwitz we don't accept payment for letters! And I'll bring the reply, if I can."

So I go to see him again in the evening. The reverse procedure takes place: the electrician reaches inside his shoe, produces a card from you, hands it to me with a bitter frown. Because the electrician has no sympathy for our love. Besides, I am sure he is very unhappy living in a bunk — that one by one-and-a-half meter cage. Since the electrician is very tall, it must be quite uncomfortable for him.

So, first of all — the tall electrician. Secondly — the wedding of the Spaniard. The Spaniard fought defending Madrid, then escaped to France and ended up at Auschwitz. He had found himself a Frenchwoman, as a Spaniard would, and had had a child by her. The child grew. The Spaniard stayed on and on behind the barbed-wire. So the Frenchwoman started clamoring for a wedding. Out goes a petition to H. himself. H. is indignant: "Is there no *Ordnung* in the new Europe? Marry them immediately!"

So they shipped the Frenchwoman, together with the child, to the camp, hurriedly pulled the stripes off the Spaniard's back, fitted him into an elegant suit pressed personally by the Kapo in the laundry room, carefully selected a tie and matching socks from the camp's abundant supplies, and married them.

Then the newlyweds went to have their pictures taken: she with the child at her side and a bouquet of hyacinths in her arms, he standing close to her on the other side. Behind them — the orchestra *in corpore*, and behind the orchestra the SS man in charge of the kitchen, furious:

"I'll report this, that you're playing music during working hours instead of peeling potatoes! I've got the soup all ready, and no potatoes! I fuck all weddings!"

"Calm down . . . 'some of the other "bigwigs" tried to pacify him. "It's orders from Berlin. We can have soup without potatoes."

The newlyweds, meanwhile, had finished the picture-taking ceremony and were sent to a Puff suite for their wedding night. The regular Puff residents were temporarily exiled to Block 10. The following day the Frenchwoman returned to France, and the Spaniard, again in his stripes, returned to a labor Kommando.

But now everyone at the camp walks proudly, head high.

"We even have weddings in Auschwitz!"

So, first of all — the tall electrician. Secondly — the wedding of the Spaniard. And thirdly — school is almost over. The FKL girls were the first to finish. We bade them farewell with a chamber music concert. They sat at the windows of Block 10 and out of our windows flowed the sounds of the saxophone, the drum, the violins. To me, the loveliest is the saxophone, as it sobs and weeps, laughs and giggles!

What a pity Słowacki* died so early, or he would most certainly have become a saxophone player.

After the women it was our turn. Everybody assembled in our attic classroom. *Lagerarzt* Rhode (the "decent" one who makes no distinction between Jews and Aryans) came in, took a look at us and our work, said he was very pleased and quite certain that the situation in Auschwitz would greatly improve from now on, and left quickly, for the attic was cold.

All day they have been saying goodbye to us here in Auschwitz. Franz, the fellow from Vienna, gave me a last-minute lecture on the meaning of war. Stuttering a little, he spoke of the people who build, and the people who destroy. Of victory for the former and defeat for the latter; of the comrades from the Urals and London, Chicago and Calcutta, on land and sea, who are fighting for our cause. Of the future brotherhood of all creative men. Here, I thought to myself, is a messianic vision emerging out of the surrounding death and destruction — a characteristic process of the human mind. Then Franz opened the package which he had just received from Vienna and we had our evening tea. Franz sang Austrian songs and I recited poems that he did not understand.

Then I was given some medicine and a few books for the road. I squeezed them inside my bundle, underneath the food. Would you believe it — the works of Angelus Silesius! So I am quite pleased, because of everything combined: the tall electrician, the Spaniard's wedding, the school being over. And in addition — I received letters from home. They had strayed a long time, but found me at last.

I had not heard a word from home for almost two months and I worried terribly. Fantastic tales have been circulating as to the conditions in Warsaw, and I had already started writing desperate letters. And then yesterday, just think, two letters! One from Staszek and one from my brother.

Staszek writes very simply, like a man who wishes to convey something straight from the heart in a foreign tongue. "We love you and think of you," he says, "and we also think of Tuska, your girl. We live, we work and write." They live, work and write, except that Andrzej has been shot and Wacek is dead.

What a pity that the two most talented men of our generation, with the most passionate desire to create, were the ones who had to die!

* A Polish romantic poet.

You probably remember how strongly I always opposed them — their imperialistic conception of an omnivorous state, their dishonest approach to society, their theories on state art, their muddled philosophy, their futile poetry, their whole style of living and their unconscious hypocrisy.

And today, separated as we are by the barrier between two worlds, the barrier which we too will cross some day, I reopen our dispute about the meaning of the world, the philosophy of living, and the nature of poetry. And today I shall still challenge their acceptance of the infectious idea of the all-powerful, aggressive state, their awe for the evil whose only defect is that it is not our own. And even today I shall challenge their unrealistic poetry, void of all human problems.

But across the barrier that divides us I can still see their faces, and I think about them, the young men of my generation; and I feel a growing emptiness around me. They went away while still so much alive, so much in the very center of the world that they were building. I bid them farewell, my friends on the opposite side of the barricades. May they find in that other world the truths and the love that they failed to find here!

Eva, the girl who recited such beautiful poems about harmony and stars, and who used to say that "things aren't really that bad . . ." was also shot. A void, an ever-growing void. And I had thought that all this would be limited to us. That when we return, we should be returning to a world which would not have known the horrors and the atmosphere that are killing us. That we alone had hit bottom. But it seems that they too are being taken away . . . out of the very center of life.

We are as insensitive as trees, as stones. And we remain as numb as trees when they are being cut down, or stones when they are being crushed.

The other letter was from my brother. You know how affectionate Julek has always been in his letters. This time too he tells me that they are thinking of us and waiting, that they have hidden all my books and poems . . .

When I return I shall find on my shelves a new little volume of my poems. "They are your love poems," writes my brother. I think it is somehow symbolic that our love is always tied to poetry and that the book of poems which were written for you and which you had with you at the time of your arrest is a kind of victory *in absentia*. Perhaps they were published in memory of us? But I am grateful to the friends who keep alive our poetry and our love and recognize our right to them.

Julek also writes about your mother, that she prays for us and trusts that we shall return and that we will always be together . . . Do you recall what you wrote in the very first card I received from you, only a few days after arriving at the camp? You wrote that you were sick and were desperate because you felt responsible for my being thrown into the concentration camp. That had it not been for you, etc. . . . Do you want to know how it really happened?

It happened this way: I was waiting for your promised telephone call from Maria's. That afternoon, as on every Wednesday, the underground school held a class at my place. I spoke, I think, about linguistics, and I think that the paraffin lamp went out.

Then again I waited for you to call. I knew you would, because you had promised. But you did not. I cannot remember if I went out to dinner. If so, then on returning I sat again by the telephone, afraid I might not hear it from the other room. I looked through some newspaper clippings and read a story by Maurois about a man who weighed human souls in order to learn how to keep them captive for ever in imperishable receptacles, and thus find a way to unite his own soul with that of his beloved for all eternity. But he only succeeded in accidentally capturing the souls of two circus clowns, whereas his own soul and the soul of the woman in question continued to float separately in space . . . It was getting light when I fell asleep.

In the morning as usual I went home with my briefcase and books. I had my breakfast, said I must rush off but would be back for dinner, ruffled the ears of the dog, and went to see your mother. She was worried about you. I took the trolley-bus to Maria's and on the way down looked long and intently at the trees of Łazienki Park, of which I am very fond. Then I walked up Puławska Street. The staircase was covered with cigarette butts, and, if I remember correctly, had some traces of blood. But it may have been only my imagination. I went up and rang the doorbell, using our code. Men with revolvers in their hands opened the door.

Since then, a year has passed. But I am writing about it so that you will know I have never regretted that we are here together. It has never even occurred to me that it could be any other way. And I often think about the future. About the life we shall have, if . . . About the poems I am going to write, the books we shall read together, the objects that will be around us. I know these are small things, but I think about them nevertheless.

IX

We are back. As in the old days, I went over to my Block, rubbed some of the patients with mint tea and stood around for a while, a knowing expression on my face, watching the doctor operate. Then I helped myself to the last two shots of Prontisil which I am sending to you. Finally I went to see our Block barber, Hank Liberfreund (a restaurant owner from Kraków), who decided that I shall certainly be the best writer among the orderlies.

Apart from that, I spent all day long snooping around the camp, carrying my letter to you. In order to reach their destination, these few pieces of paper must have a pair of feet. It is the feet that I have been hunting for. I finally located a pair — in high, red, laced-up boots. The feet, besides, wear dark glasses, have broad shoulders, and march daily to the FKL to collect corpses of male infants which must be processed through our office of male statistics and our male mortuary, and examined personally by our S.D.G. Order is the essence of the universe, or, less poetically — *Ordnung muss sein!*

And so the feet march to the FKL and are, for a change, fairly sympathetic. They too, they tell me, have a wife among the female prisoners, and understand how it is. They will deliver my letter free of charge. And perhaps smuggle me in too, should an opportunity arise. Actually, I feel rather in the mood for travelling, though my colleagues suggest I take along a heavy blanket and — wrap it around me where it may afford the most protection . . . With my luck and resourcefulness, they figure, I am bound to be caught on the first try. I told them to go and smear themselves with Peruvian itch ointment!

I am still examining the surrounding landscape. Nothing has changed, only there is somehow even more mud. Spring is in the air. Soon people will start drowning in mud. The breezes from the forest now carry a whiff of pine, now of smoke. Cars drive by, now loaded with bundles, now with muzulmen from Buna; now with dinner for the offices, now with SS men on their way to change the guard.

Nothing has changed. Yesterday was Sunday and we went to the camp for a delousing inspection. The barracks seem even more terrible in the winter! The dirty bunks, the black, damp earth floors, swept clean, the stale odor of human bodies. The Blocks are packed with people, but there is not one louse inside. The never-ending delousing treatments have not been in vain. After the inspections, just as we started to leave, a *Sonderkommando* marched back to camp returning from the cremo. Black with smoke, looking fat and prosperous, the men were loaded down with heavy sacks. There is no limit to what they may take; anything except gold, but this is what they smuggle the most of.

Small groups of people began stealing out of the barracks, rushing over to the marching column and snatching the awaited packages from their hands. The air became filled with shouts, cursing and the sound of blows. At last the *Sonder* disappeared behind the gate leading to their quarters, which are separated from the rest of the camp by a stone wall. But it was not long before the Jews started sneaking out to trade, organize and visit with friends.

I cornered one of them, an old pal from my pervious Kommando. I became ill and landed at the K.B. He was "luckier," and joined the *Sonder*, which is certainly better than swinging a pickaxe on nothing but one bowl of soup a day. He shook my hand warmly.

"Ah, it's you! Want to buy anything? If you've got some apples . . ."

"No, I haven't any apples for you," I replied affectionately. "So, you're still alive, Abram? And what's new with you?"

"Not much. Just gassed up a Czech transport."

"That I know. I mean personally?"

"Personally? What sort of 'personally' is there for me? The oven, the barracks, back to the oven . . . Have I got anybody around here? Well, if you really want to know what 'personally' — we've figured out a new way to burn people. Want to hear about it?"

I indicated polite interest.

"Well then, you take four little kids with plenty of hair on their heads, then stick the heads together and light the hair. The rest burns by itself and in no time at all the whole business is *gemacht.*"

"Congratulations," I said drily and with very little enthusiasm.

He burst out laughing and with a strange expression looked right into my eyes.

"Listen, doctor, here in Auschwitz we must entertain ourselves in every way we can. Otherwise, who could stand it?"

And putting his hands in his pockets he walked away without saying goodbye.

But this is a monstrous lie, a grotesque lie, like the whole camp, like the whole world.

THE PEOPLE WHO
WALKED ON

On 24 March 1944, President Roosevelt expressed concern that the Hungarian Jews would be murdered and warned Germany against committing a new crime. On 17 May, the first transports from Hungary arrived in Auschwitz, and from then on came without a break throughout the summer. As usual, about 10 percent of the healthiest people "went to the camp," and continued on transports west, to other camps.

Thanks to organizing, the period of the Hungarian transports was the richest period in Auschwitz.

It was early spring when we began building a soccer field on the broad clearing behind the hospital barracks. The location was excellent: the Gypsies to the left, with their roaming children, their lovely, trim nurses, and their women sitting by the hour in the latrines; to the rear — a barbed-wire fence, and behind it the loading ramp with the wide railway tracks and the endless coming and going of trains; and beyond the ramp, the women's camp — *Frauenkonzentrationslager*. No one, of course, ever called it by its full name. We simply said FKL — that was enough. To the right of the field were the crematoria, some of them at the back of the ramp, next to the FKL, others even closer, right by the fence. Sturdy buildings that sat solidly on the ground. And in front of the crematoria, a small wood which had to be crossed on the way to the gas.

We worked on the soccer field throughout the spring, and before it was finished we started planting flowers under the barracks windows and decorating the Blocks with intricate zigzag designs made of crushed red brick. We planted spinach and lettuce, sunflowers and garlic. We laid little green lawns with grass transplanted from the edges of the soccer field, and sprinkled them daily with water brought in barrels from the lavatories.

Just when the flowers were about to bloom, we finished the soccer field.

From then on, the flowers were abandoned, the sick lay by themselves in the hospital beds, and we played soccer. Every day, as soon as the evening meal was over, anybody who felt like it came to the field and kicked the ball around. Others stood in clusters by the fence and talked across the entire length of the camp with the girls from the FKL.

One day I was goalkeeper. As always on Sundays, a sizeable crowd of hospital orderlies and convalescent patients had gathered to watch the game. Keeping goal, I had my back to the ramp. The ball went out and rolled all the way to the fence. I ran after it, and as I reached to pick it up, I happened to glance at the ramp.

A train had just arrived. People were emerging from the cattle cars and walking in the direction of the little wood. All I could see from where I stood were bright splashes of color. The women, it seemed, were already wearing summer dresses; it was the first time that season. The men had taken off their coats, and their white shirts stood out sharply against the green of the trees. The procession moved along slowly, growing in size as more and more people poured from the freight cars. And then it stopped. The people sat down on the grass and gazed in our direction. I returned with the ball and kicked it back inside the field. It travelled from one foot to another and, in a wide arc, returned to the goal. I kicked it towards a corner. Again it rolled out into the grass. Once more I ran to retrieve it. But as I reached down, I stopped in amazement — the ramp was empty. Out of the whole colorful summer procession, not one person remained. The train too was gone. Again the FKL blocks were in unobstructed view, and again the orderlies and the patients stood along the barbed-wire fence calling to the girls, and the girls answered them across the ramp.

Between two throw-ins in a soccer game, right behind my back, three thousand people had been put to death.

In the following months, the processions to the little wood moved along two roads: one leading straight from the ramp, the other past the hospital wall. Both led to the crematoria, but some of the people had the good fortune to walk beyond them, all the way to the Zauna, and this meant more than just a bath and a delousing, a barber's shop and a new prison suit. It meant staying alive. In a concentration camp, true, but — alive.

Each day, as I got up in the morning to scrub the hospital floors, the people were walking — along both roads. Women, men, children. They carried their bundles.

When I sat down to dinner — and not a bad one, either — the people were walking. Our Block was bathed in sunlight; we threw the doors and the windows wide open and sprinkled the floors with water to keep the dust down. In the afternoons I delivered packages which had been brought that morning from the Auschwitz post office. The clerk distributed mail. The doctors dressed wounds and gave injections. There was, as a matter of fact, only one hypodermic needle for the entire Block. On warm evenings I sat at the barracks door reading *Mon frère Yves* by Pierre Loti — while the procession continued on and on, along both roads.

Often, in the middle of the night, I walked outside; the lamps glowed in the darkness above the barbed-wire fences. The roads were completely black, but I could distinctly hear the far-away hum of a thousand voices — the procession moved on and on. And then the entire sky would light up; there would be a burst of flame above the wood . . . and terrible human screams.

I stared into the night, numb, speechless, frozen with horror. My entire body trembled and rebelled, somehow even without my participation. I no longer controlled my body, although I could feel its every tremor. My mind was completely calm, only the body seemed to revolt.

Soon afterwards, I left the hospital. The days were filled with important events. The Allied Armies had landed on the shores of France. The Russian front, we heard, had started to move west towards Warsaw.

But in Birkenau, day and night long lines of trains loaded with people waited at the station. The doors were unsealed, the people started walking — along both roads.

Located next to the camp's labor sector was the deserted, unfinished Sector C. Here, only the barracks and the high voltage fence around them had been completed. The roofs, however, were not yet covered with tar sheets, and some of the Blocks still had no bunks. An average Birkenau Block, furnished with three tiers of bunks, could hold up to five hundred people. But every Block in Sector C was now being packed with a thousand or more young women picked from among the people on the ramp . . . Twenty-eight Blocks — over thirty thousand women. Their heads were shaved and they were issued little sleeveless summer dresses. But they were not given underwear. Nor spoons, nor bowls, nor even a rag to clean themselves with. Birkenau was situated on marshes, at the foot of a mountain range. During the day, the air was warm and so transparent that the mountains were in clear view, but in the morning they lay shrouded in a thick, icy mist. The mornings were cold and penetrating. For us, this meant merely a refreshing pause before a hot summer day, but the women, who only twenty yards to our right had been standing at roll-call since five in the morning, turned blue from the cold and huddled together like a flock of partridges.

We named the camp — Persian Market. On sunny, warm days the women would emerge from the barracks and mill around in the wide aisles between the Blocks. Their bright summer dresses and the gay kerchiefs on their shaved heads created the atmosphere of a busy, colorful market — a Persian Market because of its exotic character.

From afar, the women were faceless and ageless. Nothing more than white blotches and pastel figures.

The Persian Market was not yet completed. The Wagner Kommando began building a road through the sector, packing it down with a heavy roller. Others fiddled around with the plumbing and worked on the washrooms that were to be installed throughout all the sectors of Birkenau. Still others were busy stocking up the Persian Market with the camp's basic equipment — supplies of blankets, metal cups and spoons — which they arranged carefully in the warehouses under the direction of the chief supervisor, the assigned SS officer. Naturally, much of the stuff evaporated immediately, expertly organized by the men working on the job.

My comrades and I laid a roof over the shack of every Block Elder in the Persian Market. It was not done on official order, nor did we work out of charity. Neither did we do it out of a feeling of solidarity with the old serial numbers, the FKL women who had been placed there in all the responsible posts. In fact, we used organized tar-boards and melted organized tar, and for every roll of tar-board, every bucket of tar, an Elder had to pay. She had to pay the Kapo, the *Kommandoführer*, the Kommando "bigwigs." She could pay in various ways: with gold, food, the women of her Block, or with her own body. It depended.

On a similar basis, the electricians installed electricity, the carpenters built and furnished the shacks, using organized lumber, the masons provided metal stoves and cemented them in place.

It was at that time that I came to know the anatomy of this strange camp. We would arrive there in the morning, pushing a cart loaded with tar-sheets and tar. At the gate stood the SS women-guards, hippy blondes in black leather boots. They searched us and let us in. Then they themselves went to inspect the Blocks. Not infrequently they had lovers among the masons and carpenters. They slept with them in the unfinished washrooms or the Block Elders' shacks.

We would push our cart into the camp, between the barracks, and there, on some little square, would light a fire and melt the tar. A crowd of women would immediately surround us. They begged us to give them anything, a penknife, a handkerchief, a spoon, a pencil, a piece of paper, a shoe string, or bread.

"Listen, you can always manage somehow," they would say. "You've been in the camp a long time and you've survived. Surely you have all you need. Why won't you share it with us?"

At first we gave them everything we happened to have with us, and then turned our pockets inside out to show we had nothing more. We took off our shirts and handed them over. But gradually we began coming with empty pockets and gave them nothing.

These women were not so much alike as it had seemed when we looked at them from another sector, from a distance of twenty metres.

Among them were small girls, whose hair had not been shaved, stray little cherubs from a painting of the Last Judgment. There were young girls who gazed with surprise at the women crowding around us, and who looked at us, coarse, brutal men, with contempt. Then there were married women, who desperately begged for news of their lost husbands, and mothers trying to find a trace of their children.

"We are so miserable, so cold, so hungry," they cried. "Tell us, are they at least a little bit better off?"

"They are, if God is just," we would answer solemnly, without the usual mocking and teasing.

"Surely they're not dead?" the women asked, looking searchingly into our faces.

We would walk away without a word, eager to get back to work.

The majority of the Block Elders at the Persian Market were Slovak girls who managed to communicate in the language of the new inmates. Every one of these girls had behind her several years of concentration camp. Every one of them remembered the early days of the FKL, when female corpses piled up along the barracks walls and rotted, unremoved, in hospital beds — and when human excrement grew into monstrous heaps inside the Blocks.

Despite their rough manner, they had retained their femininity and human kindness. Probably they too had their lovers, and probably they too stole margarine and tins of food in order to pay for blankets and dresses, but . . .

. . . .but I remember Mirka, a short, stocky "pink" girl. Her shack was all done up in pink too, with pink ruffled curtains across the window that faced the Block. The pink light inside the shack set a pink glow over the girl's face, making her look as if she were wrapped in a delicate misty veil. There was a Jew in our Kommando with very bad teeth who was in love with Mirka. He was always running around the camp trying to buy fresh eggs for her, and then throwing them, protected in soft wrapping, over the barbed-wire fence. He would spend many long hours with her, paying little attention to the SS women inspecting the barracks or to our chief who made his rounds with a tremendous revolver hanging from his white summer uniform.

One day Mirka came running over to where several of us were laying a roof. She signalled frantically to the Jew and called, turning to me:

"Please come down! Maybe you can help too!"

We slid off the roof and down the barracks door. Mirka grabbed us by the hands and pulled us in the direction of her shack. There she led us between the cots and pointing to a mass of colorful quilts and blankets on top of which lay a child, she said breathlessy:

"Look, it's dying! Tell me, what can I do? What could have made it so sick so suddenly?"

The child was asleep, but very restless. It looked like a rose in a golden frame — its burning cheeks were surrounded by a halo of blond hair.

"What a pretty child," I whispered.

"Pretty!" cried Mirka. "All you know is that it's pretty! But it can die any moment! I've had to hide it so they wouldn't take it to the gas! What if an SS woman finds it? Help me!"

The Jew put his arm around her shoulders. She pushed him away and suddenly burst into sobs. I shrugged, turned around, and left the barracks.

In the distance, I could see trains moving along the ramp. They were bringing new people who would walk in the direction of the little wood. One Canada group was just returning from the ramp, and along the wide camp road passed another Canada group going to take its place. Smoke was rising above the treetops. I seated myself next to the boiling bucket of tar and, stirring it slowly, sat thinking for a long time. At one point a wild thought suddenly shot across my mind: I too would like to have a child with rose-colored cheeks and light blond hair I laughed aloud at such a ridiculous notion and climbed up on the roof to lay the hot tar.

And I remember another Block Elder, a big redhead with broad feet and chapped hands. She did not have a separate shack, only a few blankets spread over the bed and instead of walls a few other blankets thrown across a piece of rope.

"I mustn't make them feel," she would say, pointing to the women packed tightly in the bunks, "that I want to cut myself off from them. Maybe I can't give them anything, but I won't take anything away from them either."

"Do you believe in life after death?" she asked me once in the middle of some lighthearted conversation.

"Sometimes," I answered cautiously. "Once I believed in it when I was in jail, and again once when I came close to dying here in the camp."

"But if a man does evil, he'll be punished, won't he?"

"I suppose so, unless there are some criteria of justice other than the man-made criteria. You know . . . the kind that explain causes and motivations, and erase guilt by making it appear insignificant in the light of the overall harmony of the universe. Can a crime committed on one level be punishable on a different one?"

"But I mean in a normal, human sense!" she exclaimed.

"It ought to be punished. No question about it."

"And you, would you do good if you were able to?"

"I seek no rewards. I build roofs and want to survive the concentration camp."

"But do you think that they," she pointed with her chin in an indefinite direction, "can go unpunished?"

"I think that for those who have suffered unjustly, justice alone is not enough. They want the guilty to suffer unjustly too. Only this will they understand as justice."

"You're a pretty smart fellow! But you wouldn't have the slightest idea how to divide bread justly, without giving more to your own mistress!" she said bitterly and walked into the Block. The women were lying in the rows of bunks, head to head. Their faces were still, only the eyes seemed alive, large and shining. Hunger had already started in this part of the camp. The redheaded Elder moved from bunk to bunk, talking to the women to distract them from their thoughts. She pulled out the singers and told them to sing, the dancers — and told them to dance, the poets — and made them recite poetry.

"All the time, endlessly, they ask me about their mothers, their fathers. They beg me to write to them."

"They've asked me too. It's just too bad."

"Ah, you! You come and then you go, but me? I plead with them, I beg them — if anyone is pregnant, don't report to the doctor, if anyone is sick, stay in the barracks! But do you think they believe me? It's not good, no matter how hard you try to protect them. What can you do if they fall all over themselves to get to the gas?"

One of the girls was standing on top of a table singing a popular tune. When she finished, the women in the bunks began to applaud. The girl bowed, smiling. The red-headed Elder covered her face with her rough hands.

"I can't stand it any longer! It's too disgusting!" she whispered. And suddenly she jumped up and rushed over to the table. "Get down!" she screamed at the singer.

The women fell silent. She raised her arm.

"Quiet!" she shouted, though nobody spoke a word. "You've been asking me about your parents and your children. I haven't told you, I felt sorry for you. But now I'll tell you, so that you know, because they'll do the same with you if you get sick! Your children, your husbands and your parents are not in another camp at all. They've been stuffed into a room and gassed! Gassed, do you understand? Like millions of others, like my own mother and father. They're burning in deep pits and in ovens . . . The smoke which you see above the rooftops doesn't come from the brick plant at all, as you're being told. It's smoke from your children! Now go on and sing." She finished calmly, pointing her finger at the terrified singer. Then she turned around and walked out of the barracks.

It was undeniable that the conditions in both Auschwitz and Birkenau were steadily improving. At the beginning, beating and killing were the rule, but later this became only sporadic. At first, you had to sleep on the floor lying on your side because of the lack of space, and could turn over only on command; later you slept in bunks, or wherever you wished, sometimes even in bed. Originally, you had to stand at roll-call for as long as two days at a time, later — only until the second gong, until nine o-clock. In the early years, packages were forbidden, later you could receive 500 grams, and finally as much as you wanted. Pockets of any kind were at first strictly taboo, but eventually even civilian clothes could sometimes be seen around Birkenau. Life in the camp became "better and better" all the time — after the first three or four years. We felt certain that the horrors could never again be repeated, and we were proud that we had survived. The worse the Germans fared at the battle front, the better off we were. And since they fared worse and worse . . .

At the Persian Market, time seemed to move in reverse. Again we saw the Auschwitz of 1940. The women greedily gulped down the soup which nobody in our Blocks would even think of touching. They stank of sweat and female blood. They stood at roll-call from five in the morning. When they were at last counted, it was almost nine. Then they were given cold coffee. At three in the afternoon the evening roll-call began and they were given dinner: bread with some spread. Since they did not work, they did not rate the *Zulage*, the extra work ration.

Sometimes they were driven out of the barracks in the middle of the day for an additional roll-call. They would line up in tight rows and march along the road, one behind the other. The big, blonde SS women in leather boots plucked from among them all the skinny ones, the ugly ones, the big-bellied ones — and threw them inside the Eye. The so-called Eye was a closed circle formed by the joined hands of the barracks guards. Filled out with women, the circle moved like a macabre dance to the camp gate, there to become absorbed by the great, camp-wide Eye. Five hundred, six hundred, a thousand selected women. Then all of them started on their walk — along the two roads.

Sometimes an SS woman dropped in at one of the barracks. She cased the bunks, a woman looking at other women. She asked if anyone cared to see a doctor, if anyone was pregnant. At the hospital, she said, they would get milk and white bread.

They scrambled out of the bunks and, swept up into the Eye, walked to the gate — towards the little wood.

Just to pass the time of day — for there was little for us to do at the camp — we used to spend long hours at the Persian Market, either with the Block Elders, or sitting under the barracks walls, or in the latrines. At the Elders' shacks you drank tea or dozed off for an hour or two in their beds. Sitting under the barracks wall you chatted with the carpenters and the bricklayers. A few women were usually hanging around, dressed in pretty little pullovers and wearing sheer stockings. Any one of them could be had for a piece of bright silk or a shiny trinket. Since time began, never has there been such an easy market for female flesh!

The latrines were built for the men and the women jointly, and were separated only by wooden boards. On the women's side, it was crowded and noisy, on ours, quiet and pleasantly cool inside the concrete enclosure. You sat there by the hour conducting love dialogues with Katia, the pretty little latrine girl. No one felt any embarrassment or thought the set-up uncomfortable. After all, one had already seen so much . . .

That was June. Day and night the people walked — along the two roads. From dawn until late at night the entire Persian Market stood at roll-call. The days were warm and sunny and the tar melted on the roofs. Then came the rains, and with them icy winds. The mornings would dawn cold and penetrating. Then the fair weather returned once again. Without interruption, the trains pulled up to the ramp and the people walked on . . . Often we had to stand and wait, unable to leave for work, because they were blocking the roads. They walked slowly, in loose groups, sometimes hand in hand. Women, old men, children. As they passed just outside the barbed-wire fence they would turn their silent faces in our direction. Their eyes would fill with tears of pity and they threw bread over the fence for us to eat.

The women took the watches off their wrists and flung them at our feet, gesturing to us to take them.

At the gate, a band was playing foxtrots and tangos. The camp gazed at the passing procession. A man has only a limited number of ways in which he can express strong emotions or violent passions. He uses the same gestures as when what he feels is only petty and unimportant. He utters the same ordinary words.

"How many have gone by so far? It's been almost two months since mid-May. Counting twenty thousand per day . . . around one million!"

"Eh, they couldn't have gassed that many every day. Though . . . who the hell knows, with four ovens and scores of deep pits . . . "

"Then count it this way: from Koszyce and Munkacz, almost 600,000. They got 'em all, no doubt about it. And from Budapest? 300,000, easily."

"What's the difference?"

"*Ja*, but anyway, it's got to be over soon. They'll have slaughtered every single one of them."

"There's more, don't worry."

You shrug your shoulders and look at the road. Slowly, behind the crowd of people, walk the SS men, urging them with kindly smiles to move along. They explain that it is not much farther and they pat on the back a little old man who runs over to a ditch, rapidly pulls down his trousers, and wobbling in a funny way squats down. An SS man calls to him and points to the people disappearing round the bend. The little old man nods quickly, pulls up his trousers and, wobbling in a funny way, runs at a trot to catch up.

You snicker, amused at the sight of a man in such a big hurry to get to the gas chamber.

Later, we started working at the warehouses, spreading tar over their dripping roofs. The warehouses contained mountains of clothing, junk, and not-yet-disembowelled bundles. The treasures taken from the gassed people were piled up at random, exposed to the sun and the rain.

Every day, after lighting a fire under the bucket of tar, we went to organize a snack. One of us would bring a pail of water, another a sack of dry cherries or prunes, a third some sugar. We stewed the fruit and then carried it up on the roof for those who took care of the work itself. Others fried bacon and onions and ate it with corn bread. We stole anything we could get our hands on and took it to the camp.

From the warehouse roofs you could see very clearly the flaming pits and the crematoria operating at full speed. You could see the people walk inside, undress. Then the SS men would quickly shut the windows and firmly tighten the screws. After a few minutes, in which we did not even have time to tar a piece of roofing board properly, they opened the windows and the side doors and aired the place out. Then came the *Sonderkommando* to drag the corpses to the burning pits. And so it went on, from morning till night — every single day.

Sometimes, after a transport had already been gassed, some late-arriving cars drove around filled with the sick. It was wasteful to gas them. They were undressed and *Oberscharführer* Moll either shot them with his rifle or pushed them live into a flaming trench.

Once, a car brought a young woman who had refused to part from her mother. Both were forced to undress, the mother led the way. The man who was to guide the daughter stopped, struck by the perfect beauty of her body, and in his awe and admiration he scratched his head. The woman, noticing this coarse, human gesture, relaxed. Blushing, she clutched the man's arm.

"Tell me, what will they do to me?"

"Be brave," said the man, not withdrawing his arm.

"I am brave! Can't you see, I'm not even ashamed of you! Tell me!"

"Remember, be brave, come. I shall lead you. Just don't look."

He took her by the hand and led her on, his other hand covering her eyes. The sizzling and the stench of the burning fat and the heat gushing out of the pit terrified her. She jerked back. But he gently bent her head forward, uncovering her back. At that moment the *Oberscharführer* fired, almost without aiming. The man pushed the woman into the flaming pit, and as she fell he heard her terrible, broken scream.

When the Persian Market, the Gypsy camp and the FKL became completely filled with the women selected from among the people from the ramp, a new camp was opened up across from the Persian Market. We called it Mexico. It, too, was not yet completed, and there also they began to install shacks for the Block Elders, electricity, and windows.

Each day was just like another. People emerged from the freight cars and walked on — along both roads.

The camp inmates had problems of their own: they waited for packages and letters from home, they organized for their friends and mistresses, they speculated, they schemed. Nights followed days, rains came after the dry spells.

Towards the end of the summer, the trains stopped coming. Fewer and fewer people went to the crematoria. At first, the camp seemed somehow empty and incomplete. Then everybody got used to it. Anyway, other important events were taking place: the Russian offensive, the uprising and burning of Warsaw, the transports leaving the camp every day, going West towards the unknown, towards new sickness and death; the revolt at the crematoria and the escape of a *Sonderkommando* that ended with the execution of all the escapees.

And afterwards, you were shoved from camp to camp, without a spoon, or a plate, or a piece of rag to clean yourself with.

Your memory retains only images. Today, as I think back on that last summer in Auschwitz, I can still see the endless, colorful procession of people solemnly walking — along both roads; the woman, her head bent forward, standing over the flaming pit; the big redheaded girl in the dark interior of the barracks, shouting impatiently:

"Will evil be punished? I mean in normal, human terms!"

And I can still see the Jew with bad teeth, standing beneath my high bunk every evening, lifting his face to me, asking insistently:

"Any packages today? Couldn't you sell me some eggs for Mirka? I'll pay in marks. She is so fond of eggs . . ."

WITHIN THE GREAT
POSTENKETTE

The working day was starting within the Great *Postenkette*. Long rows of people in stripes were leaving through the gates of the camp under the careful gaze of the guards and moving at a slow pace beyond the fences: to Könisberg, to dig the main drainage trench; to Kiesgrube, to gather gravel; to *Kompostierung*, to pick through manure. The penal company went by in tight groups of five, smartly beating out a rhythm (whoever didn't beat it, had his teeth beaten in), and went to its piecework — the digging of a trench. Apart from digging, those of the Königsberg also dealt in vodka; those of Kiesgrube, also brought eggs and butter; and those of *Kompostierung*, rings and money they found in the manure.

Along all the roads of Birkenau the work Kommandos moved from inside the great *Postenkette*. Women's Kommandos, dressed in dirty dresses with stripes painted in oils on their backs, went to the Effects to sort through the belongings of those who had been gassed. The Canada Kommando went by in red kerchiefs and, behind them, blue kerchiefs, white ones, green ones — a meadow of flowers, a flowing river. Kommandos of men went by: the daily shift of *sonder* to the crematorium, people going to spade, pickax, truck. Kommandos went to the *Frauenlager*, and, passing the ramp dividing the first and second section of the camp, walked through the gate into the women's camp and after being inspected, melted between the Blocks, distributing letters, cigarettes, and vodka.

The orchestra in the work camp was still playing loudly around the Kommandos that were leaving; the camp gate was wide open; and the sweaty, busy *Arbeitsdienst* with the black band on his arm was still bustling around the guardhouse window. The SS man with his clipboard in his hand was still standing in front of the window, noting down the numbers of the outgoing Kommandos. And inside the Great *Postenkette*, people had grabbed their spades; the fires in the crematoria had been stoked. In Effects, the Blocks containing goods had been opened, and everybody else — those from the firm of Wagner and of *Wasserleitung*, as well as those of *Gleisbau* — had bent over the ground, pushed trucks. Outside the Great *Postenkette*, the working; day had started. Earth was being poured from one place to another; endless rows of barracks were being erected, surrounded with barbed wire, and connected to the electrical grid.

The *Vorarbeiter* were writing down the number of people in their groups, and every two hours checking to see that they were all there. The Kapos were wandering over the entire area checking on the tempo of work. Those who knew how to work so as not to drop weren't doing anything. Behind the coal piles of the Blocks, the SS men watched for those who were lazy, weak, and unobservant.

At the same time, out of the line of vision, money, civilian clothing, and valuables changed hands. SS cigarettes, spirits, butter . . . Prominents crept around the women's Kommandos, and from time to time couples disappeared into the bushes or into the empty guard towers of the third area, which was still being built.

And at the same time, along the wide roads that extended like shoulders out of the ramp, was the other stretch of Birkenau, in the birch wood by the side of the crematorium and the little white house where the last of the Hungarian transport was going to the gas, carrying flesh to be burned and baggage to be sorted.

The working day was starting within the Great *Postenkette*.

The Great *Postenkette*, on the other hand, was standing still, was alert. It surrounded with chains of guard towers the huge area of the camp and looked with SS men's eyes onto the crowd milling inside, onto the verdure of trees and the mud of the trampled earth. The carbines, arranged on posts, stood ready to fire.

Behind the *Postenkette* stretched a line of bunkers that could close the whole area off with cross fire. Patrols with dogs walked there. Every ten minutes or so, noncommissioned officers checked on the watchfulness of the Great *Postenkette*.

A mouse couldn't slip through, a bird couldn't fly over it.

Yet people escaped.

They dug holes in the ground, camouflaged them so that no eye could spot them; they hid in them and, covered over by other people, lay there the whole day so that only the following night, when the Great *Postenkette* — which, after each escape stood without a break until dawn and throughout the following day — had withdrawn, would they leave the bunker, and, crossing the Sola, go back to their own country with a wellpaid guide.

They hid in the *DAW* among piles of airplane parts — in enormous containers, in imaginatively constructed dugouts — and escaped by night in the same way. Those who had helped them stayed behind, awaiting their turn, their luck — with their own plans.

Because everyone who had a healthy body and wasn't hungry dreamed at least once of running away from the camp and made more or less realistic plans. The *Pfleger* who worked in the Gypsy camp had a wild plan to some night break the back of the driver who came in a truck with a trailer filled with corpses from the *FKL,* the Quarantine, and Heavy Labor; take his place at the wheel; and drive out the gate (where they didn't control the corpse carriers) to the little town, or, even farther, to Kraków, instead of to the crematorium, and spill the corpses out like pears in the marketplace.

The person who returned at night from the ramp wanted to jump into the deep-as-ocean darkness, and then, opening his eyes, would notice the silhouettes of the guards' automatics lowered at the ready.

People dreamed about freedom and knew how to pay for it. There were tens of unsuccessful escapes for each successful one. Those sniffed out of bunkers by dogs, spotted by the SS men, betrayed by their colleagues were not infrequently clubbed to death on the spot. Their corpses, propped up on spades, stood in front of the camp gates opposite the playing orchestra and looked at the living returning to the camp, with the free eyes of the dead.

Yet people escaped.

But on the day about which I am going to tell you, my friend Tadek escaped from the camp. Escaped, and ended up in Kraków.

We had long spoken with him about escaping. Tadek had money, ways, means, and imagination. It was he who thought about twisting the neck of the chauffeur and driving away in the truck of corpses. It didn't succeed. But it was completely clear that if we escaped, it would be together: Tadek, Janusz, and I.

It happened differently. Tadek escaped with other people, and we who had helped him remained, awaiting our turn, our luck, and with our own plans. We stayed — to the end.

I

The day about which I am going to tell you, began with me clearing the table after breakfast. The electric machine went into its hiding place under the top of the table. I put the rest of the kielbasa and bread neatly on a plate and pushed it into the hidey-hole under the beam, opened the window to air out the room, which was filled with the smell of onions, and thought that I should go organizing, bring back some new products and some of the silk underwear that had come into fashion. And who was supposed to be fashionable if not the *Baubiuro* worker, a Prominent who sat through rain and wind under the roof poring over drawings and in fine weather wandered with an important expression through the camp, as though he had planned it and built the crematoria? We'll lower the weight into the well, here; we'll lower the weight into the well, there; we'll measure the level of the water, and, at the same time, we'll see to the margarine, the kielbasa, and the silk.

I dried my hands, threw the briefcase containing the plans onto my shoulders, and went to Tadek's. He was sitting behind the table, a little preoccupied, and dangled from a string in his hand a scale made out of a pencil. He was weighing gold teeth, popularly known in the camp as *gryzioki*, on the ingeniously made scales.

Tadek didn't even look at me.

"What do you need?" he asked through clenched teeth.

"I'm going to the Quarantine. Do you need me to bring you something? Margarine, kielbasa? After that, I'll be at the Zauna," I offered shortly.

"No thanks. When you're at the Quarantine give the Insurgents my regards," he said, lowering the hand that held the scales, "and tell them to go to hell for not fighting against the Germans."

"What do you want," I responded, "they're civilians."

"What does civilian mean? Attached to his rags, his bedding, his yard, and his vodka. They drank the whole war away and now they are surprised that it came back on them. We have to expect some moral standards from them, don't we?"

Through the walls came the sounds of girlish laughter and the noise of planks being moved. Tadek nodded his head:

"They're already licking the walls. They're starting early today."

They had constructed a double wall in the *Baubiuro*, a moveable one like in the novels of Leblanc. A table piled with soft Canadian blankets stood in the niche — all of it for the obvious use of the office workers as well as the noteables of the camp. Bernard, the Kapo of the *Baubiuro*, drew a decent, and, what's more, a steady, profit from this moveable wall.

"I'm curious who that is?" I said, listening. "The *Oberkapo* from the kitchen?"

"He usually comes after dinner," Tadek replied, absorbed in the plans lying on the table. "It's most likely the *Bauleiter*'s secretary."

A disheveled blonde with an angular body came from freedom to do clerical duties. She had a variety of jobs in the office. Her work in the wall was undoubtedly beyond the call of duty, but — like Bernard's profits — steady.

"Actually, if you look at it straight, that Uprising isn't a bad thing," said Tadek. "It depends who you ask. You're from Kraków. I'm from Warsaw. My mother's in Warsaw."

"Believe me, that's sad. But perhaps she left town? Do you know how many people are wandering the roads? It's probably easy to cross."

"Please God," I said, turning toward the door.

I bumped into Janusz on the way out. Loaded with stuff, he was also apparently heading out for the field. Tadek watched with interest.

"Are you going into the field? You as well? What a shame!"

"So what?" Janusz said in surprise, "Have you got some pressing business? I've eaten breakfast, the weather's good, so I'm going out. Anyway, I've got reasonably interesting work with the electricians. But if . . ."

"No, no," Tadek interrupted. "Nothing special. Please come to lunch. I'd like you both to be here for lunch. Okay? I've got important business."

"If it's important to you . . ."

"It's very important to me," Tadek stressed. "You'll help me with a transaction."

And he bent over the table covered with maps of the camp and on which lay a pile of gold teeth and a scale carefully made out of pencils.

Janusz and I walked out and meandered across the fields of the third area, which was in the process of being built, toward the main road between the camps.

"What plans do you have for today?" I asked Janusz.

"I'm putting up an installation with the electrians. It's incredibly nerveracking: a triangle of posts stands at the mercy of the wind; it's completely unattached to the ground, and you have to climb up and hoist several hundred kilos of metal onto the Block. A transformer. Good work. And you?"

"Measuring water in the area. I'll see if any of our acquaintances are in Quarantine — God forbid."

The September sun shone brightly here. Through the delicate mist to the south could be seen the distant mountains, gray forests, and patches of green meadows looking like craters among bands of gray. Nearer at hand, lay a verdure of trees, and quite close by, countless straight rows of barracks divided by camp roads, filled to the brim with crowds of people.

To the west, lay a completely dark, nearly black, forest, and closer by, a birch wood full of smoke and screams and tall pines out of which poked crematoria; to the east, the red roofs of a town out of which a slender church spire pointed to the sky.

"How much longer are we going to look at that?" I sighed. "It's time for us, Janusz."

"We'll see what Tadek does," Janusz answered. "But . . . he's been planning for months, poking around, and nothing. But let's wait: it's easier for him than for us. On the other hand, drop by our bunker. Only if you have the time, of course," he added immediately. "We should check that things are in order."

Our bunker had become ours by accident. One of our friends had once noticed a group of Russians, far away from their Kommandos, loitering aimlessly without work by a certain trench. He noticed them one day, he noticed them another day, and when some people from that group escaped, and again, he decided it was worth examining that area.

He kept the secret of the trench to himself for six months, but when, however, all the Russians escaped and the bunker, which was well camouflaged, stood empty, he let me in on it. After that my friend went into the *KB*, he settled down comfortably, and no longer had the desire to escape. By the nature of things, the bunker became our property. One had to be careful, however: every few days we checked to see whether the branch accidently thrown onto the expanse of grass covering the entrance to the bunker had been moved.

I, unfortunately, did not know whether I would have time to be here and there, at the Quarantine, the Zauna, Mexico, and back at the bunker.

"As you wish," Janusz replied reluctantly, "I don't recommend that you go to Mexico. You'll be turned off, that's all. Am I to expect you for lunch?"

I nodded my head in reply, and we parted. Without a word, Janusz turned left to his transformer station while I, as regulations required, reported to the guard at the gate — who wrote down my number and was curious as to what I was going to measure and why — and went into the Quarantine.

The Quarantine was chock-full of "refugees" from Warsaw. Lots of unshaved, pale people in crumpled clothes between the Blocks and at the wires, as usual. They mill from one corner to another not knowing what to do with themselves. A shapeless, nameless mass of people who only a month ago had been cabdrivers, shopkeepers, lawyers, worked in offices or "even" at the city hall. People who rode the trams, ate in a normal way with knife and fork, went to sleep when they wanted to. People who could be our parents or friends; one just has to look at their faces carefully. Now, the normal pattern of their lives broken, they don't know anything, they understand nothing. They are only very roughly sorted now, not sorted according to sex or age, loaded into the Quarantine without a selection because there's no room anywhere else. Everything's overcrowded.

They look at the striped clothing of the people from Birkenau with fear and contempt; they've been told that these people are criminals. We in our stripes regard them with disdain, as the person who, having understood the real, bitter meaning of life, looks at the person who is just testing that meaning — in short, as a professional looks at the work of a bungling dilettante.

We know that you can't telephone the women's camp from here to ask about your wife's health, that there are no mailboxes in which to post letters to Częstochowa or Radom, that there's no one to complain to about having been given, for no reason, a triangle signifying "political prisoner." But they don't know that and gaze distrustfully at the white strips of material freshly sewn onto the left breast and decorated with a number and triangle, desperately asking each other and us.

"Mister, we're not politicals; we didn't fight the Germans."

"That's exactly why," reply those who own all the wisdom of the world. One or another even has some relation from Łódz in the *Werkschutz* or somewhere else. They hang on to it like a drunkard a lamppost. They've done nothing, maybe he could help.

"Wait, the war's going to last a while, your cousin'll come here," those wise ones prophesy. "What's with that Uprising," they ask, searching the faces for people they know.

"Everyone knew there'd be an Uprising, and the Germans were the first to know. They placed units in the streets and waited."

"And our people had nothing?"

"They did. Of course they did. Take me, for example, I come from Narutowicz Square. They made their way into our house with acetylene lamps, supposedly with grenades, one had a rifle. Kids, all of them! Was this necessary? To destroy the town like that."

"Everything was destroyed? What about the town center? Marszałkowska Street?"

"Rubble. Just chimneys and paving stones. Piles of brick."

"But you didn't fight?"

No, they hadn't fought.

"What was it all for? We could live, everybody had stacks of money. Lots of cafés, theaters . . . And now" — they look disapprovingly at their crumpled clothes and touch their unshaved faces — "we have to wander around like beggars. No one knows what's going to happen. They didn't give us any blankets, nor food. They even steal from our servings."

"The camp stands on robbery," I reply philosophically.

"But from our servings? What'll become of us?"

"Nothing. The wood will suffice," I add casually, thinking about the piles of wood warehoused diligently and with foresight near the crematorium by the camp administration. It's clear that the coal will get used up, so we'll use wood for fuel.

"My good people" — I shake my head not for the first nor last time — "do you really understand what freedom is? To live without a gong, without an Appel, not to have a number? To move around without a guard? Not to look up at the chimneys? Why didn't you run?"

They hadn't known where they were going, had been told to civilian labor, and in any case . . .

"The war will be over soon, in three weeks at most. When the Americans take France, the Germans will be finished."

Every transport to Auschwitz, without exception, brought with it this faith in a quick and immediate end to the war.

People thrown into a different world in which time was kept differently, could not imagine that a person could live here for longer than a month or six weeks. And because they didn't think about their own deaths, the only salvation seemed to be an end to the war. The common law of human thought.

"And if it doesn't end, and winter comes? Do you know how many of you will be finished?"

I take a small weight out of my pocket, lower it into some well, note down the levels with serious expression, and distance myself from these people.

They're from another world, one from which I, too, once came, but to which I will not return. Is it at all possible to go back, I wonder, to that other world of shopkeepers, racketeers, and moralizers? Thrifty people who are concerned about the hole in their socks and the morality of their daughter? So that's my city? I don't believe it. But I check the level of the water and avoid these people. I've had enough of them.

My friend, Józek, who's listing them, has also had quite enough. His eyes are puffy and his head is drooping sleepily.

"A damn pile of work. Do you know that some of them are passing themselves off as officers? It's a good job it's going through me and I'm tearing up the forms, otherwise they'd have the entire political department at their throats. But I have a certain profit from it."

He does have a profit, and it isn't a good one. The profit has nice legs and went through the rollers of the disinfection with no harm to itself. It even kept its hair because shaving had gone out of style.

"My secretary, what a body! A machine not a person!"

So I promise to carry a letter to her in the *FKL*.

"And you know what's the most interesting thing? Luck smiles on the stupid! Imagine, yesterday one of the Warsaw crew crawled through the wires and vanished into thin air. A wild rush for freedom! We don't understand that any more — taking such a risk."

The crowd spills across the roads of the Quarantine. The SS doctor looks over the candidates for transport. Straight rows of naked men stand in front of the Block. But empty baby carriages move down the whole width of the road on the other side of the Quarantine's wires. Thousands upon thousands upon thousands. They stretch along the newly packed road from the crematorium to the station — to be sent out.

We stand upright and silent.

Just then two from "the Uprising" came up to us carrying a barrel of soup to the Block. They put the barrel down, and one of them turned to Józek: "I'm an upholsterer from Grojeck. Do you think they'd take me into the baby carriage factory? I really am a good craftsman."

It wasn't until I'd left the Quarantine that I remembered that I had bought neither margarine nor kielbasa. It's always like that when you get talking, I thought angrily. I wonder what Tadek wanted us for?

II

Very lively lines of communications operate across the third *Bauabschnitt*. Margarine, kielbasa, and meat carefully hidden in corners of clothing flow that way from the SS potato storage: "good" German cigarettes from the civilians; English chocolate stolen from POW packages by the SS and "palmed off" by us for the obvious items. Newspapers, eggs, vodka flow from there. Cigarettes and vodka flow away from the camp to the above potato storage, and clothing, gold, money (albeit increasingly rarely — the exchange rate is falling) to the civilians. It's hardly surprising, therefore, that the route is heavily guarded by the SS — especially from the Political Department — and full of ambushes. A second similarly lively road leads to the Effects. One goes along a broad comfortable tract the length of all the parts of the camp, passing the crematoria hidden behind a hedge.

The hedge consists of half-dead branches stuck into the earth. The branches stand out jarringly against the green wood, harmonizing with nothing, neither with the pines, nor the crematorium on the left, nor the crematorium on the right. Nonetheless, of necessity they hide the pit on the right. But even that wood is not natural, it's filled with rancid, blue smoke and smells of burned human beings. It's not surprising; the pits are full of melted human fat that burns incessantly.

One turns left after the crematoria and through a gate guarded by a bribed, but very diligent guard to whom one has to show ten passes and at least twenty cigarettes, and one arrives at Auschwitz's Spice Islands — the Effects.

Truth to tell, bad SS men bustle about even here, guarding the accumulated treasures, but there is treasure! Who wouldn't take the risk, especially since the bargaining chip is vodka, valued as highly as beads were by primitive peoples.

This then is the Effects: on the right, the big Zauna — a brick building, washroom, de-lousing chamber, and temporary store room for the personal clothing of a transport. And on the left: barracks, barracks, barracks. I no longer remember how many there were of those barracks, but I can still see the insides — heavy, stuffed to the top like pirate ships filled with booty.

In some, lay already sorted things: bundles of women's underwear, men's suits, bulging suitcases. In others, heaps of things were piled higgledy-piggledy awaiting a human hand to restore them to order. Inanimate objects pile themselves up between the Blocks as well. There's a certain gradation here: a pile of shoes, a hill, a mountain of lost, orphaned, single, unpaired shoes. Helpless women in pink headscarves rummage through this pile, picking out approximately matched pairs, putting together, like a matrimonial agency, an unhappy, unsuited married couple of shoes.

Tied together by their laces, these misalliances wander into freight cars, fill the insides of trucks, and blunder somewhere into the depths of Germany marked out for some charitable cause. Because the camp cannot officially take anything from Effects, the camp Kommandant once ordered several thousand shoes for the prisoners and got them: his own freight cars, which having wandered like Sinbad around the Reich, returned to their point of origin. The shoes, in the meantime, had rotted through, gone into the fire, and the prisoners walked around in ones they'd organized. Those who didn't have the means to organize quickly died and, therefore, didn't need shoes.

Right behind the shoes, lay pots, bowls, basins, pans, baskets, children's carriages, enamelled dishes of the oddest shapes, and every kind of implement used in Hungarian houses. Closer to the hospital wires, bundles of still unpacked underwear and boundless treasures: marmalade, butter, bread. As a rule, bracelets were hidden in marmalade, rings in butter, and money in bread.

The girls in Effects are pretty and clean. They smell of fresh silk underwear and the latest perfumes. They throw watches and gold to the men, but they know how to exact love and its physical tokens — this isn't their first day in the Lager. They also know how to make the correct gesture.

And so, here I stand at the doors to the Block next to girls who are sorting through the underwear. I look around for the lady Kapo. She's there, lying on a couch in the shadow of the barracks.

"Kapo," I say right out, "I'm from the *Baubiuro* and want some underwear for myself and my colleagues."

The woman opens her dark-circled eyes and looks me over

solemnly from head to toe. I repeat my request. She beckons toward a girl:

"Give him some. *Reizhosen*, understand?" and closes her eyes.

The girl flashes her teeth in a smile and goes into the depths of the Block. We squeeze our way through bundles.

"How many do you want?"

"Oh, give me about five. That'll give us some in reserve."

The girl rummages along the shelves and throws silk down on my head. I look at it with embarrassment. Wearing women's underwear has recently come into fashion. But this? I hold a pile of women's high-cut briefs in my hand.

"These'll be the best for you!" The girls bursts out laughing. "Loose and comfortable. Anyway, it's what the Kapo ordered."

They do exchange them for me, but the Kapo mustn't see. I hide the silk under my trousers and leave, smiling pleasantly at the girls, the Kapo, and the Effects — Auschwitz's Spice Islands.

And that's how it is. Now here, now there, drop a weighted string into some well, measure the level, note it down; stroll down one road, then another; avoid the *Raportführer* lying in wait on the tower; turn back; chase dazed couples out of the bushes; glance at people who are going to the gas without knowing it; doff your cap at a passing SS man; now here, now there drop a weighted string into the depths of a well . . .

Now I'm walking through Mexico, a camp of eleven thousand Hungarian Jewish women who live in the flimsy Blocks of an unfinished camp. The *Postenkette* — a couple of old gendarmes dozing over their machine guns, sheltered by paper roofs. Bread is unloaded onto the ground here, water brought in cisterns — fascinatingly primitive. Whoever cares to, comes to Mexico.

And so I walk across Mexico. Autumnal clouds of an angry blue tint move across the sky and are torn into shreds by a cutting crosswind. Sometimes the wind tears across the ground and then the women, who have been chased out of the Blocks, huddle together. They're wearing low-cut summer dresses, tatters smeared with oil paint. They do nothing; their main occupation is the Appel. Every day there are either thirty too many or twelve too few. They are counted and counted and counted. Sometimes an SS woman comes and, in a tried and tested way, takes the sick and pregnant to the doctor. They leave and never come back — the gas chamber gives no one back.

When it's sunny, they lie naked on the damp earth like animals. They're probably as cheerful and patient as a person who has gotten to know the taste of bread and water and the earth's good silence.

And so I, an ordinary, living being, walk across Mexico. Prominents weave between the women: in their celluloid capes and rubber boots, the Kapos and Block Elders combine function with elegance.

The wind tears the paper from the roofs, rips it into shreds, and throws it back down. But beneath is a window, and at the window little muslin curtains (those curtains still haunt me) are now being pulled back and some hand is waving to me through the pane. Out of habit, I glance at the guard. The guy's asleep in the hut, and the machine gun is lying on its base, a fixed piece of iron. By the walls of the Block, girls are lying, as apathetic as felled trees or broken flowers.

But the Block Elder's quarters are clean and pleasant. The small room is decorated warmly and cosily — a carpet, drapes at the window, a couch with little pillows, women's knickknacks on the table, and an electric coffee machine. How did that get here, I wonder; there's no electricity yet in Mexico. I look at the unknown owner of these quarters, of this cosily set-up room. She's a young Hungarian with big dark eyes and lightly madeup lips. She doesn't know German well, but after a second hazards, "Do you speak French? You do? Oh, that's wonderful!"

She's a student from the art school in Budapest, and draws even here.

"Take a look . . ."

I look at this woman I don't know but who beckoned me in with her hand. She's graceful, her breasts are small, and as hard as apples, probably. Her hips are well constructed, and her muscles move harmoniously beneath her tight skirt.

I look at my unknown woman, glance around the room, and take stock: the *Zimmers* had her for the couch; those from *Bekleidungskammer* for the carpet and covers; those from Canada for the coffee machine; those from Electricals for the current; the glaziers for the windowpanes.

"Why don't you take a look? It's a study of my sister. Do you like it?"

The sketch is good: a kneeling naked girl, her back to the viewer, holding her hair in both hands, as though in despair. The flesh is deliciously drawn, a human mass, tense with expectation.

"But you know, I haven't a single pencil. Show me the briefcase."

She takes out a drawing pad with sketches in it, even takes single sheets of paper.

"Bring me colored crayons, will you? You must have plenty of everything in the *Baubiuro. N'est ce pas?*"

She spreads out a whole gamut of drawings before me. As she lowers her head, her kerchief slips off. It's only now I see that her hair is shorn to the skin. Of course, they're still shaving the Jewish women. She catches my eye and blushes:

"Forgive me," she says with tears in her eyes and pushes the kerchief back on her forehead.

"But why?" I say clumsily, blushing as well. I try to cover my confusion by praising her little room. "It's so tasteful."

"Yes, I'm particularly happy that I finally covered all the walls with blue blankets. I love the color blue. And apart from that, I can't hear the noise from the Block. Imagine, one thousand eight hundred filthy women behind that wall screaming the entire night. I couldn't close an eye. They were quarrelling about the blankets, so I took them all. They're very happy about that. It's better that no one has anything, than that only some should. The Judgment of Solomon, don't you think?"

I don't think so, but say I do, and add:

"It's true that one can get used to the camp? It draws in, absorbs, imbibes, imposes its stronger laws on people. Segregates to the left and the right, and, as here, divides the wall of this room. Haven't you noticed?"

The dark brows rise thoughtfully. No, no, she hasn't noticed, perhaps because she's only recently come to the camp. But would like a drink of black coffee, perhaps, real coffee?

"Black coffee in the fifth year of the war in a concentration camp? Where did you get it?" I feign sincere surprise.

"A gentleman shouldn't ask, but I'll tell you anyway. From your packing department. Try a cake" — she pushed a plateful toward me — "*specialité de la maison.* And the apricot jam comes from Canada, in case you're interested."

Someone knocked at the door. A fat, chubby-faced *Stubedienst* came in.

"Shall I spread the blankets on the floor? They're wet and they'll rot."

"No, let them lie without blankets. Tell them I want silence. Take the sick to the hospital immediately; I don't want them moaning like they did yesterday, or I'll strangle them. I've had enough of it. Listen," she added as the other was walking out, "keep five cubes of margarine and two kielbasas back today. When my sister comes, give her soup. And now you're to stand at the door and let no one in? Understand?" And with an impatient gesture she sent her out the door, then turned to me.

As I left Mexico, the Kommandos were already forming into groups and going to their huts for lunch. Scattered implements pointed up at the sky. Then I remembered that I didn't have time to go to the bunker. I realized that the camp was pulling me further into itself, and, as that room was separated from the Block, a wall divided me from the world beyond the great *Postenkette*. As I walked into the office, I wondered what Tadek wanted from us. Was he . . .?

III

Tadek grabbed me by the arm, and looked me right in the face.

"I'm going, right away I think. You'll help, of course."

I leaned against the wall.

"Of course," I said quietly, "I'll help."

"Good. You know the barracks' parts in the fields behind the offices? A truck will pull up there. Go so no one in the office notices. Later you can say that you know nothing. I'm going to fetch Janusz so he doesn't show up here."

"All right, Tadek," I said, calm now. "Who's going with you?"

"Władek Piłat and Janek. Spirits up!"

He always had a tendency to pathos. I sneaked out of the office and carefully, trying not to overdo caution and draw someone's attention, slipped between the bushes and among the prefabricated pieces of barracks. My heart was hammering.

This is no longer messing about with people; he's really going all out, I thought. But it's not for me, I added with unwarranted bitterness. Far off, the SS men were sitting motionless in the towers looking down onto the field. The roads were empty and dead. It was lunchtime everywhere. We were hidden from the rest of the camp by anemic bushes and the goodwill of those who were looking. Behind the *Postenkette* the world stretched all the way to the horizon. Suddenly, I felt a wild yearning for space and my jaws started to tremble. The pain in my muscles made me realize how tightly I was clenching them. Tough, I thought, perhaps we'll make it through the bunker. But the leader? We'll have to go all the way, like madmen. I was furious with myself that I hadn't checked on the bunker before lunch, as though that would have helped, that it was Tadek fleeing and not me.

Tadek and Janusz finally showed up, emerging from the other side of the boards. Tadek explained in hushed tones:

"Andrzej is watching on the road. Władek and Janek in the bushes. They're already waiting. The truck is on its way."

Janusz was pale and silent. He wrinkled his brow and moved his jaw nervously. It's odd how in such moments of tension and anticipation an absurd silence descends and one can practically hear one's blood flowing.

The silence was suddenly broken by the growl of the truck. A huge truck, fueled by wood gas, it smoked and stank.

"It's time," Tadek said.

He pulled two bottles of spirits out of hiding, slipped them into his pocket, and disappeared between the trees. Janusz explained in a whisper:

"He took that for the carpenters' Kapo to expedite the arrival of the truck. That driver always brings vodka."

We started to load prefabricated door units onto the truck. They were lying in one pile near the truck.

"Did Tadek choose the place?"

Janusz nodded his head.

After setting down four panels we had an empty space inside for people.

"Wait," Janusz whispered when we'd jumped off the platform, "was that Andrzej whistling?"

"No," I answered, "don't get hysterical. Maybe they saw us? They could have on this tall truck."

"We'll see."

We held our breath and listened. The truck was rumbling steadily, and the driver's eyes were closed; he was pretending to be asleep.

It was all absurd. SS men were looking down from the guard towers. Nobody was working except for us two. Around us the Kommandos were eating lunch. The windows of the painters' barracks gave out straight onto our truck. The sides of the truck rose sky high, taller than the bushes. It had to be visible from afar. We hid three people in it in plain view of the entire camp. If they check carefully, they'll tumble to the fact that we had to have been helping. They won't squeal, for sure. But when they realize that it was us? Then . . .

Tadek finally arrived. He was now dressed in a civilian suit with a camp number tacked on and with stripes painted on with toothpaste, which could easily be removed. The other two came out of the bushes. We squeezed hands. Without saying a word, the three crawled inside. We covered them with two ordinary wall panels, and, for camouflage, threw a few boards, window frames, circles, beams on top — in a word, created an artistic mess. We loaded the truck with a heap of wood. The driver crawled out of the cabin and looked it over critically.

"Ready?"

"This as well." Janusz handed him a bundle with gold in it. I recognized Tadek's handkerchief. Probably the teeth he was weighing in the morning. And a lot more besides. The driver took the bundle and hid it in the gas engine. If they catch them, they'll beat them and put them into a *Sonderkommando*. Maybe they'll survive. If they catch them with gold, it's the gallows. Not for escaping but for smuggling. Better not to have gold on you.

"Ready?" asked the driver.

"Ready."

The truck rumbled louder, skidded in the mud, and rolling from side to side, drove off.

At that point, we stared at each other for a long time.

"Let it succeed. Let it succeed. And . . . us?"

Janusz shrugged his shoulders.

"Let's get out of here as quickly as possible. The atmosphere's bad. Were you at the bunker?"

"No, in Mexico."

"I'll go this afternoon. I don't want to be in the office."

We stop by the carpenters' on the way, to show ourselves. The Kapo is red in the face and is talking loudly, a sign he's been drinking.

"Where's Tadek?" he asks. "I didn't give him money for the vodka. Since when has he been giving on tick?"

"He's already so rich that apparently he can give vodka on a few hours' tick. Maybe it was a keepsake?" Janusz jokingly replied, and we both burst out laughing at the jest. It was obvious that Tadek could outmaneuver ten and had only one firm business rule: from hand to hand.

"Tadek would skin his own father," the Kapo concluded, "Have you been at the office?"

"No, in Mexico," Janusz said.

"I saw such a beautiful girl," I threw in, "the Block Elder on that Block in the middle, Kapo, short, dark, sketches."

"I know her. I told them to make a table for her. A good body."

He took a cigarette out and lit it.

"It's boring in this camp," he sighed. "When's it going to end, this damned war?"

"A year from today, Kapo."

We left the hut. Our tension relaxed. We sat down to one side and were silent for a long time. Then Janusz got up and walked off in the direction of the trench. I went back to the office.

I drew and drafted, marked the levels of the water I had measured in the morning with colored lines, and waited for the row.

First, Jewish women came to see Tadek on business. Very surprised that he wasn't there, they came to me. I said I didn't know, and would they clear off, I had important work to do. Then, someone from the *Unterkunft* came, saying that he'd managed to organize some quilts for him but he'd have to pay right away. They were sent to me. I acted on his behalf, as was our custom, but deep down I was furious at him.

Then they started to worry about him in the office.

"He hasn't escaped, has he?" somebody said casually.

I mechanically sorted through the maps and held my face in half-shadow so as not to reveal my tense nerves.

"No, I don't think so; he goes nowhere without Krystyn and Janusz. They're a gang."

"There are no gangs in an escape. You don't tell even your closest friend."

"Tadek had too many business deals to escape. Who'd cream the Jews?" Everyone laughed, but the wait grew tenser.

Around four, Bernard, a Kapo, arrived. He was amazed and confused when I told him I knew nothing.

"Do you really not know anything about Tadek?"

"How should I know? I was at the Quarantine and the Effects the entire morning, and then I went to Mexico. I've got a Block Elder there. Maybe he went to the women's camp?" I suggested. Bernard shook his head.

"I don't think so. He's not like that. I was going to give him the news from the latest communication from London."

"You fixed the radio?" I asked with interest.

"The electricians came and did it. D'you know how they're fighting near Arnheim? You have no idea! The English have landed in gliders, and when they capture the bridges across the Rhine, *alles* will be *verloren*. There's no Siegfried line there!"

"The Siegfried line goes to the sea," I said firmly. I started sharpening my pencil, but my hands were shaking.

"That's not true. There's no Siegfried line there. When they capture the bridges . . ."

"And if they don't capture them?"

"If they don't capture them, then six more months."

"Or longer."

"No longer, I'm telling you. Where could he have gone?"

"Perhaps to the *Truppenlazarett*? Actually, I've no idea."

Bernard scratched his head.

"We'll see," he said at last.

"What will we see?" I asked casually through my teeth, in which I was holding a pencil. But Bernard left without replying.

It was already dusk in the room, soon it would be time to *Antreten* for the *Appel*. I could relax my facial muscles.

Tadek's absence worried the whole office. Every once in a while doors slammed and questions crisscrossed about him. I'd mutter that I didn't know, and, finally, that I wasn't his nursemaid, and that once I'd set myself to work I wanted to finish it. I wouldn't have time tomorrow — I had the *FKL* and the Hungarian camp — and the plans had to be finished.

"Giez stung him," said an old engineer ironically who was busy cooking up all sorts of dishes. "He's going to build the Lager, damn it, win the war.

"I'd be angry, too, if my friend had escaped and left me stranded."

I smashed my ruler down on the table just as the doors opened and Janusz came in.

"Come to *Antreten*. D'you know that Tadek's still not here? Bernard told me."

"The whole office here is shaking," I replied. "He's probably got caught up somewhere."

Talking loudly, we push to our places through the fives that are being formed.

"He didn't get caught up anywhere. Bernard said he'd escaped."

"But," I said in disbelief, "Tadek wouldn't escape without us."

At the same time, the bunker through which we had to go without a guide, without the quarter kilogram of gold necessary for the road, rose before my eyes. We'd have to sit twenty-four hours in a tight, basement grave, and then go — like madmen.

Our bunker, I thought, we'll manage. Others don't even have that. We started moving into the camp. At that moment, from the main guard tower, a long drawn out siren started to sound a high-pitched single note.

"So he really escaped," someone next to me said. "He was a good fellow. Let's hope he succeeds; I won't mind standing longer on Appel."

Janusz glanced at me briefly.

"Now it's going to start in earnest. Look out for yourself."

I suddenly remembered that Janusz was supposed to have been to the bunker today. I seized his arm.

"Did you go?"

"I did."

"It's okay?"

Janusz turned his face toward me.

"It's okay. Overturned. Somebody snitched."

"So that's it? It's all for nought. Nothing to be done — this way?" I nudged him as though he could do something. He shrugged impatiently.

"Watch out. Keep in step. *Links, links.*"

The drum beat out a strong rhythm. In straight lines, our heads turned to the right, we walked into the camp.

Walked into the camp.

WE START OVER

One day was just like another. Transports went neverendingly to the gas. Thousands of people evacuated from Warsaw, contemptuously referred to as "Insurgents," arrived. But trains left from the ramp every day, filled with prisoners. They went west — to Gross Rosen, to Sachsenhausen, to Buchenwald, to Natzweiler — went and melted into "small" camps whose names no one knew as yet.

But one day was just like another and the work continued in its age-old fashion. The camp was still being enlarged, wood was still being carried to the crematoria. Rows of enormous wells were being hastily completed. The construction of new high-tension wires was started; the western transformer station was erected. Settling tanks for the main sewage system were laid out. Roads were paved, ground levelled, posts driven in for new barracks. Old work was completed, and materials brought in for new.

But, increasingly, in the camp offices people whispered about the complete liquidation of the camp and carefully prepared themselves for future transports by getting small and compact bundles of gold and valuables ready. From one day to the next, the liquidation was awaited, but when it came, it struck like a thunderbolt. The system was collapsing, and the play for life was beginning anew.

One day, our chief burst into our electrician's hut, out of breath.

"We're rolling up the third *Bauabschnitt*. Liquidation."

There was a moment of silence, and then we went out, each one of us taking his tools. The chief came out after us, slamming the hut door.

"It probably won't be needed. But roll it up quickly. That's an order!"

And he went with us, explaining the ins and outs as we walked. We had to take down the electric fence, take down the barbed wire, unscrew the isolators, lamps, and God knows what else. Dismantle, load, send off. Where to? It's obvious — to the nearest *KZ* — to Gross Rosen. Very pressing work — send out a set of sets for building fences five-hundred-meters long. Why? Gross-Rosen is being enlarged. Understood? Do it!

So we do it. We do it in a typically Auschwitz spirit: people are going to the gas; huge piles of wood lie by the cremo, probably for us; the camp has been so surrounded with machine guns that not even a mouse can get out; a few bombs'll drop, and that'll be that. What do we have to lose? If any one needs the barbed wire, they can come and get it. If a coil offers resistance, wire cutters to its head, then, a hammer. The insulators are made out of good, prewar porcelain; let's see if we can break them with a single blow. You're tired? Why do you have to carry bundles of wires to the road? Drown them in the trench; the water's muddy in there; no one will see.

In this fashion, we dismantled two kilometers of fence, and there was still not enough.

"So, chief, do we dismantle it all the way?" we asked, when the unfortunate sets of sets departed for Gross-Rosen.

"Actually, no," the chief replied, "because you are going to Budy. That camp has to be electrified. Quickly! That's an order!"

Budy was a "small" camp, let's call it an agricultural one, consisting of cattle, barns, wagons, SS men, and prisoners. But it had no light, even though the posts had already been erected in spring 1943.

We took the detailed electrification plans out of the building office, but when we came to the area we started by looking for the nearest electrical line and, when we'd found it, took it upon ourselves to lay out the sidings. The plans went up in smoke.

We hung a few new kilowatts to the already overloaded lines, but so what? They said let there be light, there's light, and if it all blows at once, so much the better. There'll be new work. And, because it's good work, it has to be respected. In the final analysis, we had survived the Lager in just this fashion, not in any other.

We had been working for two days and were doing fine. The natural world (with its inseparable element — the guard); organizing; good spirits. We left our tools, overalls, exchangeable goods at Budy. But on the third day, the order came to lock the camp tight and not one Kommando went out to work. Obviously — fear, confusion, gossip: if it's the gas, we're going to resist, let them shoot us, but not that. And we'll kill a few of them, too. What a joke — liqui dation, transport, evacuation! Because of partisans, because of the offensive, and because of who knows what else . . . they'll transport the skilled workers . . . perhaps they'll leave the skilled workers . . . we're as smart as we ever were, and, after all, we're skilled workmen. Gossip was gossip, but in the afternoon all the Poles were led out to the neighboring section, where the Gypsies had been, then the

Hungarians, now us and, after us, women were supposed to be kept. But that's already another story.

So we were transferred to a new area. It was a bigger deal than a move from one city to another, or from one country to another. Everything had to be organized from square one, nothing was a given except for cunning and relationships.

The most important thing was togetherness. Tygrys is already standing by the barbed wire and shouting across the whole width of the ramp to the women's camp:

"Senka, Senka, give me Senka!"

"I'm on the transport," a girl's shout floats in from over there, carried like a leaf in the wind. They wave good-bye and move away from the barbed wire, perhaps forever.

Krystyn, at the other barbed wire, requisitions goods from our previous accommodations. They throw over blankets, clothing, food to him. It's those Poles who have stayed in their old places. There are a few like that, there really are — Prominents, or with relationships or luck. But I have the most important role — renewing relationships. Why else was I a Prominent here for a year? So I bring a bucket of potatoes, a bit of kielbasa, a few sticks of margarine. Finally, pots. Krystyn cooks dinner. "After all, it's not so bad, it could be worse," I say. The potatoes are excellent.

"Of course, we concentration campers are not going to let them get us."

"The worst is behind us," I throw in, remembering past years.

"Surely we won't be starting over," Tygrys adds in an uncertain tone.

In the evening, we lie comfortably on the bunk. We have stolen a light bulb, we have screened an area off with blankets, we are protecting our "privacy." We reminisce, tell stories. Youthful escapades are good, but better yet are crime stories. We fall asleep; it's warm and cozy.

The following day we give the Old Man, the *Rottenführer* from the Political Department, a hundred English cigarettes, and in spite of the strict *Lagersperre* we go through the barbed wire to rescue what we left behind in the shop. We bring it back; we have money for food and a bit for the road.

We wait yet another day.

The first transport was supposed to go to Czechoslovakia for excellent work, they said. Only metallurgists, experts, real ones. Of course, we should go with them! But the crowd was mixed; we ran away from there.

For the next one, the SS made the selections and separated us. Immediately, however, we recongregated into the same group and tried to figure out how to take our things, because we couldn't leave the rows. Because of that, Tygrys took the watch off his wrist and, accompanied by a guard, went to the Block. The expedition was expensive, because the camp Kommandant was there with his entire retinue. Despite that, however, we got what we needed. We stand until evening. Deep at night, we march out to the washrooms. Delousing, a bath, fresh clothes, an inspection of packets. The "fresh clothes" are, in reality, old rags, and in them, we walk over to our familiar part of the camp, to the special Block. It is night, we cannot leave the Block, but after a couple of hours we have better clothing and more food for the journey. Even now, as we are about to leave, all our avenues are still open.

They say that a big transport — a thousand people — is "bad," but one that has three hundred people is *prima*, because it is going to a small, "excellent" camp. Obviously, we immediately switch Block and group — we'll go where it's "better."

Before dawn, they drive us out of the Block, arrange us in fives, in groups, in columns. They count, count, count. A fine, autumn rain comes down in the darkness. We stand for an hour, two, our clothes get soaked, the cold penetrates our skin. We start to shake with cold. We stand without moving for an eternity.

The three of us hold each other up by the arms. The old, hopeless Appels in the mud and the rain come back to us. Are we starting over once more? From behind come snatches of conversation silenced by the wind:

"The evacuations have jammed all the camps. You're not going to get a "function," brother. It'll be the spade, my friend, or the stones. There won't be packages from home either, and you won't be able to organize gold teeth for butter. Canada will be over for us! I'm telling you, we're still going to suffer!"

"Don't panic, don't panic, we've gone through so much already, we'll survive somehow until the war ends."

"How many of us survived the camp? Only a small percent. And now the counting is going to start over."

"Listen, so many have left before us; they've sent civilian *meisters* to build new camps; our *Kommandoführer*'s haven't gone to the front either. There'll be people we know everywhere."

"Don't be so naive, what *meister* or SS man's going to help if he's not paid in gold or dollars? As for our companions, they're going to be wielding spades as well. We're starting over all right."

"Oh, we'll manage. Is a camp for people, or what?"

At last, we walk out of the gates of the camp and march past lamps shining above the wire. In the darkness lie rows of black barracks. Here and there, a fragment of a door, or an empty window, is etched and illuminated by a stray reflector. Here and there, beneath the windows shine rusty puddles of mud. The dark silhouettes of the guard towers are black against the somewhat lighter sky. The crematoria burn, the smoke moves in a wide river across the sky. The rest of the world disappears into darkness.

The thin, trampled mud spatters around our feet and pours over the tops of our shoes. A train, its engine smoking, is already waiting on the ramp. The doors of the cattle wagons stand wide open.

AUSCHWITZ TERMS

The isolation and extraordinariness of the surroundings, the mix of many languages, and the official German language all combined to produce a distinctive camp language, which, like the language of conspiracy, still needs to be codified. We provide here the meanings of some of the terms used in Auschwitz, which may make it easier to understand the text.

ABGANG — A group leaving one Block for another, going from the hospital to the camp, from the camp to the hospital. Also, a single individual. "An *abgang* of thirty people left our block today." "How many *abgangs* do you have?"

ANTRETEN — Assembly. Camp life consisted of two moments: when a prisoner went somewhere by himself and when he went in a line. "Can't you hear it's *Antreten*? "We're going to an *Antreten*."

APPEL — Roll call, the daily tally of the strength of the camp. A sacrosanct event. Also the strength of the Block relative to the camp at the roll call. "Let's go to the *Appel*." "Does the *Appel* tally?" — *block-elder* to clerk. Often, the *Appel* dragged on and the prisoners had to stand at attention for hours. The longest *Appel* in Auschwitz lasted two days.

BLOCK — Camp barracks. In so-called Old Auschwitz, these were solid, two-story constructions built by the prisoners. In Birkenau, they were almost without exception wooden horse stables. Every prisoner was assigned to some Block in front of which he had to stand for Appel. Specific Kommandos occupied specific Blocks. The Prominents slept in Blocks they chose for themselves: "Out of the block and to the Appel!" "Block Six to delousing!"

BLOCK ELDER — The prisoner in charge of a Block. Saw to it that the Block was in order, supervised the distribution of food, parcels, and so on. Was responsible for numbers tallying at Appel. Other duties included: searching for escapees (within the great

Postenkette), meting out corporal punishment at official executions, and so on. Surrounded by a halo of criminality (some had several thousand murders on their conscience), they limited themselves in time to the comfortable function of representing the Block to the SS, leaving actual governance to the *Schreiber* and *Stubedienst*. The Block Elders of the Quarantine in Birkenau were famous, mostly Poles (e.g., Number 1825 Franek Karasiewicz).

BLOCK ELDER'S ROOM — For the Block Elder and *schreiber*, constructed at the front of a Block. Usually very luxuriously appointed by any standard. Entrance forbidden to the prisoners on the Block. "Don't make a racket, *muzulmen*, the Block Elder's sleeping in his room."

BUNK — Two-story structure for sleeping. In the absence of other structures, and of space for them, all human functions, except excretion, were performed here: eating, killing lice, scraping off mud, writing letters home, and organizing. The bottom and first floors of this structure were like open drawers — you had to use them in a lying-down position. On the top, however, you could stand, sit, hang your clothes from a beam, and so these bunks were occupied by the so-called better people.

BUNKER — Hideaway dug out of the ground by prisoners planning an escape. Also, a cement cell in which a prisoner "arrested" in the camp for breaking the law — trading, a torn blanket on one's back for protection against the cold, attempted escaped, an illegal letter — stood with his back touching the ceiling for long weeks, days, and nights. Also a shelter for the camp guard, what the English call a "pill box." "As long as there's a bunker we can escape." "Yes, but if they catch you, it's the bunker — guaranteed." "Especially since they've built bunkers all round the camp, how are you to get past them at night?."

CANADA — Symbol of the camp's prosperity. Also, the Kommando working with transports coming to the camp and the gas. "It's Canada in the camp now; you should have been here sooner to know what it used to be like." "Canada's going to the ramp."

CHIMNEY — Symbol of the crematorium and death in the gas chamber. "Why are you pushing like a Jew to the chimney?"

DAW — *Deutsche Abrüstungswerke.* A hard Kommando, chiefly employed in dismantling planes lost over Germany. The classic place for escapes. "The siren's sounding, someone must have escaped from DAW again."

DURCHFALL — Diarrhea, dysentry — the classic camp sickness and the fear of all prisoners. In most cases, untreated and incurable. Everyone was on his own in the battle against *Durchfall*. That battle is one of Auschwitz's unwritten stories. "Don't drink the water, you'll get *Durchfall*." "Bread baked to a cinder is the best cure for *Durchfall*."

EFFECTS — Initially, a storage room for prisoners' personal belongings. Later, a whole separate part of the camp in whose Blocks riches taken from transports going to the crematorium lay — and disappeared. "Bring me back a nice shirt if you're going to Effects."

FLECK — Spotted typhus, the third classic Auschwitz sickness. Until 4 April 1943, all those sick with fleck went, without exception, to the gas chamber. In the memory of many, fleck is associated with the figure of Dr. Zenkteller, the untiring bloodhound of lice, and to those suffering from typhus who had been hidden on other, typhus-free hospital Blocks by friends of the *Pflegers*.

FUNCTION — A good position, not in a Kommando. Not necessarily one that was officially good like Block Elder's *pipel*, runner, hospital *pfleger* and so on were. "The guy's lucky, he got a function."

GASKAMMER — Gas chamber. In the space of only a few years, several million people went through some not very large halls of Auschwitz and left "in the shape of smoke through the chimneys," as was said ironically in the camp. Since each larger concentration camp had its own gas chambers and crematoria, their number can be estimated in the hundreds. The architectural achievement of the twentieth century! "The whole transport went to the gas." "Why worry, we're going to the gas anyway."

GONG — Reveille, signal for work, Appel, sleep. "Get up people, it's past the second gong."

GREEN — SS man. Rarely used.

HOLZHOF — The notorious muzulman kommando, the lumber yard.

KAPO — Prisoner in charge of a work detail. Supervised the work, distributed soup, bonuses, and beatings. Had unlimited power over prisoners. The merits of a Kommando were measured chiefly by whether the *Kapo* was good, although essentially bad Kommandos did exist — *Weichseldurchtich,* for example — as did essentially good ones, the ones working in the women's camp. As a rule, each *Kapo* had his own hut in the field, a place to rest, sleep, trade, drink, and collude with the SS, and for obvious reasons with their *pipels.* "When the *Kapo* tells you, you do it." "I'll tell the *Kapo* you don't want to work."

KOMMANDO — Work detail. Working at a specific job in a specific place, with its own Kapo and SS supervisor (*Kommandoführer*).

KRANKENBAU — Hospital, the famous *KB.*

LAGER — Camp ("concentration" understood).

LEICHENHALLE — Camp morgue, where the day's harvest was laid out in exemplary order (corpse by corpse; layer upon layer; head to toe; tall person on top of tall person). Each corpse had its own death certificate; before being taken to the crematorium, the corpses were laid in rows on the camp road by the hospital so that their numbers, tattooed on the left hand, were clearly visible to the SS checking the identity of the dead. In the evening, the corpses were loaded onto trucks with raised platforms; they were tipped out automatically at the crematorium; the rest was up to the Jews of the so-called *Sonderkommando* and the fire.

MELDUNG — Denouncement, penal report. The system of informing was widespread among prisoners, particularly when it wasn't a matter of a torn piece of blanket, a cigarette smoked at work, or an unwashed bowl — although such things also brought bad consequences — but rather a matter of accounts being settled between old numbers — of profitable functions, of women, of gold hidden in the beams.

MUZULMAN — Literally, Muslim — a physically and mentally totally depleted human being who no longer had the strength or the will to fight for life. Usually suffering from *Durchfall*, phlegmon, or scabies, and more than ripe for the chimney. No account can adequately render the contempt in which the *muzulman* was treated by his fellows in the camp. Even prisoners delighting in camp autobiographies are reluctant to admit that they, too, had once been *muzulmen*.

OLD NUMBER — Low number, denoting a camp old-timer. Source of honor and respect from other old numbers and young numbers, latecomers to the camp, also known as millions. They staffed the camp's best functions, possessed excellent knowledge of camp life and were filled with Lager patriotism. "What do you millions know about the camp! Ask an old number (!), he'll be able to tell you what's he's been through."

ORGANIZING — The acquisition in any way possible of means of survival beyond the daily ration, whether honestly — from the SS kitchen, the Effects, the ramp — or dishonestly, from your colleague's ration. The organizer, a person used to this way of life, often had enormous wealth and always enjoyed the full respect and envy of the camp.

PFLEGER — Nurse in the hospital, corresponding, more or less, to the position of the *stubedienst* in the Lager. "Water, *Pfleger!*" "The *Pfleger's* more important than the doctor."

PHLEGMON — Intramuscular boil, the other classic Auschwitz sickness; for many years, like *Durchfall*, it sentenced people to the gas chamber.

PIPEL — *Blockelder's* or Kapo's errand boy. Usually a child who had survived a Jewish transport. Female equivalent: *kalifaktor*.

POST — Guard. An SS man. *Blockführers*, those, that is, who oversaw the internal life of the camp, were sent to the Post for misdemeanours such as trading, relations with women, and so on, if they were caught.

POSTENKETTE — Chain of guards surrounding the camp or workplace. A small *Postenkette* stood by the camp wires at night. The great *Postenkette* stood during the day (in the case of escapes, for the whole day), surrounding the camp for a radius of several kilometers.

REVIER — Hospital, but only in the Women's Camp's jargon, which did not include the term *KB*.

ROLLWAGON — A wagon pushed by people. There were no draught animals in the camp. People were used to convey soup, bread, clothing, garbage, corpses from camp to hospital.

SCABIES — The fourth classic Auschwitz sickness. Often, infected Blocks (from the *FKL*, for example) went to the gas in their entirety. "Have you got scabies? Rub yourself with tea."

SCHUTZHÄFTLING — A political prisoner, "in protective custody," locked up just in case. Like the number, this was an official camp title.

SELECTION — That is, the selecting of muzulmen for the gas. It took place regularly, more or less every two weeks, although there were periods — 1944, for example — when selections were not made because the crematoria and gas chambers were overloaded.

SŁUPEK — A prisoner's hands were tied behind his back, a rope was threaded through them and attached to a ring at the top of a stake, or to a cross beam in the Block. The rope would be used to pull the prisoner into the air. He would hang like this for one hour, two. His arms were eventually pulled out of their sockets, his tendons torn. The entire operation was called "słupek."

SONDERKOMMANDO — Special Kommando, consisting entirely of Jews, and working at the crematorium gassing and burning people. "Who's going to have gold if not the *Sonderkommando*?"

STRIPES — Camp clothing made out of special, gray-blue striped material (nettlefiber, it was said). Well-cut, form-fitting stripes were a sign of well-being, function, and self-esteem on the part of the prisoner who wore them.

STUBE — A room, or section, of a Block. "I'm on Block six, third *Stube*, top bunk."

STUBEDIENST — The *"Kommandant"* of a *Stube*. Distributed food, saw to the cleanliness of the *stube*, and, clearly, did not go out on kommandos. Unlimited power over prisoners.

SZPIA — Needle, an injection of phenol into the heart, the means by which muzulmen were put to death in the early years of Auschwitz. "They all went to the needle."

TOTENMELDUNG — Death report issued by the hospital, or by the Block Elder when the death took place within the camp. Showed time and cause of death. The reports for the gassed prisoners read: "sent for special treatment."

TRAGER — Stretcher. And a box for carrying bread, and a "handbarrow" for hauling soil.

TRUPPENLAZARETT — SS hospital situated within the great *Postenkette*. It remained unfinished right to the end of the camp.

UNTERKUNFT — Camp storerooms, warehouses, name of a Kommando.

VERNICHTUNGSLAGER — Extermination camp. The official designation of Auschwitz.

VERTRETER — Block Elder's deputy. The actual authority figure in the Block at those times when the Block Elder was representing the Block.

VORARBEITER — Kapo's assistant, what the English call "foreman."

WASCHRAUM — In essence, a washroom; often, however, it served other purposes. The *Waschraum* in Old Auschwitz served as an arena for boxing matches and wrestling. The *Waschraum* in Birkenau was used for staging reviews that, for a time, were organized by the hospital. Throughout the hospital's entire existence, the *Waschraum* was the assembly point for muzulmen who were brought there after being selected from all the hospital Blocks, and who were taken by truck to the gas in the evening.

WINKEL — Colored triangle indicating the type of crime the prisoner was supposed to have committed, worn on the left breast in front of the number. "He's got a red *winkel*, but he's worse than a criminal."

ZAUNA — Shower, delousing. Because things brought by transports and used by prisoners were deloused there as well, people working in the *Zauna* had everything from gold to books. Women were shaved to the bare skin and disinfected exclusively by men.

ZIGUENER — The Gypsy camp. Gypsies from all of Europe who were interned in Auschwitz soon lost all the rights and semblance of rights due to interned people, and fell victim en masse to hunger, filth, disease, and barbaric treatment at the hands of the SS and the camp personnel. "I'm going to the *Ziguener*."

ZULAGE — Extra portion of food for workers. "There's a *Zulage* today; it'll be easier to last until tomorrow lunchtime."

ZYKLON — The gas used in the gas chambers. In 1944, for economic reasons the single dose was lowered. Jews from the so-called *Sonderkommando* reported that instead of in five minutes, death ensued in from fifteen to twenty-five. This gas was manufactured by a private German firm.

3 powojenna publikacja Oficyny Warszaw-
skiej na obczyźnie, która założona w 1938
roku przez Anatola Girsa i Bolesława
Barcza w Warszawie spalona została w
powstaniu Warszawskim, podczas którego
zginął Bolesław Barcz. Praca niniejsza na-
pisana jest przez byłych więźnów politycz-
nych niemieckich obozów koncentracyj-
nych. Rozpoczęto ją wkrótce po uwolnieniu
z obozu Allach-Dachau przez wojska 7 Armii Amerykańskiej. Druk ukończono w
czerwcu 1946 roku. Odbito 10 000 numero-
wanych egzemplarzy. Część nakładu opra-
wiono w »pasiaki« wycięte z orginalnych
ubrań więziennych.

3 rd post-war publication by Oficyna Warszawska abroad. Oficyna Warsawska was established in 1938 by Anatol Girs and Bolesław Barcz in Warsaw and burned during the Warsaw Uprising in which Bolesław Barcz perished. The present work is written by former political prisoners of German concentration camps. It was started shortly after camp Dachau-Allach was liberated by the 7th American Army. Printing was completed in June 1946. 10,000 numbered copies were made. Part of the edition was bound in concentration camp "stripes" cut from original prison garments.